JN110607

The Academic Canon of Arts, Humanities, and Sciences

The Rissho International Journal
of Academic Research
in Culture and Society **3**

The Academic Canon of Arts, Humanities, and Sciences

Edited by The Rissho University
International Journal Committee

RISSHO University

Editing / Publishing: Rissho University
4-2-16 Osaki, Shinagawa Ward, Tokyo 141-8602, Japan
Sales: Heibonsha Limited, Publishers
3-29 Kandajinbo-cho, Chiyoda Ward, Tokyo 101-0051, Japan

The Rissho International Journal of Academic Research in Culture and Society 3
The Academic Canon of Arts, Humanities, and Sciences
Edited by The Rissho University International Journal Committee

© Rissho University 2020
All rights reserved.
Printed in Japan

Contents

Message From The President: The Rissho International Journal of Academic Research in Culture and Society

Rissho University's roots go back to the year 1580, when the Iidaka Danrin seminary was established in Sosa, in what is now Chiba Prefecture. It was an educational institution of the Nichiren School of Buddhism, which was founded by Nichiren (1222 - 1282) around the middle of the Kamakura period in Japan. Today, Rissho's history and traditions are among the most illustrious of all of the nearly 800 universities in Japan. Our university is one of the largest in Japan, too, with a student body of more than 10,000.

As an educational institution we have developed steadfastly over the centuries, while experiencing the vicissitudes of history. Maintaining optimism for the future, Rissho University actively promotes a wide range of original, forward-looking academic research projects, publishing and promulgating research results, thereby fostering the global advancement of knowledge and contributing to sustainable social development.

Rissho is a multi-disciplinary university with eight undergraduate faculties and seven graduate school research departments. Taking advantage of its strengths in various academic fields and its unique characteristics, the university has restructured advanced data intelligence systems that store the results of our research activities. To promote comprehensive and integrated innovative thinking in the humanities, social sciences and natural sciences, we are enhancing our research systems to make them more effective. We intend of course to continue enriching the practical and sustainable nature of those systems, while also contributing to the development and communication of an even more extensive store of knowledge for Japan and the world at large. With these goals in mind, we have decided to publish *The Rissho International Journal of Academic Research in Culture and Society* as a compendium of outstanding and influential research results.

At Rissho University, our pedagogical and research reforms are alert to world standards. At the heart of those reforms lies an ideal espoused by

Ishibashi Tanzan, who served as the 16th president of our university and also Japan's 55th Prime Minister. He was a man with a great soul, famed for his integrity as an individual, his lionhearted style as an orator, and his rare skills as a journalist and politician espousing the Small Japan policy (or "Small Japanism"). But above all else he was a principled philosopher and a great thinker who synthesized theory and practice. He always prized world peace and order, and as an upright man of learning he dedicated himself to the en-noblement of the human spirit, always exhibiting a glimmer of hope for the future. His emphasis on philosophical anthropology lives on today as part of the enlightenment pedagogical ideals of Rissho University.

Rissho University intends to use the opportunity provided by publication of this *Journal* to instill further intellectual momentum into the trends driving this tumultuous age of globalization. But even more, as an educational and academic research institution, we shall pursue a bold mission: contributing through our university's various pedagogical endeavors to the creation and development of sustainable human communities for a brighter tomorrow. This will help us to continue our own sustainable growth. These ideals are in keeping with the 2030 Agenda for Sustainable Development, adopted at the UN Summit in 2015, and promoting these ideals has a direct positive impact on improving quality assurance in each area covered by the Goals.

Hiroshi Yoshikawa
The 34th President of Rissho University

Traces of Nichiren in Early Modern Kamakura

Eichi Terao

Abstract

Nichiren spent his main period of activity in Kamakura. As Nichiren was active in Kamakura for more than ten years, there are a great many historical landmarks there associated with him. These have been designated as sacred places by subsequent successors of Nichiren and deemed as places that commemorate his life and allow visitors to relive his experiences. In the early modern age, it has become commonplace for the public to visit a variety of temples and shrines. People of all social classes travel great distances to visit sacred mountains, famous temples, and shrines, or even local temples and shrines. These and other scenic sites of historical interest have become places visited for pleasure and recreation rather than only out of religious belief. In light of these social developments, what role is played by the sacred sites associated with Nichiren? In this paper, I will first examine the perception of Sacred Sites Associated with Nichiren in Regional Chronicles and Records of Famous Places held by the intelligentsia, the common people, and others as described in early modern regional chronicles and records of famous places. Following this, I will examine how temples themselves described the sacred sites associated with Nichiren based on the construction of stone monuments and documents describing their origin and history.

Introduction

Nichiren (1222–1282), one of the noted founders of Japanese Buddhism, spent his main period of activity in Kamakura. Following the so-called *kai-shu-sengen* (the Proclamation of the Beginning of the Ministry) in April

1253 (the year *Kenchō* 5) at Seichō-ji Temple in what was then known as Awa Province (present-day Chiba Prefecture), Nichiren went to Kamakura in August 1256 (*Kenchō* 8).[1] Thereafter, until Nichiren's arrest during the Tatsu-no-Kuchi Persecution (*tatsu-no-kuchi honan*) in September 1271 (*Bun'ei* 8)—and except for the period from May 1261 (*Kōchō* 1) to February 1263 (*Kōchō* 3), during which Nichiren was exiled in Izu— his main base of activities was believed to be Kamakura. The major earthquake of 1257 (*Shōka*1) and the presentation in 1260 (*Bun'ō* 1) of the "*Treatise on Spreading Peace Throughout the Country by Establishing True Dharma*" (*Risshō Ankoku-ron*) to Hōjō Tokiyori, the supreme leader of the Kamakura Shogunate, both occurred in Kamakura. In February 1274 (*Bun'ei* 11) the Sado Exile was ended and Nichiren returned to Kamakura, but in May he left for Minobu and would never again return to Kamakura.

As Nichiren was active in Kamakura for more than ten years, there are a great many historical landmarks there associated with him. These have been designated as sacred places by subsequent successors of Nichiren and deemed places that commemorate the life of Nichiren and allow visitors to relive his experiences.

In the early modern age, it has become commonplace for the public to visit a variety of temples and shrines. People of all social classes travel great distances to visit sacred mountains, famous temples and shrines, or local temples and shrines. These temples and shrines and other scenic sites of historic interest have become places visited for pleasure and recreation rather than only out of religious belief.[2]

In light of these social developments, what role is played by the sacred sites associated with Nichiren? In this paper, I will first examine the perception of Sacred Sites Associated with Nichiren in Reginal Chronicles and Records of Famous Places held by the intelligentsia, the common people, and others as described in early modern regional chronicles and records of famous places. Next, I will examine how temples themselves described the sacred sites associated with Nichiren based on the construction of stone monuments and documents describing the origin and history of the sites.

1. Sacred Sites Associated with Nichiren

In the early modern age, a wide variety of locations have been recorded in regional chronicles. Among these are works produced by regional clans and the Shogunate (central government), such as the *Aizu Fudoki*, the *Chikuzen-no-kuni Zoku-fudoki*, and the *Shinpen Musashi-no-kuni Fudoki-ko*. In Sagami Province, which includes Kamakura, the Shogunate compiled the *Shinpen Sagami-no-kuni Fudoki-ko*. However, this document was formally published only after the advent of the Meiji Period. The regional chronicles of Kamakura, known as the *Kamakura Monogatari* and the *Shinpen Kamakura-shi*, which included topographic, geographic, and demographic data about the region, were published early and thus have been used frequently as reference works. As it became increasingly popular for people to visit temples and shrines throughout Japan, regional chronicles describing other regions were soon being published and read. In this section of the paper, I will focus on the *Shinpen Kamakura-shi* as the regional chronicle of reference and the *Kamakura Meisho-ki a*nd the *Tōkaidō Meisho Zue* as references for famous and scenic places to establish how the sacred sites associated with Nichiren were depicted.

The *Shinpen Kamakura-shi*[3] is a regional chronicle of Kamakura that was compiled as a result of an order issued by a powerful *daimyō* (feudal lord), Tokugawa Mitsukuni, to Kawai Tsunehisa and other subjects during the *Enpō* era (1673–1681) and published in 1685 (*Jōkyō* 2).[4] This work lists eleven Nichiren-shū temples and four historical sites associated with Nichiren himself. Table 1 shows a list of these fifteen sites. As some of their locations are not mentioned in the work; only those that are known are indicated.

Fig. 1 *Shinpen Kamakura-shi,* Precincts map of Kōsoku-ji; National Diet Library Digital Cillections, Japan

Table 1—*Nichiren-Shū Temples and Historical Sites Associated with Nichiren*

Location	Site	Associated with Nichiren's biography
Nishi Mikado	Kōshō-ji (associated with Taihei-ji site)	
Hase	Kōsoku-ji (associated with the Yadoya Mitsunori site)	yes
	Ryōzen-ga-saki	yes[5]
	Nichiren Kesakake-no-Matsu	yes
	Yukiai-gawa	yes
Koshigoe	Ryūkō-ji	yes
Komachi	Myōryū-ji	no
Komachi	Daigyō-ji	no
Komachi	Hongaku-ji	no
Ōmachi	Myōhon-ji (associated with Hikigayatsu, the Hiki Yoshikazu site, and the Take-no-Gosho site)	yes
Nagoe	Ankoku-ji (associated with Matsubagayatsu)	yes
Nagoe	Chōshō-ji (associated with Ishii)	yes
Nagoe	Nichiren-no-Koimizu (associated with Kamakura Gosui)	yes
Kunoya	Osarubatake-yama (associated with the Sannō-dō site and Hosshō-ji)	yes
Mutsu'ura	Jōgyō-ji	no

Of the fifteen temples and historical sites listed, a total of ten (six temples and four historical sites) are related to the biography of Nichiren. Here, I will provide simple descriptions of the sites related to the biography of Nichiren in the order they appear in the text.

- Kōsoku-ji: This is the site of Yadoya Nyūdō's residence. When Nichiren was subjected to the Tatsu-no-Kuchi Persecution, believers and disciples who were arrested were held by Yadoya Nyūdō and placed in a dungeon-like prison. Nyūdō later became a believer of Nichiren's teachings.
- Ryōzen-ga-saki: When Ninshō of Gokuraku-ji prayed for rain, Nichiren also prayed for rain in the same location.
- Nichiren Kesakake-no-Matsu: This marks a *matsu* (pine tree) on which Nichiren hung his stole during the Tatsu-no-Kuchi Persecution.
- Yukiai-gawa: During the Tatsu-no-Kuchi Persecution, the messenger whose mission was to inform Kamakura that a miracle had occurred at

Tatsu-no-Kuchi met another messenger here—the one whose mission was to inform those holding Nichiren of the stay of execution ordered by Hōjō Tokiyori.

· Ryūkō-ji: This temple was built by the Rokurōsō (the Six Senior Disciples) after Nichiren's death (this is also the site where Nichiren was made to sit for his execution during the Tatsu-no-Kuchi Persecution).[6]

· Myōhon-ji: This temple is on the site where Nichiren started preaching. It was built by Hiki Daigaku-Saburō, one of Nichiren's followers.

· Ankoku-ji: This cave, written the *Risshō Ankoku-ron* where Nichiren came from Bōshū-Kominato, is where Nichiren began preaching the sutra (it is currently known as Ankokuron-ji).[7]

· Chōshō-ji: This is the location where Nichiren built a hut to live in.

· Nichiren-no-Koimizu: This is the spring from which water suddenly gushed forth when Nichiren wanted a drink while on his way from Awa to Kamakura.

· Osarubatake-yama (Go-Enpaku-Zan): When Nichiren first came to Kamakura, he lived in a cave on this mountain. Monkeys gather in a field where they offer food to Nichiren.

The Nichiren Kesakake-no-Matsu, Yukiai-gawa, Ryūkō-ji, Osarubatake-yama (Hosshō-ji), and Jōgyō-ji are located outside Kamakura. According to the *Genroku-Gōchō* (Translator's note:book of maps of every region of Japan created in the *Genroku* era [1688–1704]), the following fourteen villages were within the borders of Kamakura: Gokurakuji-mura, Ōgigayatsu-mura, Ōmachi-mura, Nishimikado-mura, Jōmyōji-mura, Midarebashi-mura, Zaimokuza-mura, Yamanouchi-mura, Yukinoshita-mura, Komachi-mura, Nikaidō-mura, Jūniso-mura, and Sakanoshita-mura.[8]

The *Kamakura Meisho-ki*, which may be thought of as a kind of tourist information book, was published in multiple editions during the Edo period. Of all the editions still known to be extant today, the one dated 1713 (*Shōtoku* 3) is the oldest, followed by 23 subsequent editions up to the one produced in the *Ansei* era (1854–1860: three editions). One of the characteristics of these books is that in just a limited number of pages (6–9 pages) they provided concise descriptions of the famous sites they listed. As detailed study of the *Kamakura Meisho-ki* has been conducted by others, that work may be referred to for further details.[9]

The famous sites listed in the *Kamakura Meisho-ki* are slightly different depending upon the edition. However, the Nichiren-shū temples number 12 and the historical sites associated with Nichiren total six. Table 2 shows a brief listing of these sites.

Table 2—*Nichiren-shū Temples and Historical Sites Listed in the Kamakura Meisho-ki*

Site	Associated with Nichiren's biography
Meuriu-ji (Myōryū-ji)	No
Daigyō-ji	No
Honkaku-ji (Hongaku-ji)	no
Nichiren Koshikake-ishi	yes
Myōhon-ji (site associated with Hiki-no-Hangan)	yes*
Jiyauyeiji (Jōei-ji)	yes
Myōhō-ji	yes
Daihō-ji	no
Ankoku-ji	yes*
Chōshō-ji	yes*
Koimizu	yes*
Osaruhatake	yes*
Hoshiyou-ji (Hosshō-ji)	no
Kausokuji · Nichirau Shōnin tsuchi-no-rau (Kōsoku-ji · Nichirō Shōnin tsuchi-no-rō)	yes*
Nichiren Shōnin Kesakake-no-Matsu (and mound)	yes*
Reusen-ga-saki · Nichiren Amakohi (Ryōzen-ga-saki · Nichiren Amagoi)	yes*
Yukiai-gawa	yes*
Ryūkō-ji · Myōjin	yes*

Thirteen of the eighteen temples and historical sites listed are associated with the biography of Nichiren. Of those listed above, the ones that were not listed in the 1713 (*Shōtoku* 3) edition were Nichiren-Koshikake-Ishi, Jōei-ji, Myōhō-ji, Daihō-ji, Hosshō-ji, and the Nichiren Kesakake-no-Matsu mound. Of the sites not listed in the 1713 edition, Hosshō-ji was once again listed in the 1784 (*Tenmei* 4) edition, and Jōei-ji, Myōhō-ji, Daihō-ji, and the Nichiren Kesakake-no-Matsu mound were listed as of the *Kansei* era (1789–1801) edition. Only Nichiren-Koshikake-ishi was first listed in the *Ansei* era edition.

It has been pointed out that the *Kamakura Meisho-ki* referred to regional chronicles such as the *Kamakura Monogatari* and the *Shinpen Kamakurashi*, which preceded it. Thus, the locations of sites associated with Nichiren included in the *Shōtoku* 3 edition of the *Kamakura Meisho-ki* are identical to those in the *Shinpen Kamakura-shi* in terms of both temples and historical sites (See*). As each edition was updated to the *Kansei* edition and the *Ansei* edition, the sites that followed the *Shōtoku* 3 edition of the *Shinpen Kamakura-shi* gradually increased in number. However, Hosshō-ji was listed as being affiliated with Osarubatake-yama in the *Shinpen Kamakura-shi*, but was listed independently in the *Kamakura Meisho-ki*.

Next, I will take up the issue of the *Tōkaidō Meisho Zue* (Collection of Pictures of Famous Sites along the Tōkaidō Route).[10] This work is a guide of the famous sites and ancient ruins that were considered the standard sites along the post road from Kyoto to Edo (modern-day Tokyo). As is indicated from the term *zue* ("collection of pictures") in the name of the work, *Tōkaidō Meisho Zue* includes illustrations of major sites and ruins along with the text. It was written by Akisato Ritō and published in 1797 (*Kansei* 9).[11] Although Kamakura was not one of the post towns along the Tōkaidō route, it was included as a famous site with historical ruins. *Tōkaidō Meisho Zue* includes nine Nichiren-shū temples that are historical sites associated and Nichiren (Table 3). The sites written about in the text are listed and the name of the temple is, when necessary, shown beside it within parentheses.

Table 3—*Historical Site Nichiren-shū Temples Associated with Nichiren*

Site	Associated with Nichren's biography
Ryūkō-ji	Yes
Yukiai-gawa	Yes
Kōsoku-ji	Yes
Ubume-tō (Daigyō-ji)	No
Myōhon-ji	Yes
Osarubatake-yama (Go-Enpaku-Zan, Hosshō-ji)	Yes
Nichiren-sui	Yes
Ishii (Chōshō-ji)	No
Ankoku-ji	Yes

The number of sites listed in *Tōkaidō Meisho Zue* is about two-thirds the number listed in the *Shinpen Kamakura-shi* and the *Kamakura Meisho-ki*. However, since the objective of the work was to describe the famous sites and historical ruins in the post towns along the Tōkaidō route, it seems reasonable that the number that could be listed would be somewhat limited. Of the nine temples and historical sites listed, seven are associated with the biography of Nichiren, and all nine are also listed in the *Shinpen Kamakura-shi* and the *Kamakura Meisho-ki*. No mention of Nichiren's life is made, however, in the entry for "Ishii (Chōshō-ji)."

The above overview suggests that the entries in the *Kamakura Meisho-ki* and the *Tōkaidō Meisho-zue* that refer to historical sites related to Nichiren were made either in direct reference to the *Shinpen Kamakura-shi* or in the tradition of that work. Thus, we will examine the specific listings in the *Shinpen Kamakura-shi* and the *Tōkaidō Meisho-zue* relating to historical sites associated with Nichiren. The *Kamakura Meisho-ki* lists the names of the sites but in general does not provide explanations of them. Even when it does, these explanations are limited to a single line of text.[12]

The sites the two works have in common are Kōsoku-ji, Myōhon-ji, Ankoku-ji, and Nichiren Koimizu. The accompanying texts are contrasted in Table 4 and described in the following sections. All are temples or historical ruins located within Kamakura. The text in the *Tōkaidō Meisho-zue* was not simply copied from the *Shinpen Kamakura-shi*; the descriptions are some-what simplified versions that nonetheless follow the order of the *Shinpen Kamakura-shi*. This is particularly evident in the entries for Myōhon-ji and Ankoku-ji. Text unique to the *Tōkaidō Meisho-zue* and not seen in the *Shinpen Kamakura-shi* appears only in the description of Myōhō-zakura in the third entry, Ankoku-ji.

Fig. 2 *Shinpen Kamakura-shi*, Precincts map of Myōhon-ji; National Diet Library Digital Collections, Japan

Table 4

Shinpen Kamakura-shi	Tōkaidō Meisho-zue
①Kōsoku-ji, the Site of Yadoya Mitsunori's Residence (pp. 101–102)	①Kōsoku-ji (pp. 850–851)

Kōsoku-ji, also known as Gyōji-san, lies on the left of the road en route to the Great Buddha. The site is also known as the "Yadoya" as it was inhabited by a vassal of Taira Tokiyori known as Yadoya Saemon Mitsunori who, as a nyūdō [lay priest], went by the moniker Saishin.

Kōsoku-ji is situated on the left side of the road that leads to the Great Buddha. It is the site of the residence of Yadoya Saemon Mitsunori, a nyūdō [lay priest] and a retainer of Hōjō Tokiyori; hence, the area is called Yadoya-machi ["Yadoya's town"].

When Nichiren was on the verge of being beheaded at Tatsu-no-Kuchi, Yadoya Mitsunori was entrusted with the custody of Nichiren's disciples, Nichirō and Nisshin, along with the follower Shijō Kingo and his three sons, following their capture at Ankoku-ji. Mitsunori held these individuals in earthen cages.

Nichiren Shōnin met with tribulation at Tatsu-no-Kuchi and was handed over to be imprisoned, along with his disciples Nichirō and Nisshin, and the follower Shijō Kingo and his three sons. They were placed in the custody of Mitsunori, and held captive in earthen cages.

It was only after Nichiren was spared his fate by a miraculous occurrence that Mitsunori started to believe in him. He built a thatched dwelling on his estate, where he asked Nichirō to be a founding priest. Apparently, the temple's sangō [the name of a metaphorical mountain associated with a temple] was named after Mitsunori's late father [Gyōji being the onyomi reading of Yukitoki], while the jigō [the main name of a temple] was named after Mitsunori [Kōsoku being the onyomi reading of Mitsunori]. More recently, the dowager of Furuta Shigetsune, the hyōbu shōyū [junior minister of war], re-established Daibai-in. Hence, Kōsoku-ji is now also known as Taibai-ji.

Nichiren Shōnin was delivered from harm by a miraculous occurrence. Following the miracle, Mitsunori himself started to believe in Nichiren. He donated his estate to Nichirō and allowed him to found a sect. Hence, the temple's sangō [the name of a metaphorical mountain associated with a temple] was named after Mitsunori's late father, while the jigō [the main name of a temple] was named after Mitsunori.

The temple is main hall enshrines wooden images of Nichiren and Nichirō, Mitsunori, and Shijō Kingo and his three sons.	Enshrined in the temple's main hall are Nichiren Shōnin, Nichirō, Mitsunori, Shijō Kingo, and others.
The temple is a branch temple of Myōhon-ji.	
North of the temple, on the hillside, lies the earthen cage in which Nichirō was held captive.1	Nichirō Shōnin's earthen prison lies on the hillside north of the temple.
②Myōhon-ji Hikigayatsu, historic site associated with Hiki Yoshikazu, Take-no-Gosho site (p.123)	②Myōhon-Ji (pp. 855–866)
Myōhon-ji was named Chōkōzan. It was the temple in which Nichiren began to preach. It is said that one of Nichiren's lay devotees called Hiki Daigaku-Saburō had built it. While Nichiren was still alive, he had passed it down to Nichirō, who is considered to be the founder.	Situated in Hikigayatsu, Myōhon-ji shares the same abbot as the Nichiren-affiliated temple, Ikegami Honmon-ji. Nichirō Shōnin founded this temple here, as this was the place from which Nichiren Shōnin preached his sermons.
The commemoration of its founding takes place on January 21st. The abbot of this temple is also the abbot of Ikegami Honmon-ji. […]	
The main temple: The hall used to enshrine a statue of the Amitabha [Buddha]. That statue was a private statue of Daigaku-Saburō. […] The statue of Shakyamuni [Buddha] was said to be made by Chin Nakei. When Nichiren was exiled to Izu, he took the statue of Buddha with him. Later, the statue came into the custody of Nichirō. This statue is now in Honkoku-ji. Therefore, another statue of Shakyamuni is said to be enshrined here […]	The object of devotion was a statue of the Buddha: Following his demotion, Nichiren Shōnin took that statue of Buddha with him. Subsequently, the statue came into the custody of Nichirō and now stands in Honkoku-ji, in the old capital [Kyoto]. However, the temple's object of devotion is a replica of the said statue.

18

③Ankoku-ji, situated in Matsubagayatsu (p. 135)	③Ankoku-ji (p. 862)
The temple Ankoku-ji, known honorifically as Myōhō-zan, is situated east of Nagoe-mura, and is subordinate to Myōhon-ji. An inscription at the mongate states the following: "Ankoku-ron Cave, October 13, Year 1 of *Taiei*, Year of the Snake [1521], [signed] Yūken."	Situated in Matsubagayatsu, Ankoku-ji is a temple of the Nichiren denomination.
Those who enter the gate will find a cave to their right. It was in this cave that Nichiren wrote *Ankoku-ron* ["Peace for the Country"] after coming from Kominato in Bōshū. It is clear from *Chūgasan* (*Nichiren Shōnin Chūgasan*) that Nichiren started the project in *Shōka* Year 1 [1257] and finished writing it in *Bunnō* Year 1 [1260]. It was here that Nichiren began to advocate the main teachings of the Lotus Sutra. Apparently, things started to propagate from Hosshō-ji. "Matsubagayatsu" refers to this location.	A cave lies within the precincts. After arriving from Bōsō, Nichiren Shōnin confined himself in this cave and wrote *Risshō Ankoku-ron* ("Treatise on Spreading Peace throughout the Country by Establishing True Dharma").
	In front of the temple stands a noted tree named Myōhō-zakura.
④Nichiren-no-Koimizu (pp. 135–136)	④Nichiren-sui (p. 862)
Nichiren-no-Koimizu is a small well on the southern side of the road, about one and a half ri from Nagoe-zaka toward Kamakura.	Nichiren-sui is situated in a town to the south of Nagoe-zaka.
Folklore states that when Nichiren travelled from Awa province to Kamakura, he sought water from this hillside, and the water suddenly gushed forth. Though small, this spring never dried—even in times of drought—and the water remained ever cool.	Nichiren Shōnin would seek water here when he passed by during hot weather. Water sprung forth here, like a waterfall, from the hillside road. The volume of water remained consistent, whether hot or cold; it is a clear and holy spring.
Locals say that there are five significant wells of Kamakura, namely, Kinryū-sui, Furō-sui, Zeni Arai-mizu, Nichiren no Koi-mizu, and Kajiwara Tachi-arai-mizu.	Nichiren no Koi-Mizu is one of the five noted wells of Kamakura, including Kinryū-sui, Furō-sui, Zeni Arai-mizu, and Kajiwara Tachi-arai-mizu.

They are all listed in both the *Shinpen Kamakura-shi* and the *Tōkaidō Meisho-zue*, but, as mentioned above, the mentions of them listed in the biography of Nichiren differ in the entries for Chōshō-ji (Ishii). The text of the *Tōkaidō Meisho-zue* and the first half of the *Shinpen Kamakura-shi* contain the entries in question. Simplified summaries are listed with their order of appearance slightly altered. Among these entries are those that are abbreviated excerpts from the biography of Nichiren, such as "This was formerly where the hut in which Nichiren lived was located." The *Shinpen Kamakura-shi* includes the main parts of the entries related to Nichiren's life that have to do with the items listed in Table 4. However, the entries for Chōshō-ji (Ishii) differ. This is likely why the entries in the *Tōkaidō Meisho-zue* that relate to the life of Nichiren are also abbreviated. In addition, *Tōkaidō Meisho-zue* entries that should use the name "Nichijō" instead mistakenly used "Nichirō."

Table 5

Shinpen Kamakura-shi	Tōkaidō Meisho-zue
Chōshō-ji, an Annex to Ishii (p. 135)	Ishii (p. 862)
Known honorifically as Shakusei-zan, Chōshō-ji lies in a valley to the south of the road passing through Nagoe-zaka.	Ishii is situated in a valley south of the Nagoe-zaka road. The temple is named Chōshō-ji.
Within the precincts, a spring gushes forth from a cleft in the rock, forming one of the ten wells of Kamakura. This is why the temple became commonly known as Ishii Chōshō-ji [translator's note: ishii literally means "stone well"]. Chōshō-ji is of the Hokke-shū [Lotus school].	
The temple grounds formerly housed Rakuyō-Honkoku-ji and the present temple is the branch temple of the same.	It is the site of the former Nichiren school of the old Kyoto temple, Honkoku-ji.
According to the temple's priest, Nichiren once had his dwelling here. It subsequently became the home of Nichirō, Nichi'in, and Nichijō. Because Nichijō was the uncle of Minamoto-no-Takauji [Ashikaga Takauji], the temple was relocated to Kyoto and named Honkoku-ji.	Because Nichirō was the uncle of Takauji [Ashikaga Takauji], the temple was relocated to the old capital [Kyoto]. Within the precincts, a spring gushes forth from a cleft in the rock. A noted spring, this is one of the ten wells of Kamakura.

Chōshō-ji was passed on to Nichiei the disciple, whereupon it was renamed Myōhō-ji. This is because Nichiei was known as Myōhōbō. The temple was subsequently relocated to Ōkura Tō-no-tsuji, and then to Tsuji-machi. According to the temple's priest, in its present Tsuji-machi location, the temple is now known as Keiun-ji, having previously been known as Myōhō-ji. Conversely, in the Nagoe-zaka location, the temple now has the honorific name of Myōhō-ji having previously been known as Keiun-ji. The reasons for these circumstances are unknown. The present Chōshō-ji lay in disrepair earlier, when a priest named Chūhi Nichiryū Hosshi cherished the temple ruins, and so built a temple here and named it, Chōshō-ji. Hence, Nichiryū became known as Chūkō Kaizan [translator's note: it means "revitalizing priest"]. He was a man of the Kominato of Bōshū. It is uncertain when the temple was restored and when Nichiryū passed. [...]

As can be seen, the sacred sites associated with Nichiren that are listed in regional chronicles and records of famous places are based on the entries found in *Shinpen Kamakura-shi*, which were then later utilized in the *Kamakura Meisho-ki* and the *Tōkaidō Meisho-zue*. In addition, new entries were added to the *Kamakura Meisho-ki* each time it was revised.

2. Stone Tower Signposts and Their Origins

The next issue is how the sacred sites associated with Nichiren were marked so that they could be identified. Here, I would will focus on the construction of stone towers at these sites. In the early modern age, one of the methods used to inform the masses on ordinances involved the use of street-side bulletin boards (*kōsatsu-ba*).[13] While these bulletin boards were also raised in front of the gates of temples and shrines when announcing events during the year or when sacred objects from other temples or other locations came to be

21

placed on display, it could be said that the stone towers that were erected in front of the gates, as well as those within the grounds, served more as permanent signs and landmarks.

The types of stone towers used to mark the holy sites associated with Nichiren and erected at the Nichire-shū temples in Kamakura are shown in Table 6. Among the temples where the stone towers are located, those listed in the *Shinpen Kamakura-shi* as being associated with the sacred sites of Nichiren were Ankokuron-ji (Ankoku-ji), Myōhō-ji, and Chōshō-ji. A temple listed in the same text that as not being associated with Nichiren was Hongaku-ji. Finally, temples that did not appear at all in that work were Myōhō-ji, Jōei-ji, and Myōchō-ji. Those that were later added to subsequent editions of the *Kamakura Meisho-ki* were Myōhō-ji and Jōei-ji.

The shapes of the stone towers can be categorized as follows: (1) Daimoku towers, which have the mantra "*daimoku* (namu-myōhō-renge-kyō)" inscribed in the center front portion of the tower; and (2) towers that have the name of the sacred site inscribed on their front.[14] The types of towers are indicated in Table 6.

Table 6—*Stone Towers Used to Mark Sacred Sites Associated with Nichiren*

Year (Western Calendar)	Name	Type	Location No.[15]
Jōkyō 3 (1686)	Nichiren Daibosatsu tower	2	Ankokuron-ji 1
Genbun 4 (1739)	Nichiren Go-shōan (hut) tower	2	Myōhō-ji 2
Kan'en 2 (1749)	Daimoku (mantra) tower	1	Hongaku-ji 1
Kan'en 3 (1750)	Daimoku (mantra) tower	1	Ankokuron-ji 2
An'ei 9 (1780)	Tower commemorating the 500th anniversary of the Passing of Nichiren	1	Myōhō-ji 1
Tenmei 5 (1785)	Daimoku (mantra) tower	1	Myōhon-ji 2
Kansei 4 or later (1792)	Daimoku (mantra) tower	1	Chōshō-ji 1
Kansei 12 (1800)	Daimoku (mantra) tower	1	Jōei-ji 3
Bunsei 3 (1820)	Daimoku (mantra) tower	1	Myōhō-ji 3
Bunsei 11 (1828)	Temple name Tower	2	Jōei-ji 6
Tenpō 9 (1838)	Daimoku (mantra) tower	1	Myōchō-ji (lost)[16]
Tenpō 11 (1840)	Tower marking the Sacred site of Matsubagayatsu	2	Ankokuron-ji 3
Tenpō 14 (1843)	Tower erected in gratitude to Nichiren	1	Jōei-ji 2
no details known; Edo period	Matsubagayatsu Honkoku-ji Honorary Monument	1	Chōshō-ji 3

The earliest known stone tower that indicated a sacred site associated with Nichiren is the Founder Nichiren Daibosatsu tower at Ankokuron-ji (Ankokuron-ji 1; see Fig. 3). This monument was erected in 1686 (*Jōkyō* 3), but the front of the tower says,

> This is Nagoe Cave, where *Risshō Ankoku-ron* was written. The hermitage was originally located here in the location of Matsubagayatsu Ankokuron-ji Temple.

Thus, it refers to the cave where Nichiren wrote the *Rissho Ankoku-ron*, in which he referred to his hut at Matsubagayatsu. The Daimoku (mantra) tower (Ankokuron-ji 2) erected at this temple in 1750 (*Kan'en* 3) has the following inscription on its right side:

> This is a sacred site of the Great Founder, who resided in this temple's Matsubagayatsu hermitage, and preached the Dharma day and night over the course of many years. It was also the place where, according to legend, Nichiren was beaten with wooden sticks and pelted with pieces of roof tiles and stones. It was here that the six senior disciples as well as all the other disciples entered the monastic life and received the Dharma.

Thus, the tower indicates that this was a place where Nichiren spread Buddhist teachings and was persecuted after presenting the *Rissho Ankoku-ron*. The tower Marking the Original Sacred Site at Matsubagayatsu erected in 1840 (*Tenpō* 11) (Ankokuron-ji 3; see Fig. 4) says "Original Sacred Site of Matsubagayatsu" on its front and has the following inscriptions on its rear and right sides:

> The Sacred Cave at this temple is the place where our great founder, the great Bodhisattva spread the four famous phrases and propagated at the risk of his life from the middle of Kenchō era / received. Natural disasters continued one after another from the first year of *Shōka* (1257) and as a result the *Rissho Ankoku-ron* was written and presented on July 16 of the first year of *Bun'ō* (1260). / Hōjō Tokiyori in order to warn him but late at night on August 27, some thousands attacked and burned Nichiren's hut in an attempt to kill him, but he escaped and from this place on May 12 the following year. / He was then exiled to Izu-no-kuni and subsequently came to live here. He tried to correct others' wrong teachings frequently / and on

September 12 of the 8th year of *Bun'ei* (1271), Yoritsuna approached with a hundred men to capture Nichiren, tried to behead him at Tatsunokuchi, but he escaped. / Nichiren was exiled to Sado-no-kuni, where he spent four years in misery, after which in the spring of the 10th year of *Bun'ei* (1273), he was released. / Afterward he preached at this cave with his disciples at his side, during which time he taught the words of the Lotus Sutra / so that it would spread throughout the world for the happiness of all. This place here at this temple / is known as the original Go-shōan or Go-sōan (the holy grass hut), the town nearby is called Nagoe, and the cave is called Matsubagayatsu. Here, he lived for twenty something years until his death, until which time he taught the sutra and wrote the *Ankokuron*, and for this reason it is a sacred site. At Nichiren's direction, Nichirō founded the Myō-Hokke-zan-Ankokuronkutsu-ji temple here. Thus, it is a sacred site / for the priests of the religions of Japan and laypeople alike, and therefore we should visit and express our great appreciation to the Great Bodhisattva here.

As you see, it shows detailed history with 13 lines about this temple. According to the text, Nichiren spent more than twenty years to propagate there, and asked Nichirō to found a temple there after Nichiren's death. Examination of historical texts on Ankokuron-ji shows that the 1689 (*Genroku* 2) edition of the *Kamakura Matsubagayatsu Ankokuron-ji Brief History*[17] contains an entry describing the same information with more details.

Fig. 3

Fig. 4

Fig. 5

At Myōhō-ji, where a signpost marks Nichiren's hut at Matsubagayatsu (as in Ankokuron-ji), the monument marking Nichiren's hut (Myōhō-ji 2) was erected in 1739 (*Genbun* 4; see Fig. 5). The front side of the tower has the following inscription:

This is the first sacred site at the Nichiren Shū temples in Japan—the location of the Founder's hermitage—and the former site of the Honkoku-ji, the one of the three major temples. Honkoku-ji was eventually moved from Kamakura to Kyoto.

Thus, it identifies Nichiren's hut as the first temple of Nichiren Buddhism. The reverse side of the tower has the following inscription:

Hokke-dō of Ryōgon-san Myōhō-ji which is located in Matsubagayatsu, Nagoe, Kamakura of Sagami Province, is a sacred location where the Great Founder (Nichiren Shōnin) first began to propagate and spread the teachings of the Nichiren sect. In the fifth year of the *Kenchō* era (1253), when Nichiren Shōnin founded the sect on Mt. Kiyosumi, he chanted the Daimoku for the first time at Dōzen-bo, and tried to convert the lord of the

25

country to follow the true Law of Buddhism. For this purpose, he moved from Awa Province and came to reside in Kamakura, where he spent his time spreading the teachings of the Lotus Sutra and subdued heretical sects. This is the very spot where Daikōzan Honkoku-ji Temple in Rokujō of the capital used to stand, the place where he bestowed the teachings and spread the message of the Lotus Sutra.

Thus, the inscription indicates that this was the place in Kamakura where Nichiren stayed after beginning his ministry in 1253 *(Kenchō* 5). Examination of the tower commemorating five hundred years since Nichiren's passing that was erected in 1780 (*An'ei* 9) (Myōhō-ji 1) reveals the following inscription on its side:

Former site / Matsubagayatsu Go-sōan, Honkoku-ji in Kyoto.

This indicates that the Matsubagayatsu hut stood at that location. The history of Myōhō-ji included in the 1795 (*Kansei* 7) revised edition by Nichiō an entry entitled "*Kamakura Kosaka-no-gō Nagoe-san-chū Matsubagayatsu Myōhō-ji Ryaku-engi*" summarized history. The text of this entry is more detailed than the history inscribed on the stone tower.[18]

Asat Ankokuron-ji and Myōhō-ji, Chōshō-ji also has a marker indicating that it was the location of the Matsubagayatsu hut. The Daimoku (mantra) tower, erected sometime after 1792 (*Kansei* 4) (Chōshō-ji 1), is inscribed with the words "Matsubagayatsu" on its base and both sides of the tower itself are inscribed with the following text:

The Founder—who spent his life chanting the Sūtra—was enshrined. His statue was carved by Nichiryū Shōnin, Nagakatsu, in the first year of *Kōchō* (1261), here, at the former site of the original Hokke-dō of Honkoku-ji Temple, Shakusei-zan, Chōshō-ji Temple.

Thus, the inscription indicates that the site is the former location of the Kyoto Honkoku-ji, where Ishii Nagakatsu gave alms to Nichiren Shōnin. However, it does not identify the site as the location of Nichiren's Matsubagayatsu hut (see Fig. 6). The results of a lawsuit in which it was argued that Myōhō-ji is the rightful location of Nichiren's hut made it impossible for Chōshō-ji to claim that it is the location of the hut. Prior to 1781 (*An'ei* 10), there was a stone monument at the gate identifying it as the location of the Matsubagayatsu hut, but that same year people from Myōhō-ji destroyed the monument.[19] There is also a monument known as the Matsubagayatsu Honkoku-ji Commemorating Monument (Chōshō-ji 3) that was erected in the Edo period, but it does not identify the location as the former site of the Matsubagayatsu hut.

Fig. 6   Fig. 7

Jōei-ji is not mentioned in the *Shinpen Kamakura-shi*. But the Daimoku (mantra) tower there, erected in 1800 (*Kansei* 12), indicates that offerings of *mochi* (rice cakes) were made to Nichiren at that location at the Tatsu-no-Kuchi Persecution. The old woman who made the rice cake offerings was later worshipped as Sajiki-Daimyōjin, and the item worshipped there is the *bota-mochi* (a kind of rice cake) offering of the Sajiki-no-Ama (the Sajiki nun). There is an inscription describing the history of this patron goddess that reads as follows:

The old woman who, at the Tatsu-no-Kuchi Persecution on September 12 of the 8th year of *Bun'ei* (1271), / came to? with an offering to the Founder of mochi rice cakes with sesame seed powder, / so says a letter. Afterward, she was worshipped at a small shrine as Saijiki-Daimyōjin. / She is the patron of this temple, There is a detailed historical record.

The monument erected in 1828 (*Bunsei* 11) (Jōei-ji 6) was also inscribed with the temple name, which does not indicate Jōei-ji as the formal temple name. Rather, it calls the temple "Bota-mochi Temple," and that it is a sacred site associated with Nichiren. The Nichiren Commemorative tower, erected in 1843 (*Tenpō* 14) (Jōei-ji 2) calls it the "Former site of Sajiki-Daimyōjin."

The story about the offering of the *bota-mochi* is also included in the entry dated September 12 of the Myōhon-ji Annual Events document compiled by Nichiga of Hoda-Myōhon-ji in 1545 (*Tenbun* 14). It reads as follows:

Kakimochi was brought from the temple into the presence of the statue of Buddha. The maidservant offered rice, sake, and kakimochi. The question was asked, "Why the kakimochi?" The response was that it was a present from a noble woman called Mrs. Sajiki live in Kamakura, and was received when the great sage went to Tatsunokuchi that evening. The maidservant thus brought the kakimochi herself and presented it as an offering.[20]

This appears to be the earliest record of this event. This text identifies the offering not as *bota-mochi* but as *kaki-mochi*.[21] Investigation of all the works containing biographical information on Nichiren reveals that the "bota-mochi offering story" does not appear in the *Ganso Kedō-ki*, the *Nichiren Shōnin Chūga-san*, the *Ganso Renkō Satta Ryaku-den*, the *Hokke Reijō-ki*, the *Nichiren Dai-Shōnin Godenki*, or the *Honge Betsuzu Kōso-den*, which suggests that the story was not circulated until at least the end of the first half of the Edo period, when it appeared in the *Honge Betsuzu Busso Tō-ki* written by Nitchō. This work was completed in 1730 (*Kyōhō* 15), but it was not published until 1797 (*Kansei* 9).[22] Thereafter, it appeared in some form in the *Kōso Nenpu Kōi* by Nittai and Nichigi, the *Nichiren Shōnin Ichidai Zue* by Nakamura Keinen, and the *Kōso Ruisai Roku* by Fukami Yōgon, among others. The fact that Jōei-ji is referred to as "Bota-mochi Temple" and the story about the offering of *bota-mochi* are contained in the Myōhon-ji temple history at the head temple of Jōei-ji, known as *Chōkō-zan Myōhon-ji Shi*.[23] Although the date of publication of this work is unclear, it is thought to have been completed no later than 1832 (*Tenpō* 3).[24]

Hongaku-ji is not listed in the *Shinpen Kamakura-shi*, the *Kamakura*

Meisho-ki, or the *Tōkaidō Meisho-zue* as being a sacred site associated with Nichiren. The Daimoku (mantra) tower that was erected at this temple in 1749 (*Kan'en* 2) (Hongaku-ji 1) has a detailed history spanning 12 lines of text on three sides of the tower (see Fig. 7):

Regarding the beginning of Tōzan, in autumn of the eighth year of *Bun'ei* (1271), the Great Founder Bodhisattva avoided the Tatsu no kuchi persecution and was exiled to Sado Province. During the thousand-day period, he suffered from harassment but was not harmed. Finally, in the spring of 1274, he unexpectedly received a pardon from Hōjō on the twenty-sixth day of the third month and once again returned to Kamakura. He then resided at this hermitage in Ebisu-dō until midsummer. He widely spread the teachings of the Sūtra to overcome the material and the immaterial, with the desire of repaying the four favors—there were no further events after this. On the eighth day of the fourth month, he came into contact with Taira no Yoritsuna. Our Founder spoke eloquently of the profound truths of the teachings and moved those in attendance. The security of a nation is dependent on the correctness of the Dharma therein. That is, through the text and logic of the Sūtra, the immediate realization of enlightenment was exhibited. He repeatedly admonished the lord of the province, and Vice-General Hōjō Tokimune subsequently heard the wonderful Dharma and suddenly believed it. Out of joy, on the second day of the fifth month, permission of propagation was issued, and he praised Nichiren highly. In the all over the world there is none like him, and he can indeed be called a great monk. These words are true. Their meaning is profound. Bodhisattva marked the spread of the teachings across the land. After the death of the Buddha, mankind entered declining latter age of the Dharma, and then appeared the teacher who spread the Law. Thus, there appeared the great benefit of the Lotus Sūtra, and there was great merit realized by the Honge Sect. On the twelfth day, he finally left the hermitage to visit the true Ryōzen, wonderful land with tranquil light, where he lived as a hermit in the mountains of Kai Province, Koma District, Hakiri Town, which is now this sacred site. From ancient times, Hiruko-no-mikoto (i.e., Ebisu) was worshipped, and a shrine was erected in his honor. At that time, the shrine was colloquially called Ebisu-dō. Furthermore, the bridge over the river in front of the shrine was also called Ebisu-dō; the name has a connection with our temple.

Nichiren, who was pardoned from his exile in Sado, returned to Kamakura on March 26, 1274 (*Bun'ei* 11). Subsequently, on May 12 he headed for Minobu, where he stayed for a month and a half in the hut at Ebisu-dō. This Ebisu-dō is said to have been the Ebisu-dō at Hongaku-ji.

The history related to Ebisu-dō is also seen in the postscript of the *Komachimura Nichiren-shū Hongaku-ji Engi-utsusi*, which was written by the 11th abbot of Hongaku-ji, known as Nichie, during the *Keichō* era (1596–1615). Specifically, the postscript states the following:

When the Great Founder, Nichiren, Great Bodhisattva desired to enter Minobu-san and create the first sacred site, it was designated the land of the third admonition. The reason is that on the twenty-sixth day of the third month of the eleventh year of *Bun'ei* (1274), when he returned to Kamakura from Sado, six senior disciples and followers—one being Shijō Kingo—built a hermitage and presented him with it. On the eighth day of the fourth month of the same year, he Yoritsuna about the country; this was the third such time. The lord of the country was not willing to agree, but on the twelfth day of the fifth month of the same year, he left that place, entering Kai Province, Hakiri Town. On the seventeenth day of the sixth month, he first created a hermitage on Minobu-san, and after, he left the hermitage in Ebisu-dō, where Nisshin Shōnin resided. After Hōjō Takatoki died, the hermitage completely decayed. In the past, this temple had Ebisu-dō (where it enshrined the statue of Ebisu carved by Unkei). For this reason, the bridge in front of the gate was named Ebisu-dō Bridge.[25]

To this text, at the beginning of the Edo period the history of the place as a sacred site associated with Nichiren was already known. However, regarding the naming of Hongaku-ji as Higashi-Minobu-san, there is another text saying the following:

Nitchō Shōnin later moved to Minobusan, made this temple as a propagation point in Kamakura, spreading the teachings to a place called East Minobu-san. Subsequently, Myōden-ji Temple in Kyoto was established and called West Minobusan by Nichii Shōnin.

However, further investigation regarding the year this text was completed is required.

Regarding the link between Ebisu-dō and Nichiren's hut, no mention is made in any of the texts dealing with the biography of Nichiren such as the *Ganso Kedō-ki* or the *Nichiren Shōnin Chūga-san*, and not even in the *Honge Betsuzu Busso Tōki*, which was written in the mid-Edo period. In the *Nichiren Shōnin Ichidai Zue* of 1858 (*Ansei* 5), the following is included:

On March 26 the Founder was reunited in Kamakura with Nisshō and other priests and laymen, which made him so happy that everyone cried. In order to teach his disciples, he moved to the place where Ebisu-dō was located which he made his residence for a time so that he could fulfill his role as teacher. This place was located at the current location of Myōgon-zan Hongaku-ji.[26]

Myōhon-ji, which is located on the far side of the Nameri-kawa river across from Hongaku-ji and Ebisu-dō bridge, is identified as the first temple founded by Nichiren. The Daimoku (mantra) tower erected in 1785 (*Tenmei* 5) (Myōhon-ji 2) has inscriptions on both sides:

Left side: "Former site of Hikigayatsu Daigaku Saburō Yoshimoto Hongyō-in Nichigaku Shōnin"
Right side: "The original location of the Honge Jōgyō Saitan Nichiren Daishi Dōjō"

Thus, it is identified as the site of the residence of the follower Daigaku Saburō and as the original location of the Nichiren's Dōjō. In other words, it is the first temple (see Fig. 8). The Daimoku (mantra) tower erected in 1820 (*Bunsei* 3) (Myōhon-ji 3) has the following inscription on its right side:

At this temple, the Great Founder, Great Bodhisattva continually chanted the daimoku. At the age of 53, on the twenty-sixth day of the third month of the eleventh year of *Bun'ei* (1274), he returned from Sado Province to Kamakura and Myōhon-ji Temple, the sacred site where he resided, and propagated the teachings. While there, he propagated the five characters constituting the mystic Law for several years through constant chanting of the daimoku and developed voiceless male and female believers who believed in it. They practiced the daimoku to realize the tower.

Here, in the description of the history of the mantra, it is indicated that Myōhon-ji is the place where Nichiren—who had returned to Kamakura after being released from his exile in Sado—taught the "Namu-Myōhō-Renge-Kyō". This same text is inscribed on the tower commemorating the 550th anniversary of Daigaku Saburō's memorial that was erected in 1835 (*Tenpō* 6).[27]

Fig. 8

This history is included in the *Kamakura Matsubagayatsu Ankokuron-ji Ryaku Engi* of Ankokuron-ji, the subordinate temple of Myōhon-ji that was mentioned above:

After the pardon of *Bun'ei* 11 (1274), Nichiren returned to Kamakura on March 26 and went to the residence at Hiki Daigaku [...]. Then, on April 12 of the same year, he went to the former location of Matsubagayatsu [...] and then went to original Hokke-dō at Hikigayatsu. At this time, Daigaku Saburō made a plea to him and he gave Nichiren a place to reside at Hikigayatsu and became Nichiren's disciple. Nichiren founded a temple at this location called Chōkō-san Myōhon-ji. This was the first temple to

32

be founded in Nichiren Shū.[28]

In addition, the *Hikigayatsu Yuisho Kudasigaki*, written by Nichigi, the 25th abbot of both Ikegami Honmon-ji and Myōhon-ji in 1730 (*Kyōhō* 15), stated the following:

Daigaku Saburō [...] founded Hokke-dō at his residence [...], which he offered to the Founder, and in the first year of *Bun'ō*, he Nichiren officiated an Opening Ceremony to celebrate the completion of construction [...]. The Founder returned to Kamakura from Sado in March of the 11th year of *Bun'ei* (1274) and afterward he began teaching with a formal permit by Tokimune, so Daigaku Saburō gave him Hokke-dō since Nichiren had nowhere to teach. Thus, Nichiren spent 50 days in Kamakura here.[29]

Thus, texts state that both Hongaku-ji and Myōhon-ji were places where Nichiren spent time in Kamakura after his release from exile in Sado.

Myōchō-ji is not mentioned in the *Shinpen Kamakura-shi*, the *Kamakura Meisho-ki,* or the *Tōkaidō Meisho-zue*. The Daimoku (mantra) tower that was erected in 1838 (*Tenpō* 9; now lost) has the following inscription on its side:

This is the area where the Great Founder left by boat when he was exiled to Izu. For this Sūtra, he did not care about his own body or life but cared only for the supreme way.

This identifies the location where Nichiren boarded a boat when he was exiled to Izu in 1261 (*Kōchō* 1). This history is also listed in the postscript to the *Yuigahama Soshi-dō Ryakuengi*[30] of 1656 (*Meireki* 2) as follows:

At the arrangement of Hōjō Shigetoki/Hōjō Nagatoki, the Great Founder was finally exiled to Ito in Izu; the time was the twelfth day of the fifth month of the first year of the *Kōchō* era (1261). The Great Founder departed alone by boat from Yuigahama to Ito in Izu. After that, on the twenty-second day of the second month of the third year of *Kōchō* (1263), he received a pardon and was allowed to return to Kamakura. He safely returned to the coast of Yuigahama. In fact, it was upon the return of the Shōnin of the Honge Sect to the area when he met great persecution. Thereafter, the Nichijitsu Shōnin built a hermitage there with the desire of showing gratitude to his master. After this hermitage was built, it was named Kaichōzan-Myōchō-ji Temple.

This indicates that Nichijitsu founded Myōchō-ji at this location. The sacred sites associated with Nichiren's exile to Izu were naturally located in Izu, but Myōchō-ji has also been named as a sacred site related to his exile in Izu. This same work of history also stated the following:

On the day that the Great Founder Nichiren was to get on the boat, the admirable Nichirō, unhappy at the departure of our master fell flat on the beach, lamenting his exile. The Great Founder said, "[Look] at the sun rising from the east and think that Nichirō is on this beach." Afterward, stopped him crying and headed to the boat.

This shows that there was a connection to Nichirō, one of the six senior disciples. This location is not only the site where Nichiren embarked on his exile, but that shows the deep connection between Nichiren and Nichirō. Also, Myōchō-ji was moved to its present location as a result of the tsunami that occurred in the *Tenna* era (1681-1684). At the former location, only Soshi-dō still stands.[31]

The preceding sections have described the stone towers located at sacred sites associated with Nichiren and erected at temples. Many of these stone towers contain histories of the locations ranging from just a few lines to dozens of lines of text in addition to the name of the sacred site. Examples are Myōhō-ji 2, Jōei-ji 3, Myōhon-ji 3, Hongaku-ji 1, and Ankokuron-ji 3. The histories inscribed on Hongaku-ji 1 and Ankokuron-ji 3 are particularly lengthy texts of over ten lines.

These stone towers were likely attempts by the temples to record ever more detailed stories of their origins as sacred sites associated with Nichiren. The histories inscribed on the stone towers can therefore be thought of as links between historical records of the temples themselves and the biography of Nichiren.

3. Conclusion

This paper has presented an examination of the early modern sacred sites associated with Nichiren that are in Kamakura. Text in the *Shinpen Kamakura-shi*, which was published in 1685 (*Jōkyō* 2) greatly influenced texts subsequently published in later regional chronicles and records of famous places. Thus, this text can be used by scholars and laypeople alike as a reference for the major sacred sites associated with Nichiren.

The *Kamakura-ki*, which was written in 1680 (*Enpō* 8), shortly before the publication of the *Shinpen Kamakura-shi*, says the following about the sacred sites associated with Nichiren in Kamakura:

> In Kamakura, there are three sites where Nichiren stayed: Matsubagayatsu, Daibai-ji Temple, and this location (Tatsu no kuchi). Moreover, there are many historical sites related to Nichiren in Kamakura that even his disciples would not know the names of if they saw them. During his life, Nichiren subdued various sects and created enemies across the country, having few supporters left. The supporters that he did retain followed him after hearing his teaching on the Dharma. For this reason, although he realized such feats, they are found only in books. It has already been written that his historical sites are greater in number in Kamakura than in other provinces.[32]

Thus, there are also sites that are not listed in any written works. The *Shinpen Kamakura-shi* was published under these circumstances.

This paper also describe temples with stone signs identifying them as sites associated with Nichiren, stone towers inscribed with histories to self-identify as sacred sites. These public displays of their origins make it clear that they are meant to be considered sacred sites. This is an effort by the temples to further their own development and one undertaken at the request of the public.

Notes

1   Eichi Terao, 2002, 2016.

2   Tsunezō Shinjō, 1982; Takashi Nakao, 1999; Shōsei Suzuki, 2001; Shinchō Mochizuki, 2002; Jun'ichirō Hara, 2007; Jun'ichirō Hara & Kazuhisa Nakayama & Yū Tsutsui & Kenji Nishigai, 2009; Shinchō Mochizuki, 2011; Jun'ichirō Hara, 2013; Keiko Oshida, 2013 et. al.

3   Koreto Ashida, 1929. The page number used in reference to the *Shinpen Kamakura-shi* refer to a version published by him.

4   Koreto Ashida, 1929. (Preface). The entry of *Shinpen Kamakura-shi* (Written by Katsuo Miura) published by the Kokushi Daijiten Editorial Board (1979-1997). The core of *Shinpen Kamakura-shi* was the *Kamakura-nikki* published in 1674 (*Enpō* 2) by Tokugawa Mitsukuni.

5   Ryōzen-ga-saki has been established as a historical site associated with Gokuraku-ji Ninshō. However, because it also mentions Nichiren, the pages related to the life of Nichiren have been indicated.

6   In the *Shinpen Kamakura-shi*, the explanation of this building contained in the passage on the Tatsu-no-Kuchi Persecution quotes from the *Nichiren Shōnin Chūga-san* only, and the statements are not particularly forceful.

7   The temple name of Ankokuron-ji is listed in some modern historical works as Ankoku-ji. Early examples of the use of the name Ankokuron-ji include the *Eitai Monpaku Chakuyō Menkyojō*, dated August 1838 (*Tenpō* 9; collection of Ankokuron-ji), and the *Matsubagayatsu Konpon Reijō Tō* of 1840. However, most historical works up to the Meiji period use the name Ankoku-ji.

8   The entry for "Kamakura" in the Kadokawa Nihon Chimei Daijiten, editorial board (1984).

9   See Tsutomu Shiraishi (1977, p. 312) and Shiori Katō (2002). The existence of the famous sites was confirmed by Katō. Although the name of the Shōtoku 3 edition of the work was the *Revised/Kamakura Meisho-ki* (publisher unknown), it is thought that other "revised editions" were published prior to this date.

10   Kan Harada, 1967. The page number used in reference to the *Tōkaidō Meisho Zue* refer to a version published by him.

11   Kan Harada, 1967; (bibliographical note by Haruhiko Asakura).

12   The four types of the *Kamakura Meisho-ki* in their entirety are reprinted by Tsutomu Shiraishi (1977).

13   Gyōon Kitamura, 1989, pp. 67–68.

14   For research on the erection of Daimoku towers in the early modern age, see Zeshū Endō (1978).

15   The location numbers refer to Eichi Terao, Naofumi Annaka, and Shumbun Homma's "4. Stone Tower Monograph" (2019). The quotes from the famous texts shown below also come from this text.

16   Kamakura-shi Bunka-zai Sōgō Mokuroku editorial board (1987, p. 101). This

tower was lost due to modern construction, so its inscription cannot be confirmed. The same is true for Myōchō-ji 1, Myōchō-ji 3, and Myōchō-ji 6 (stone column part) in the same text. A photo of what Myōchō-ji 1 and 6 looked like in the past is included in the text of Jūkichi Suzuki (1970, p. 56).

17 Takeshi Nakano, 2000.

18 Kokuchūkai Shishiō Bunko collection, it can be viewed in the Risshō University Nichiren Kyōgaku Kenkyū-jo collection photograph file. This text is the same as the history in Gyōon Kitamura (1989, p. 183, 210).

19 Gyōon Kitamura, 1989, p. 221.

20 Chibaken Shiryō Kenkyū Zaidan, 2001, p. 648.

21 Kakimochi is mochi that has been split by hand using a hammer, then dried and cut thinly (Nihon Kokugo Daijiten Editorial Board, 2nd edition, 2000–2002).

22 See Kenitsu Kanmuri (2017) for information on the completion and publication of this text.

23 Yoshiyuki Niikura, 1983, pp. 515, 518.

24 This text indicates that the Hongyō-in of Myōhon-ji In is in the 51st head priest (Yoshiyuki Niikura, 1983), p. 516). The 51st Nisshō died on May 5, 1832 (*Tenpō*3) (Hongyō-in Kako-chō, p. 464). Based on this, this text was completed prior to this date.

25 Kamakurashi Shishi Hensan Iinkai, 1987, p. 5.

26 Kanga Kikuta, 1996, vol. 4, no. 32.

27 The inscription on the left side of this monument is the introduction to the "Hikigayatsu Hakkei Shi" read by Nitchō in 1732). See Myōhon-ji Monjo Kankō-kai (2002, p. 103ff) and Kenitsu Kanmuri (2005, p. 75ff).

28 Takeshi Nakano, 2000, vol. 5, p. 124.

29 Yoshiyuki Niikura, 1983, p. 297.

30 Kamakurashi Shishi Hensan Iinkai, 1987, pp. 6-7. This history is also included in Yoshiyuki Niikura (Ed.), *Myōchō-ji Yurai*, (1983, p. 555).

31 Such progress is noted in the untitled temple history book. Yoshiyuki Niikura, 1983, p. 555.

32 Kamakurashi Shishi Hensan Iinkai, 1987, p. 126.

References

Ashida, K. (ed.) (1929). *Shinpen Kamakurashi: Kamakura Ranshōkō*. Tokyo, Japan: Yūzankaku.

Chibaken Shiryō Kenkyū Zaidan (ed.; Chiba Prefecture Historical Materials Research Foundation). (2001). *Chibaken no rekishi shiryō hen Chuse 3*. Chiba, Japan: Chibaken.

Endō, Z. (1978). "Daimoku hōtō ni miru hokke kyōdan to sono shinkou shizuokaken

Eichi Terao

fuji chiku ni tsuite", in *Nichiren Kyōgaku Kenkkyūsho kiyō*. Issue 5, 9-48.

Hara, J. (2007). *Kinsei Jisha Sankei no Kenkyū*. Kyoto, Japan: Shibunkaku Shuppan.

Hara, J. (2013). *Edo no tabi to Shuppan Bunka*. Tokyo, Japan: Miyaishoten.

Hara, J., Nakayama, K., Tsutsui, Y., Nishigai, K. (2009). *Jisha Sankei to Shomin Bunka*. Tokyo, Japan: Iwata Shoin.

Harada, K. (1967). *Tōkaidō Meisho-zue* (revised). Tokyo, Japan: Jinbutsuōraisha.

Kadokawa Nihon Chimei Daijiten (ed.). (1984). *Kadokawa Nihon Chimei Daijiten, 14 Kanagawa-ken*. Tokyo, Japan: Kadokawa shoten.

Kamakura shi Bunka Zaidan Sōgō Mokuroku Editorial Board. (1987). *Kamakura shi Bunkazai Sōgō Mokuroku–Kenzōbutsu-hen*. Tokyo, Japan: Dohosha Shuppan.

Kamakura shishi Editorial Board. (1987). *Kamakura shishi kinyou shiryou hen dai 2*. Tokyo, Japan: Yoshikawa Kōbunkan.

Kanmuri, K. (2005). *Rokugein Nitchō Shōnin Ihō*. Tokyo, Japan: Chōshi Hōen, Tokyo-shibu.

Kanmuri, K. (2017). "Rokugein Nitchō Cho 'Honge Betsuzu Busso Tōki' Seiritsu Shōkō" in *Ōsaki gaku hō, 173*, 29–64.

Katō, S. (2002). "'Kamakura Meisho-ki' Han Gyō to Sono Shūhen", Bulletin of the Graduate School, Toyo University Graduate Program. Vol. 38 Japanese Literature and Culture (Japanese Literature). 299-324.

Kikuta, K. (ed.). (1996). *Shinshaku Nichiren Shōnin Ichidai Zue*. Tokyo, Japan: Risshō Zendō Kyōkai.

Kitamura, G. (1989) *Kinsei Kaichō no Kenkyū*. Tokyo, Japan: Meicho Shuppan.

Kokushi Daijiten Editorial Board (KDEB) (eds.). (1979–1997). *Kokushi Daijiten*. Tokyo, Japan: Yoshikawa Kōbunkan.

Mochizuki,S. (2002). *Kinsei Nichirenshū no soshishinkō to shugojin shinkō*. Kyoto, Japan: Heirakuji Shoten.

Mochizuki, S. (2011). *Minobu-san shinkō no keisei to denpa*. Tokyo, Japan: Iwata Shoin.

Myōhon-ji Monjo kankōkai. (2002). *Myōhonji Monjo*. Kamakura, Japan: Honzan Hikigayatsu Myōhon-ji.

Nakano, T. (2000). *Ryakuengi shūsei* (Vol. 5). Tokyo, Japan: Bensei Shuppan.

Nakao, T. (1999). *Nichiren shinkō no keifu to girei*. Tokyo, Japan: Yoshikawa Kōbunkan.

Nihonkokugo Daijiten Editorial Board (eds.) (2000–2002). Nihonkokugojiten (2nd ed.). Tokyo, Japan: Shōgakukan.

Niikura, Y. (ed.) (1983). *Ōtakushi (Shiryō hen) Jisha 2*. Tokyo, Japan: Tokyo-to Ōta-ku.

Oshida, K. (2013). "Kamakura ni okeru dentōteki na 'koto kankō' no keishō ni kan suru kenkyū" in *Kyōdo Kanagawa, 51*, 1–27.

Shinjō, T. (1982). *Shinkō Shaji Sankei no Shakai Keizaishiteski Kenkyū*, Tokyo, Japan: Hanawashobō.

Shiraishi, T. (1977). "'Kamakura meishoki' shohan ni tsuite" in *Shidō bunko ronshū*

Vol. 14. 307-343.

Suzuki, J. (1970). *Nichiren Shōninden*, Tokyo, Japan: Kōdensha.

Suzuki, S. (2001). *Edo no Meisho to Toshi Bunka*. Tokyo, Japan: Yoshikawa Kōbunkan.

Terao, E. (2002). "Nichiren Shosha no Kakuban 'Gorinkuji-myō-himitsu-shaku' ni tsuite: Nichiren den no kentō", in Nakao, Takashi (ed.) *Kamakura Bukkyō no Shisō to Bunka,* Tokyo, Japan: Yoshikawa Kōbunkan. 289-311.

Terao, E. (2016). *Nichiren shinkō no rekishi wo saguru*. Tokyo, Japan: Sankibō Busshorin.

Terao, E., Annaka, N., Homma, S. (2019). "Nichiren Shōnin shiseki no saihakken to kenshō no rekishi" in *Kamakura Neparu kennkyū-kiyō*, Rissho University. pp. 1-53.

The Trends and Points of Issue Concerning "The Unification of Kindergarten and Nursery School Systems" after the 1990s in the Context of "Familism"

Kyoko Tanji

Abstract

The objectives of this study are to focus on childcare policies in Japan from the 1990s, sort out the trends concerning the "unification of kindergarten and nursery school systems" and its social background, and discuss these trends from the perspective of "familism." To this end, this paper explores the background of childcare policy from the 1990s through to the 2010s, providing an overview of the debates regarding the "unification of kindergarten and nursery school systems" based on information materials and previous studies on these facilities, while also extracting points of issue regarding childcare policies since the 1990s from the perspective of "familism." The results reveal two points. First, behind the debates over the "unification of kindergarten and nursery school systems" since the 1990s, there have been various changes in education policies, such as (1) countermeasures designed to address the declining birthrate and deregulation measures designed to facilitate them, (2) changes in welfare policies, mainly the reform of basic social welfare structures, and (3) increased concern for early childhood education and the provision of free early childhood education. The second point is the possibility that realization of the "unification of kindergarten and nursery school systems," which dissolves the dual structure, may transcend "familism."

1. Current Problems and the Objectives, Agendas, and Methods of this Study

1.1 Current Problems and the Objectives of this Study

The objectives of this study[1] are to address childcare policies, which are considered to have reached a turning point in the 1990s, in order to clarify the trends and the social backgrounds concerning "unification of kindergarten and nursery school systems," and to discuss these trends from the perspective of "familism." Childcare policies generally cover various forms of childcare, including childcare facilities and homelike childcare, but this paper provides a specific overview of the trends focusing on policies related to childcare facilities. This is because it is thought that policies directly related to childcare facilities which are used by over two thirds of the preschool children in Japan[2] reflect views on childrearing in Japan during infancy and early childhood.[3]

As mentioned earlier, Japan's childcare policies have been in a transition stage since the 1990s. One of the big changes surrounding the system of childcare provided by daycare institutions is the "unification of kindergarten and nursery school systems," which was realized out of concern regarding the dual structure of kindergartens and nursery schools that have been maintained since they were established during the Meiji period.

Here, I would like to review the dual structure of kindergartens and nursery schools, which forms the premise of the discussion in this paper. During the Meiji period, when modernization was proceeding, kindergartens were established as educational facilities mainly for families with housewives. By contrast, nursery schools were established as child welfare facilities for children "lacking childcare" due to work, family situation and health. Table 1 presents a comparison of the institutional differences between kindergartens, nursery schools, and accredited center for early childhood education and care called *nintei-kodomoen* (facilities unifying kindergartens and nursery schools), which were newly established in 2006. The differences in the natures of these two facilities can be clearly found in their purposes. Article 22 of the School Education Act in Japan stipulates that the purpose of kindergartens is to "provide an appropriate environment for bringing up preschoolers for healthy growth and promoting their physical and mental development for cultivating the foundation for compulsory education and the subsequent education," whereas Article 39 of the original Child Welfare Act stipulates that nursery schools are "facility intended for providing childcare services for infants and toddlers who are brought to the facility by their guardians. " The natures of these facilities can be also found in the differences concerning the age of the children receiving daycare and the operating hours of the facilities. Kindergartens whose main purpose is the "education" of toddlers are for "children aged 3 or older until they start elementary school" (Article 26 of the School Education Act). The number of education hours per day is set at "4 hours as a standard" (Course of Study for Kindergartens), and long breaks are provided. On the other hand, nursery schools serving the role of "work support" for parents are for "children aged between 0 and 5" and the length of time for providing childcare is "basically 8 hours per day" (Article 34 of the Standards for Facilities or Operation of Child Welfare Institutions). No long breaks are provided; childcare is provided almost every day except for Sundays and holidays.

Table 1—Institutional differences between kindergartens, nursery schools, and accredited center for early childhood education and care (facilities unifying kindergartens and nursery schools).

Category	Nursery school	Kindergarten	Accredited center for early childhood education and care
Underlying law	Article 39 of the Child Welfare Act (enacted in December 1947)	Articles 22 to 28 of the School Education Act (enacted in March 1947)	Act on Advancement of Comprehensive Service Related to Education, Child Care, etc. of Preschool Children (enacted in June 2006)
Jurisdiction	Ministry of Health, Labour and Welfare, municipalities	Ministry of Education, Culture, Sports, Science and Technology National school: Ministry of Education, Culture, Sports, Science and Technology Public school: Board of education Private school: Prefectures	Cabinet Office, prefectures
Establisher	Local governments (mainly municipalities), social welfare corporations, other corporations, individuals	National and local governments (mainly municipalities), educational corporations, other corporations, individuals	National and local governments, social welfare corporations, educational corporations

Kyoko Tanji

	Facilities intended for providing childcare services for infants and toddlers who are brought to the facility by their guardians (limited to facilities where the capacity of users is 20 or more, excluding accredited center for early childhood education and care) (Child Welfare Act, Article 39)	Facilities intended for providing childcare to toddlers to cultivate the foundation for compulsory education and their subsequent education, offering an appropriate environment to promote their physical and mental development (School Education Act, Article 22)	Facilities intended for providing childcare to children aged 3 or older who need education and childcare in a unified manner to cultivate the foundation for compulsory education and the subsequent education, offering an appropriate environment to facilitate their healthy growth and promote their physical and mental development, and providing childrearing support for parents (Act on Advancement of Comprehensive Service Related to Education, Child Care, etc. of Preschool Children, Article 2 (7))
Purpose			
Conditions of enrollment	When municipalities acknowledge that a guardian's work commitments, illness, or any other reasons cause a lack of daycare regarding an infant or toddler (or other children where necessary) (Child Welfare Act, Article 39) (facilities "provide daycare to infants or toddlers (or other children where necessary) lacking daycare based on entrustment from their guardians on a daily basis" before the 2015 amendment to the Child Welfare Act) Private contract (within the capacity)	When guardians wish for their toddlers to receive childcare	For children aged 3 or older and children under 3 in need of childcare
Ages covered	Infants and toddlers (other children where necessary)	Toddlers aged 3 or older before they enter elementary school	Children before the start of elementary school
When to be enrolled	When a child is in need of childcare	Beginning of the school year (April)	
When to leave	When a child is no longer in need of childcare	End of the school year (March)	

44

Hours providing childcare	Basically 8 hours per day Offer overtime childcare, nighttime childcare, and weekend childcare as well	4 hours per day as a standard The number of weeks providing education in each grade shall not be less than 39 weeks unless there are special circumstances (Ordinance for Enforcement of the School Education Act, Article 37)	Basically open for 11 hours per day and on Saturdays
Closed on and during	Sundays, national holidays, New Year holidays (From December 29 to January 3 of the next year)	Offer long breaks in spring, summer and winter in addition to the days mentioned in the column at left	
Standard of childcare to be provided	Characterized by the provision of nursing and education in a unified manner. The content is pursuant to the principles set forth by the Minister of Health, Labour and Welfare (Standards for Facilities or Operation of Child Welfare Institutions, Article 35) Childcare Guidelines for Nursing Schools	5 domains (health, human relationship, environment, language, and expression) constituting the curriculum according to the Course of Study for Kindergartens as published by the Minister of Education, Culture, Sports, Science and Technology as the standard of the curriculum Course of Study for Kindergartens	Course of Study and Childcare for accredited center for early childhood education and care
Meal service	Provide staple food and side dishes to children under 3 and provide side dishes to children aged 3 or older	Provided by each institution optionally	Obligated to provide meals to children with Type 2 and 3 Certification. Must effectively cook meals within the institution and have their own kitchen
Qualification of nursery teachers	Certificate of qualification as a nursery teacher according to the enforcement order of the Child Welfare Act	Those who have a kindergarten teacher's license according to the Education Personnel Certification Act Specialist, Class 1, and Class 2	Childcare teacher (kindergarten teacher + nursery teacher) * A transitional measure is provided.
Staff (mandatory)	Nursery teacher, contract doctor, cooking staff	Principal, teacher, school doctor	Principal, childcare teacher, school doctor, school dentist, school pharmacist, cooking staff
Staff (others)	School chief, nutritionist, janitor	Nursing teacher, school clerk	Assistance principal, head teacher, senior childcare teacher, supervising childcare teacher, etc.

Kyoko Tanji

Number of children supervised by each nursery teacher	Children aged 0 – 3:1 Children aged 2 and 3 – 6:1 Children aged 3 – 20:1 Children aged 4 and 5 – 30:1	The number of toddlers in one class should be 35 or less	- Children aged 0 to 3 – Same as nursery school - Children aged 3 to 5 – Approximately 20 to 35 children per worker Basically 35 or less in one class
Reguired facilities and equipment	Nursery schools accepting infants or children under 2: Infant room, crawling room, medical room, kitchen, toilet Nursery schools accepting children aged 2 or older: nursery room or playroom, outside playground (outside space near the nursery school equivalent to outside playground), kitchen, toilet Must have materials and tools necessary for childcare (Standards for Facilities or Operation of Child Welfare Institutions)	Faculty room, nursery room, playroom, nurse office, toilet, drinking water equipment, hand-washing facility, foot-washing facility <Facilities and equipment the institutions must try to install> Broadcast listening equipment, projection equipment, play pool, toddler washing facility, meal service facility, library, conference room The building should be no taller than two stories Must have athletic ground and the number and the type of tools and teaching materials necessary (Standards for establishing kindergartens)	According to the ordinance of each prefecture
Relationship with elementary schools	In regard to sharing information on children, documents for supporting children's growth must be sent from the nursery school to the elementary school when the children in the nursery school enter elementary school (Childcare guidelines for nursery schools, Chapter 2)	When a toddler enters elementary school, the principal of the kindergarten must send an abridged copy of the kindergarten toddler's guidance record to the principal of the elementary school (Ordinance for Enforcement of the School Education Act, Article 12 (3))	When a child of the center enters elementary school, the principal of the center must make an abridged copy of the guidance record of the child and sent it to the principal of the elementary school. (Ordinance for Enforcement of the act on Advancement of Comprehensive Service Related to Education, Child Care, etc. of Preschool Children, Article 30 (2))

(Texts added and modifications made to Ueno 2000)

46

The dual structure of kindergartens and nursery schools has been repeatedly debated since the Meiji period, when this structure was established, from the perspective of children's growth and their rights. However, the "unification of kindergarten and nursery school systems" was never institutionalized for a long time. Entering the 2000s, "accredited center for early childhood education and care," which have the functions of both a kindergarten and a nursery school, were institutionalized and positioned systematically as a third type of facility. This marked a major turning point in Japan's childcare system.

As a premise to such a dual structure, there is a tendency to prioritize the work statuses of guardians and home circumstances when choosing the facility, as opposed to the mental and physical status of each child receiving childcare. Here, the idea of "familism" (Esping-Andersen 2009–2011) can be said to exist. Familism takes family members for granted as the bearers of care labor, such as childrearing and nursing care, and depends on the self-help of family members in order to provide care. In other words, the familist idea for prioritizing family over children has supported the dual structure. This raises questions regarding how this "familism" has been maintained and how it changed as a consequence of the institutional "unification of kindergarten and nursery school systems" in the 2000s. This paper also discusses the changes in the "familism" logic behind the policy trend.

In terms of the previous studies discussing both the "unification of kindergarten and nursery school systems" and "familism," a study by Murayama (2016) discusses the policy trend related to the "unification of kindergarten and nursery school systems" from the 1990s, as well as its social background. As far as I know, however, there are no studies discussing policies related to the "unification of kindergarten and nursery school systems" since the 1990s from the perspective of "familism." In terms of "familism" in childcare policies, there are previous studies in relevant fields, such as family sociology and social welfare studies. Examples of research on childcare policies after the 1990s and their social background include a study by Nakamura (2009) discussing post-war childcare policies from the perspective of welfare regime and children's rights and an article by Shimoebisu (2015) discussing the positioning of the family in childrearing/nursing care policies. However, no studies can be found discussing the trend toward the "unification of kindergarten and nursery school systems," including early childhood education. Bearing these facts in mind, this study holds scholarly significance in its cross-sectorial approach by discussing the three phases: "education," "childcare (care)," and "family," all of which are essential in the childcare of preschool children.

Therefore, this study focuses on childcare policies from the 1990s, when the roles of kindergartens and nursery schools were questioned, and clarifies social circumstances and debates surrounding kindergartens, nursery schools, and the "unification of kindergarten and nursery school systems." It also examines the logic behind the trend of these childcare policies in terms of the prioritization of the family (familism), which serves as the foundation of the dual structure of kindergartens and nursery schools. Specifically, the first section reviews the social background surrounding kindergartens and nursery schools, the second section provides an overview of the debates surrounding the "unification of kindergarten and nursery school systems" since the 1990s, as well as policy changes, and the last section discusses the trend of these childcare policies from the viewpoint of "familism."

1.2 Methods

This study employs the methodology of a literature study using information materials and documents. Specifically, law-related documents obtained from the website of the Ministry of Education, Culture, Sports, Science and Technology, and Ministry of Health, Labour and Welfare, municipalities, brochures for the general public and practical guides of policies for childcare practitioners, are used to understand the shifts in childcare measures. In addition, the background behind the childcare policies of the 1990s and the 2010s is explored, while a comprehensive overview of the debates over the "unification of kindergarten and nursery school systems" is provided based on studies regarding women-related policies, family policies, childcare policies, and childcare systems. Using these resources, points of issue regarding childcare policies since the 1990s will be extracted from the perspective of "familism."

2. The Social and Policy Background Surrounding Kindergartens and Nursery Schools

Behind the debates over the "unification of kindergarten and nursery school systems" since the 1990s are various policy trends, such as countermeasures designed to address the declining birthrate, a relaxation of regulations aiming to facilitate this process, and the introduction of market principles, as well as shifts in welfare and education policies. Therefore, I would like to outline (1) countermeasures to the declining birthrate, (2) welfare policies, and (3) education policies in order to look into their connections with childcare policies. This will be done based on previous studies, including Yokoyama (2002), Nakamura (2009), Maeda (2014), Kondo (2016), Murayama (2016), and Morikawa (2017).

2.1 Countermeasures Designed to Address the Declining Birthrate and the Relaxation of Regulations[4]

2.1.1 Ever-declining birthrate and countermeasures designed to address this process

The "declining birthrate" became a social problem in Japan in the 1990s. The total fertility rate (the average number of children a woman gives birth to in her life) peaked in Japan during the second baby boom of the early 1970s and has been on a downward trend ever since. In 1975, it dropped below the 2.0 level to 1.91. In addition, the downward trend has become even more prominent since the late 1980s. In 1989, the fertility rate was lower than the 1966 fertility rate of 1.58, which was a Hinoeuma year known for having an extremely low fertility rate.[5] The 1989 fertility rate was called "1.57 shock," which drew attention to the "declining birthrate" as an important social issue.

The Japanese government felt a strong sense of crisis regarding this ever-declining birthrate and began to work on countermeasures designed to address the trend in cooperation with various ministries and agencies. In 1990, the government established a "liaison council concerning the establishment of an environment for giving birth to and rearing children in a healthy manner," which consisted of members from 14 relevant ministries and agencies. The report submitted by this council the following year, titled "About the establishment of an environment for giving birth to and rearing children in a healthy manner," attributed the decline in the fertility rate mainly to the rise in the percentage of unmarried women in their 20s and the lowering of the fertility capabilities of couples, pointing out that the increased burden toward marriage and childrearing constituted the "problem." Based on these factors, the government announced the "basic policy for future childcare support measures" (commonly called Angel Plan) in 1994. This

---

Kyoko Tanji

was a comprehensive childrearing support plan developed based on an agreement between the ministers of Health and Welfare, Education, Labour, and Construction at the time. The focus of the plan was the enrichment of childcare services. The initiatives it introduced included "expanded acceptance of early-age children," "spread of overtime childcare" at nursery schools, and "enhancement of the regional childrearing support centers," all of which are stipulated in the "Five-year project for urgent childcare measures" for putting the Angel Plan into practice.

Since then, the government has set out both a policy direction and a concrete plan every five years designed to facilitate childrearing support measures in an effort to counteract the declining birthrate. In 1999, a "concrete plan to implement countermeasures to the declining birthrate that should be facilitated as priority" (commonly called New Angel Plan) was formulated based on the "Basic policy for facilitating countermeasures to the declining birthrate," and then, in 2004, a "plan for supporting children and childrearing" was formulated under the "Outline of measures for a society with fewer children" and approved by the Cabinet. Furthermore, the Cabinet approved a "vision for children and childrearing" in 2010 and began to work on the concept of the new "Comprehensive Support System for Children and Childrearing," which was later introduced as a new framework from the fiscal year 2015 onward. In conjunction with these efforts, the government also expanded childcare services for early-age children to include children under 3. Focusing especially on countermeasures to the problem of "waiting-list children" since the 2000s,[6] the "zero-waiting list for nursery schools strategy" was initiated in 2001, the "new zero-waiting list for nursery schools strategy" in 2008, and the "pre-emptive plan to eliminate waiting-list children" in 2013.

However, even after the 1990s, when the countermeasures designed to address the declining birthrate were initiated, the total fertility rate continued to drop, reaching the record low of 1.26 in 2005. Since then, the number has risen slightly, but it is still at a low level compared to European countries and the United States. Since 2007, even though the total fertility rate has increased, the total number of women of childbearing age has decreased, resulting in a concurrent decline in the number of births. In 2016, the number of births dropped below 1 million, before falling to a record low of 940,000 in 2017 (National Association for Childcare Organizations, Hoiku-kenkyujo (ed.) 2018).

It is thus difficult to say that these policies have been successfully implemented; however, the countermeasures introduced to tackle the declining birthrate that have been initiated for nearly 30 years since the 1990s have gradually changed the operations of kindergartens and nursery schools. For example, in terms of kindergartens, it used to be a general rule for children to wait until April after they turned 3 years old, but now "three-year enrollment" has been institutionalized, meaning children can be enrolled from their third birthday. In addition, in order to accommodate the increased childcare needs, the "project for promoting after-hour childcare" was initiated in the fiscal year 1997 to provide "after-hour childcare" outside the curriculum of the kindergartens. As part of the countermeasures designed to address the declining birthrate, kindergartens began to partially fulfill the functions of nursery schools, offering long-hour childcare services intended to support the childcare of early-age children and the work of their guardians. As both kindergartens and nursery schools began to work on activities designed to support childrearing families of the region in an effort to support childrearing, the functions of kindergartens and nursery schools became increasingly similar as a consequence of the countermeasures designed to address the declining birthrate, which facilitated institutional unification (Tanji 2006, 2009).

2.1.2 Deregulation and the introduction of market principles

Seeing the trend of reforms in Europe and the United States, the Japanese government underwent a neoliberal policy shift following the administrative reforms that took place under the second Ad Hoc Commission on Administrative Reform in the 1980s in an effort to promote "decentralization" and "deregulation" as basic objectives.[7] This neoliberal reform, which was considered one of the methods used in implementing the countermeasures designed to address the declining birthrate, had a significant impact on childcare policies.

Since the 2000s especially, a series of deregulatory measures were initiated in relation to registered nursery schools as a way of lowering the growing number of waiting-list children. In 2000, the then Minister of Health and Welfare released a notice titled "About approval of the establishment of nursery schools," which consisted of three pillars: (1) the removal of restrictions on 'establishers' (establishment by private-sector entities (NPOs, school corporations, other corporations, business corporations) other than social welfare corporations was approved if certain standards were met); (2) a reconsideration of the requirement to self-own the facilities (the land and buildings of the nursery school must be basically self-owned but renting was now permitted); and (3) a relaxation of the capacity requirement (the minimum capacity requirement was lowered from 30 to 20).

While these deregulation measures were undertaken, the local governments of urban areas where there are many waiting-list children began to introduce their own systems. For example, Tokyo has set its own standards by relaxing the "Minimum Standards for Child Welfare Facilities" (renamed in 2011 as Standards for Facilities or Operation of Child Welfare Institutions), which stipulates national uniform standards for facilities regarding nursery room areas and staff allocation, and began the "certification system for nursery schools" in an effort to provide subsidies to nursery schools that met the standards. These frameworks, where the local governments independently provide subsidies designed to cover operational expenses, are intended for non-registered day-care facilities from a legal point of view, but they were also adopted by other local governments, mainly in the Tokyo metropolitan area including Sendai City and Yokohama City, in order to accommodate the waiting-list children (Yoshida 2002).

These efforts led school corporations to establish nursery schools by eliminating restrictions on the establishers of registered nursery schools and the certification systems of local governments. Thus, neoliberalism was one of the main factors that facilitated the "unification of kindergarten and nursery school systems."

2.2 Changes in Welfare Policies – Reform of the Basic Social Welfare Structure[8]

From the 1990s onward, an effort to reform the basic social welfare structure was enacted. This process was undertaken not only in the field of child welfare, which includes nursery schools, but also through wider welfare reforms, including welfare for the elderly and the disabled. The reform of the basic social welfare structure represented an attempt to shift from a system of "measures," administrative actions premised on actions designed to save the needy after World War II, to a system of "contract," which aims to build equal relationships between users and welfare service providers. As the national government sets national uniform standards meaning facilities are run by public funds under the principle of non-discrimination and equality, government organizations have basically decided what services to provide and

which provider should provide them. However, with the new contract-based
system, users can choose what facility or which provider they use based on
their own needs.

For example, in the field of welfare for the elderly, nursing care insurance
was introduced in 2000. This led to fundamental institutional reforms shifting from "measures" to "contracts." Here, municipalities assume the task of
certifying the need for nursing care, such as "certification of long-term care
need," while users sign contracts directly with service providers. In the field
of welfare for the disabled, the Assistance Benefit Supply System was adopted. Following this, in 2006, the Services and Supports for Persons with
Disabilities Act was also enacted.

During the course of these reforms, efforts were made to revise the Child
Welfare Act, which is the law governing nursery schools. In March 1996, the
Ministry of Health and Welfare launched a task force aiming to address the
basic problems within the Central Child Welfare Council and compiled an interim report titled "About the childcare system appropriate for a society with
fewer children." This report pointed out that in the current system, municipalities decide whether children are lacking in childcare and place those deemed
to be so in nursery schools. Thus, it is "not a framework where users could
have a choice institutionally." It also suggested that "it should be a structure
where users can choose which nursery school to go to and what childcare
services to receive" in the future.

In response to this interim report, the 1996 revised Child Welfare Act stipulated that "when there is a lack in daycare of an infant or a toddler and when
the guardian applies, a municipal government shall provide daycare to those
children in a nursery center" (Article 24 (1)), in regard to enrollment. This
amendment legally turned nursery schools into facilities that guardians "can
choose," much like kindergartens. However, because municipal governments
still assumed no responsibility for childcare and the issue of waiting-list children was becoming a problem in urban areas, users could apply for enrollment
but had virtually no choice regarding which school to attend. It was after the
deregulation policy was initiated in 2000 when various service providers appeared in the field of childcare. The direct contract method was adopted on
a full scale after the new "Comprehensive Support System for Children and
Childrearing" began in the fiscal year 2015. These results indicate that the
reform of the basic social welfare structure has had a long-term impact on the
system of childcare.

2.3 Changes in Education Policies – Free Early Childhood Education[9]

The debate over "free early childhood education" that arose in the 2000s influenced how kindergartens, as educational institutions, should provide services. Behind this debate was an increased global concern for preschool education in the latter half of the 20th century (OECD 2006–2011, Izumi, et al. (eds.) 2008). Preschool education also drew attention from the perspective of economy growth strategy, as children were considered subjects of social investment (Ikemoto 2011, Heckman 2013–2015). In response to such concern and hope for preschool education, in 2006 the Japanese government announced the "Basic Policies Regarding Economic and Fiscal Management and Structural Reform 2006," stating that "it would work on strengthening the educational functions of kindergartens and nursery schools and promoting early childhood education by expanding measures to lessen the preschool education burden placed on guardians while comprehensively considering the funding and institutional issues in conjunction with the revenue reform, in order to make early childhood education free in the future." In response to this, the Ministry of Education, Culture, Sports, Science and Technology established the "Study group for methods to promote early childhood education in the future" in 2008 in an effort to comprehensively consider how to make early childhood education free. It also compiled a report titled "About free early childhood education (interim report)" in 2009. This report states that "substantially guaranteeing opportunities for all toddlers to receive education by having the society bear the cost for early childhood education and making early childhood education free is an urgent issue in Japan's national strategies" (4). This is due to reasons such as that early childhood education's "educational and socio-economic effects are becoming evident empirically," the "lessening of financial burdens is necessary as a measure to be implemented against the declining birthrate," and that "other countries that have recognized its importance are now working on making early childhood education free." Such a policy for making early childhood education free was a suggestion that went beyond the traditional dual structure and led to the "unification of kindergarten and nursery school systems" in that it suggested all toddlers should be covered by public funds regardless of the institutional differences between kindergartens and nursery schools.

Thus, behind the debates over the "unification of kindergarten and nursery school systems" since the 1990s were wider changes in education policies, such as: (1) countermeasures designed to address the declining birthrate and deregulation measures introduced to facilitate them; (2) changes in welfare policies, mainly the reform of basic social welfare structures; and (3) increased concern for early childhood education and the provision of free early childhood education. These social and policy changes encouraged people to question the dual structure of kindergartens and nursery schools, which had been maintained since they were institutionalized.

3. Debates Over the "Unification of Kindergarten and Nursery School Systems" since the 1990s

A range of debates were held over the "unification of kindergarten and nursery school systems" since the 1990s, as well as over what kind of institutional changes were made. In this section, I will provide an overview of the kinds of debate that were held in each era, as well as how the "unification of kindergarten and nursery school systems" was institutionalized, using Morita (2000), Yoshida (2002), Nakata (2015), and Murayama (2016) as references.

3.1 Debates Over the "Unification of Kindergarten and Nursery School Systems" in the 1990s – Exploring Linkage

The debates over the institutional "unification of kindergarten and nursery school systems" in the 1990s arose during the course of exploring decentralization in conjunction with the administrative reform movement. In 1995, the Law for the Promotion of Decentralization was enacted, which led to the establishment of the Committee for the Promotion of Decentralization. In 1996, the committee offered its first recommendation, that "flexible operation must be established through shared use of kindergarten and nursery school facilities, in order to strengthen linkage between kindergartens and nursery schools and unify the relevant facilities, according to the local circumstances, so that the diverse needs of children and families could be met in a time of low birthrates" (270). To meet the needs of families with children, it was suggested to effectively use facilities and equipment according to the local circumstances without being bound by the segmentation of kindergartens and nursery schools. In response to this recommendation, in 1997 the Ministry of Education and the Ministry of Health and Welfare began discussions on the links between kindergartens and nursery schools. In March 1998, they jointly announced the "guidelines for the shared use of kindergartens and nursery school facilities." The guidelines acknowledge shared use of the facilities of kindergartens and nursery schools, provided that both the Standards for establishing kindergartens and the Minimum Standards for Child Welfare Facilities are met in terms of the reference area of the facilities and the number of staff members.

Thus, the debates over the "unification of kindergarten and nursery school systems" in the 1990s led to the "guidelines for the shared use," which contributed to partially removing the institutional barriers between kindergartens and nursery schools against a backdrop of social changes and administrative reforms. Although no discussions or policies that question the dual structure itself were found, this was when the functions and the roles of kindergartens and nursery schools changed.

3.2 Debates Over the "Unification of Kindergarten and Nursery School Systems" in the 2000s – Deregulation and Institutionalization

The neoliberal reforms progressed in the 2000s. The "Basic Policies Regarding Economic and Fiscal Management and Structural Reform 2003," approved by the Cabinet in 2003, stated that it would be possible to establish a unified comprehensive facility by regarding preschool education and childcare as one package according to the local needs (to be considered by the fiscal year 2006), and that it would be further encouraged to have both qualifications and share the use of facilities and equipment of kindergartens and nursery schools. The "comprehensive facility" presented here was institutionalized later as "accredited center for early childhood education and care" when the "Act on Advancement of Comprehensive Service Related to Education, Child Care, etc. of Preschool Children" was formulated in 2006.

The system of accredited center for early childhood education and care is a system that certifies a kindergarten or a nursery school as an "accredited center for early childhood education and care" when it has the "function of providing both childhood education and childcare to preschool children" (a function of providing education and childcare in a unified manner by accepting children regardless of the work status of the guardians), and the "function of providing childrearing support in the region." There are four types of accredited center for early childhood education and care: the "kindergarten-nursery school unified type," which can accept children aged between 0 and 5 and have the functions of both kindergartens and nursery schools; the "kindergarten type," which were transformed from kindergartens; the "nursery school type," which were transformed from nursery schools; and the "local discretion type," which includes anything other than the above. The Ministry of Education, Culture, Sports, Science and Technology had jurisdiction over kindergartens, while the Ministry of Health, Labor and Welfare had jurisdiction over nursery schools. As the Cabinet Office had jurisdiction over accredited center for early childhood education and care, some raised criticisms that the dual structure became a "ternary structure" together with both kindergartens (Ministry of Education, Culture, Sports, Science and Technology) and nursery schools (Ministry of Health, Labor and Welfare). Accredited center for early childhood education and care back then were positioned as the third type of facilities, next to kindergartens and nursery schools, and did not lead to a fundamental review of the dual structure of kindergartens and nursery schools themselves.

3.3 Debates Over the "Unification of Kindergarten and Nursery School Systems" in the 2010s – Reconsideration of the Entire Childcare System

The big topic in the 2010s has been the introduction of the new "Comprehensive Support System for Children and Childrearing" (hereinafter "New System"), which began in the fiscal year 2015 and was designed to reconsider the dual structure of kindergartens and nursery schools. This system is aimed at running accredited centers for early childhood education and care at full scale and enriching comprehensive childrearing support in order to both overcome the quantitative and qualitative shortages of childrearing support and dissolve the dual structure of kindergartens and nursery schools (vertically segmented administrative system) against the backdrop of the declining birthrate.

There are two major differences between the New System and the dual structure of kindergartens and nursery schools. One is the use of the expression "level of childcare needs" as a standard for the provision of childcare, while the other is the change in how guardians bear the expenses.

As shown in Table 1, in the previous system, one needed a certain reason causing a "lack in childcare" in order to have the children in question enrolled in a certified nursing school, and children were allowed to be enrolled only when family members or relatives living together could not provide child-care. However, in the new "Comprehensive Support System for Children and Childrearing," children receive one of the three certifications (Type 1 to Type 3) listed below, regardless of their guardians' financial circumstances, according to their "level of childcare needs" when entering an accredited early childhood care center, a kindergarten (except for some private kindergartens), or a nursery school, and choose a facility to attend according to the result of the certification.

Type 1 Certification: Early child education provided to children aged 3 or older from households that are not in need of childcare, such as households with a full-time housewife

Type 2 Certification: Childcare provided to children aged 3 or older who are in need of childcare due to the work commitments or other factors of their guardians

Type 3 Certification: Childcare provided to children under 3 who are in need of childcare due to the work commitments or other factors of their guardians

The above structure covers all preschool children who wish to receive childcare at providers' facilities, and uses the expression "level of childcare needs" relating to the children themselves as a standard for the provision of childcare. Of course, it is necessary to grasp the guardians' statuses when determining the type of certification. However, compared with the previous dual structure of kindergartens and nursery schools, where the guardians' statuses were used as a standard, the New System has a very different approach toward childcare as it sees children themselves as the main entity of childcare.

In addition, the "principle of ability to pay" (determining the childcare fee according to income) was employed in nursery schools from the perspective of work support for guardians and child welfare. On the other hand, because kindergartens were positioned as educational institutions premised on the guardians' wishes, the "benefit principle" (pay fees according to the services received regardless of income) was employed in order to collect uniform fees regardless of the circumstances of domestic finance. However, in this new "Comprehensive Support System for Children and Childrearing," this was changed to the "principle of ability to pay," where guardians' fees change according to household income (except for some private kindergartens). This is a mindset that went beyond the dual structure of kindergartens and nursery schools in that the burden placed on all preschool children receiving child-care was made equal (Tanji 2016a).

4. Discussion and Future Research

As mentioned at the beginning, in the dual structure of kindergartens and nursery schools that has been maintained since they were institutionalized, a priority was placed on family lifestyles, such as the work of guardians, rather than on mental and physical conditions of each child. Family members were taken for granted in rearing infants and toddlers, which was the premise of the dual structure of kindergartens and nursery schools. Japan's welfare regime is described as "familism" (Shimoebisu 2015), but the dual structure of kindergartens and nursery schools in particular is probably the embodiment of this "familism."

If so, the movement toward the institutional "unification of kindergarten and nursery school systems" introduced to dissolve the dual structure can be regarded as a trend that goes beyond "familism." For example, in the countermeasures designed to address the declining birthrate, along with the increased number of users of nursery schools and the provision of long-hour childcare at kindergartens and nursery schools, the functions of kindergartens and nursery schools proportionally expanded while the roles of family members in childrearing shrank. In the reform of the basic social welfare structure, nursery schools were turned into facilities that guardians can choose, just like kindergartens, while the system of "measures," where government organizations decide which service to provide and what provider to use, was turned into the system of "choice." Nursery schools were facilities used "out of necessity" due to reasons such as work, which was also reflected in the system of social welfare. However, through the structural reform, they turned into facilities that can also be used by those who want to use them. Furthermore, in education policies, early childhood education will also be publicly guaranteed for all children, regardless of their household's financial circumstances, such that if the "costs related to early childhood education are borne by society as a whole...the opportunity for all toddlers to receive early childhood education is substantially guaranteed." Thus, because the dual structure of kindergartens and nursery schools is premised on "familism," the trend concerning the "unification of kindergarten and nursery school systems" leads to an escape from "familism." Furthermore, if we look beyond this "unification of kindergarten and nursery school systems," we can get a glimpse of the issues that lie beyond such "de-familiarization in childrearing (socialization)."

The certification structure of the "level of childcare needs" in the new "Comprehensive Support System for Children and Childrearing" is modeled after the "nursing-care insurance system" introduced in 2000. This is a structure that sees the elderly as "persons concerned," determines the level of their nursing care needs based on their necessity, and provides care not premised on the presence of family members as the bearers of nursing care (Hoiku-kenkyujo 2014). In the certification standard of the "level of childcare needs" of "children" regarding the new "Comprehensive Support System for Children and Childrearing," the concept of "persons concerned" in childrearing has shifted from the family to children in an attempt to see children individually, as is the case with the domain of nursing care. This indicates a possibility of "individualization" ahead of "de-familiarization (socialization) in childrearing" beyond "familism" (Beck 1986–1998).

This paper has shown that there was an early indication that went beyond "familism," and was taken for granted in modern times during the course of the "unification of kindergarten and nursery school systems," that transcends the dual structure of kindergartens and nursery schools.

Questions remain regarding the kind of childrearing that could be achieved beyond "de-familiarization in childrearing (socialization)." In the future, I would like to explore the possibility of reaching "individualization."

Acknowledgements

This work is a portion of the findings of a study supported by JSPS KAKENHI Grant Number JP16K21425 (principal investigator: Kyoko TANJI).

Notes

1. For this article, texts were added and modifications were partially made to Tanji, K., 2019, "The trend and point of issue concerning "The unification of kindergarten and nursery school systems" after the 1990s: on "Familism" *Journal of Educational Research for Human Coexistence* 6, pp.19-30.

2. As of FY2016, over 65% of preschool children in Japan (over 95% of children aged 4 or older) go to kindergartens, nursery schools or accredited center for early childhood education and care (institutionalized as facilities for integrating the functions of kindergartens and nursery schools in the 2000s) (ed. National Association for Childcare Organizations, Hoiku-kenkyujo 2018).
3. Considering this, the findings obtained through this study can contribute to helping understand the unique context of Japan in terms of its systems and policies in the area of Early Childhood Education and Care (ECEC), which have drawn international attention.
4. I will discuss countermeasures to the falling birthrate by referring mainly to Yokohama (2002), Nakamura (2009), Maeda (2014), Kondo (2016), and Morikawa (2017).
5. Hinoeuma is one of the oriental zodiacs. Since the Edo period, there has been a superstition that those born in Hinoeuma year have fiery temperaments and that women born in this year will make their husbands die early. Because of this superstition, the fertility rate of 1966 was also low.
6. The concept of waiting-list children was introduced as "children whose application form for entering a nursery school is submitted to the municipality, who fulfill the enrollment requirements but are not enrolled currently in any nursery schools. 'Waiting-list children' also include those whose guardians are on leave and those who currently use independent projects undertaken by the local government (e.g. childcare moms) but wish to be enrolled in a nursery school," (old definition) according to the 1999 notice written by the Chief of the Day Care Division of the Children and Families Bureau. The latter half of this definition (from "and those who currently use independent projects undertaken by the local government" section onward) was modified in 2001 to "but exclude children when independent projects are undertaken by the local governments (e.g. childcare moms) and those who wish to go to a certain nursery school and are on a waiting list due to personal reasons of the guardians (new definition" (Kondo 2016). Some have pointed out that the new definition might increase the number of "hidden waiting-list children," who are not included in the number of waiting-list children even though they couldn't enter any registered nursery schools.
7. Neoliberalism refers to economic policy to relax or eliminate regulations and introduce market principles in order to facilitate growth using the free power of the private sector, under the idea of "small government," which means shrinking the role of the government.
8. Welfare policies are discussed mainly by referring to Nakamura (2009), Maeda (2014), Kondo (2016), Morikawa (2017).
9. Education policies are discussed by mainly referring to Weikart (2000=2015), Murayama (2016).

References

Beck Ulrich, 1986, Risikogesellschaft auf dem Weg in eine andere Moderne,Frankfurt am Main: Surkamp Verlag. (–1998, trans. Azuma, R. & Ito, M., *Kiken shakai atarashii kindai eno michi* [Dangerous society: A path to new modern times] Hosei University Press).

Central Child Welfare Council Task Force for Addressing Basic Problems, 1996, "Shoshika shakai ni fusawashii hoiku shisutemu nit suite" [About the childcare system appropriate for a society with fewer children] (https://www.mhlw.go.jp/www1/shingi/1203-3.html, last checked on January 30, 2019)

Committee for the Promotion of Decentralization, 1996, "Committee for the Promotion of Decentralization First Recommendation: Creation of decentralized society" (http://www.ipss.go.jp/publication/j/shiryou/no.13/data/shiryou/syakai-fukushi/606.pdf, last checked on January 30, 2019)

Council on Fiscal and Economic Policy, 2003, "Basic Policies for Economic and Fiscal Management and Structural Reform 2003" (https://www.kantei.go.jp/jp/singi/keizai/kakugi/030627f.html, last checked on January 30, 2019)

Esping-Andersen, G., 1990, The Three Worlds of Welfare Capitalism, Cambridge: Polity Press (–2001, trans. Okazawa, N. & Miyamoto, T. *Fukushi shihonshugi no mittsu no sekai: Hikakufukushikokka no riron to dotai* [Three worlds of welfare capitalism: Theory and dynamics of comparative welfare state] Minerva Shobo).

Esping-Andersen, G., 1999, Social Foundations of Postindustrial Economics, London: Oxford University Press (–2000, trans. Watanabe, M. & Watanabe, K. *Posuto kogyo keizai no shakaiteki kiso: Shijo, fukushi kokka, kazoku no seiji keizaigaku* [Social foundation of post-industrial economy: Political economic science of market, welfare state and family] Sakurai Shoten).

Esping-Andersen, G., 2009, The Incomplete Revolution: Adapting to Women's New Roles, Cambridge: Polity Press. (–2011, trans. Osawa, M. *Byodo to kouritsu no fukushi kakumei: Atarasii josei no yakuwari* [Welfare revolution with equality and efficiency: New role of women] Iwanami Shoten).

Funabashi, K., 2018, "'Kodomo kosodate shien shin-seido' ni miru kosodate shakai no shakaika no tokucho: yoroppa no senko jirei to hikakushitsutsu" [Characteristics of socialization of childrearing seen in the Comprehensive Support System for Children and Childrearing – Compared with the preceding case in Europe] *Journal of Ohara Institute for Social Research 722*, pp. 17-32.

Heckman, J.J., 2013, Giving Kids a Fair Chance, The MIT Press. (–2015, ed. Furukusa, H. *Yojikyoiku no keizaigaku* [Economic science of early childhood education] Toyo Keizai Shimposha).

Hoiku-kenkyujo (ed.), 2014, *Koredewakaru! Kodomo kosodate shien shin-seido: Seidorikai to taio no pointo* [You can understand it now! Comprehensive Support System for Children and Childrearing: To understand the system and how to deal with it] Chiisai Nakama Sha.

Ikemoto, M., 2011, "Keizaiseicho senryaku toshite chumoku sareru yojikyoiku, hoikuseisaku: Shogaikoku no doko o chushin ni" [Early childhood education and childcare policy drawing attention as economic growth strategy: With a focus on the trends seen in various countries] *Journal of Educational Sociology 88*, pp. 27-45.

Inokuma, H., 2018, "Kodomo kosodate shien shin-seido ga motarasu hoiku no shakaika to sijoka: hoiku wa dareno mononanoka?" [Socialization and marketization of childcare caused by the Comprehensive Support System for Children and Childrearing: Who does childcare belong to?] *Journal of Ohara Institute for Social Research 722*, pp. 33-57.

Izumi, C. et al. (and eds.), 2008, *Sekai no yoji kyoiku kaikaku to gakuryoku* [Early childhood education of the world, childcare reform and academic ability] Akashi Shoten.

Kondo, M., 2016, "Shoshika taisaku to hoiku shisaku" [Countermeasures to the declining birthrate and childcare measures] Japan Society of Research on Early Childhood Care and Education (ed.), *Hoikugaku koza 2 – hoiku o sasaeru shikumi: seido to gyosei* [Childcare study lecture 2 – Structure supporting childcare: Institution and administration] University of Tokyo Press, pp. 31-49.

Liaison council concerning the establishment of an environment for giving birth to and rearing children in a healthy manner, 1991, "Sukoyakani kodomo o umisodateru kankyo zukuri nit suite" [About the establishment of an environment for giving birth to and rearing children in a healthy manner] (http://www.ipss.go.jp/ publication/j/shiryou/no.13/data/shiryou/syakaifukushi/410.pdf, last checked on January 30, 2019)

Maeda, M., 2014, Minna de tsukuru kodomo kosodate shin-seido [Comprehensive Support System for Children and Childrearing created by everyone] Minerva Shobo.

Matsuki, H., 2013, *Kosodate shien no shakaigaku: shakaika no jirenma to kazoku no henyo* [Social science of childrearing support: dilemma of socialization and changes of family] Shinsensha.

Ministry of Health and Welfare, 2000, "Hoikujo no secchibninka-tou nit suite" [About approval of establishing nursery schools] (https://www.mhlw.go.jp/web/t_doc?-dataId=00ta9197&dataType=1&pageNo=1, last checked on January 30, 2019)

Morikawa, T., 2017, "Sengo hoiku taisei tankan no taido" [Signs of post-war transformation of childcare system] Shiomi, T., Matsumoto, S., Takada, F., Yaji, Y. & Morikawa, T. Nihon no hoiku no rekisi: Kodomo kan to hoiku no rekishi 150-nen [Japan's history of childcare: Views on children and 150 years of childcare history] Houbun Shorin, pp. 341-373.

Morita, A. (and eds.), 2000, *Yoshien ga kawaru hoikujo ga kawaru jichitai-hatsu: chiiki de sodateru hoiku-ichigenka* [Kindergartens are changing, nursery schools are changing, Initiated by municipal governments: Childcare unification cultivated locally] Akashi Shoten.

Murayama, Y., 2016, "Sengo no 'ichigenka-ron' 'ichigenka, ittaika seisaku' no dokoto kadai" [Trend and issues of post-war 'centralization theory' and 'centralization and unification policy] Japan Society of Research on Early Childhood Care and Education (ed.), *Hoikugaku koza 2 – hoiku o sasaeru shikumi: seido to gyosei* [Childcare study lecture 2 – Structure supporting childcare: Institution and administration] University of Tokyo Press, pp. 51-89.

Nakamura, T., 2009, *Sengo hoiku seisaku no ayumi to hoiku no yukue* [The path that post-war childcare policy has taken and the path childcare will take] Shin Dokusho Sha.

Nakata, T., 2015, "Kodomo kosodate shienho no shokai: Yoho-ichigenka ni mukete" [Introduction of Children and Child Rearing Support Act: Toward unification of kindergarten and nursery school systems] Oyobe, Y., Yamaguchi, S. & Iri, T. (and eds.) Sakaifukushi to jenda: Sugimoto kiyoe sensei taishoku kinen ronshu [Social welfare and gender: A collection of essays to celebrate the retirement of Professor Kiyoe Sugimoto] Minerva Shobo, pp. 237-245.

National Association for Childcare Organizations, Hoiku-kenkyujo (ed.), 2018, *Hoiku hakusho 2018-nen ban* [Childcare whitepaper 2018 edition] Hitonaru Shobo.

Ochiai, E., 2015, "'Nihon-gata fukushu rejimu wa naze kazokushugi no mama nanoka: 4-hokoku eno komento" [Why Does the Japanese Welfare Regime Remain Familialist?: Comments on Four Papers] *Japanese Journal of Family Sociology 27(1)*, pp. 61-68.

OECD, 2006, Starting Strong II: Early Childhood Education and Care, OECD publishing. (–2011, Hoshi, M. et al. (trans.) *OECD hoiku hakusho – Jinsei no hajimari koso chikarazuyoku: nyuyojiki no kyoiku to kea (ECEC) no kokusai hikaku* [OECD Childcare Whitepaper – Be strong at the beginning of life: International comparison of education and care during infancy and early childhood] Akashi Shoten).

Shimoebisu, M., 2000, "'Kosodate shien' no genjo to ronri" [Current status and logic of "childrearing support"] Fujisaki, H. (ed.) Oyatoko: Kosakusuru raifu kosu [Parents and children: Intermingled life course] Minerva Shobo, pp. 271-295.

Shimoebisu, M., 2015, "Kea seisaku ni okeru Kazoku no ichi" [The position of family in care policy] *Japanese Journal of Family Sociology 27(1)*, pp. 49-60.

Study Group for Methods to Promote Early Childhood Education in the Future, 2009, "Yojikyoiku no mushoka ni tsuite (chukan hokoku)" [About free early childhood education (interim report)] (http://www.mext.go.jp/component/b_menu/shingi/toushin/_icsFiles/afieldfile/2009/05/27/1267537_2.pdf, last checked on January 30, 2019)

Tanji, K., 2006, "Yochien hoikujo no kino-kakudai to yohoichigenka – kikan o taisho to shita shitsumonsi-chosa no kekka o motoni" [Expansion of the functions of kindergartens and nursery schools and unification of kindergarten and nursery school systems: Based on the results of the questionnaire survey conducted with institutions] *Research on Early Childhood Care and Education in Japan 44 (2)*, pp. 114-125.

Tanji, K., 2009, "Yochien hoikujo no 'seidoteki ichigenka' eno shikosei: 2000-nen-dainiokeru 'kinokakudai' tono kanren kara" [Orientation toward "institutional unification" of kindergartens and nursery schools: In relation with "function expansion" in the 2000s] *Journal of Child Study 15*, pp. 149-162.

Tanji, K., 2016a, "Kosodate towa ikanaru itonami ka: Sekinin ninaite no henyo kara" [What is childrearing? Based on the changes of responsibilities and bearers] Okamoto, T. & Tanji, K. (and eds.) Kyosei no shakaigaku: nashonarizumu, kea, sedai, shakaiishiki [Social science of coexistence: Nationalism, care, generation, social consciousness] TaroJiro-Sha Editus, pp. 117-138.

Tanji, K., 2016b, "Shogaikoku nihon no hoiku seido: shakaihenka no naka no hoiku" [Childcare systems in foreign countries and Japan: Childcare among social changes] Yoshida, N. (and ed.) Hoikugenri no shin-kijun [New standard of childcare principles (revised edition)] Sankeisha, pp. 25-45.

Touma, K., 2018, "Kea no tgenka to datsu-kazokuka" [Diversification and de-familiarization of care] *Journal of Ohara Institute for Social Research 722*, pp. 58-69.

Ueno, Y. (ed.), 2000, *Gendai hoiku genri* [Contemporary childcare principles], Sanko Shuppan.

Weikart, D.P., 2000, Early childhood education: Need and Opportunity, UNESCO. (–2015, Hamano, T. (trans.) *Yojikyoiku eno kokusaiteki shiza (yunesuko kokusai kyoiku seisaku sosho)* [International viewpoint toward childhood education (Fundamentals of educational planning)] Toshindo.

Yokoyama, F., 2002, *Sengo nihon no josei seisaku* [Women's policy in post-war Japan] Keiso Shobo.

Yoshida, M., 2002, *Hoikujo to yochien: togo no kokoromi o saguru* [Nursery schools and kindergartens: Exploring the attempt to unify them] Froebel-Kan.

The Life and Thoughts of Kōzōin Nisshin: His Aspiration to Establish the Teachings of a School

Daiki Kanda

Abstract

Following the death of Nichiren, the Kamakura-period Buddhist monk, his main disciples formed schools within the Nichiren sect, each one of them aiming for the legitimate inheritance of their late leader's teachings. Subsequently, major scholars of each school aspired to establish and ensure the prosperity of his teachings particular to their school as a means of ensuring the legitimacy of their intellectual lineage, doing so in the context of both historical and ideological trends of the times. The individual reception of Nichiren teachings by each school brought about the diversification of Buddhist teachings in the theological community, and disputes over their legitimacy took place on numerous occasions. The countless disputes over the legitimacy of Nichiren teachings that took place over the course of some 750 years were an accumulation of self-sacrificial efforts made by masters who put their lives on the line for the survival of their schools. This became the foundation for the continuation and development of the Nichiren sect that exists today.

This paper focuses on Kōzōin Nisshin (1508–1576) who endeavored to establish and spread the teachings of a strand of the Nichiren sect called the Nikkō School, and especially the Nichizon School, mainly located in Kyoto during the Sengoku period. At the time, disagreements on historical awareness and ideology within the Nichizon School declined the itself. In addition, the conflict with Mount Hiei had led to the annihilation of their entire community in Kyoto. Amid this crisis for the school's survival, Nisshin hoped to see its recovery brought about by the establishment of legitimate teachings and the resulting unity of the school's monk community, and thus engaged in a broad range of activities such as debating with monks belonging to other Nichiren sects. The remarkable activities undertaken by Nisshin provide a window to some aspects of the development of his sect.

Introduction

Following the death of Nichiren (1222–1282), the founder of the Nichiren sect who was most active in the eastern provinces of Kamakura-period Japan, a number of schools were formed, established by his main disciples, each basing themselves in eastern locations with connections to them. However, with the transition of political institutions and cultural centers to Kyoto during the late Kamakura period through the Namboku-chō period, the schools were pressed to secure new spheres of activity in Kyoto. Until the Sengoku period, the Nichiren sect in Kyoto reached its height of prosperity with 21 head temples firmly established in the capital, despite repeated fusion and fragmentation within each school.

A glance at the numerous splits within the Kyoto community throughout the Sengoku period reveals that the causes of the divisions sometimes secular problems such as school management policy, head temple successions, disagreements during interactions between imperial and shogunal power, etc. However, most of them were in-school disputes about the justce of the provided teachings. Each master of the Nichiren sect fostered their own awareness of each issue due to the influence of factors such as the tradition and prevailing state of the school which they belonged to. They were also influenced by the teachings of nearby schools and contemporary trends in Buddhist thinking, and, at the same time, aspiring to inherit the original and therefore legitimate teachings of the founder, Nichiren or that of the founders of their respective schools. While the masters' ideas reflected their times, their individual inheritance based on their individual awareness of the issues introduced progressive diversification in the teachings of the schools and masters.

If we survey the development of the Nichiren sect from the perspective of Kyoto's local characteristics, we can see that each school had to operate constantly while bearing other groups' ideologies in mind as they interacted with other Nichiren schools and existing religions within the confined space "inside the capital" Kyoto, the city that they all shared while seeking to secure their own power base. There were those who exchanged teachings with monks from other schools as well as those who sought to carve out a unique position for their own schools by engaging in debates in efforts to surpass other schools. The aim of my study is to examine all aspects of the ideological activities engaged in by the monks belonging to the various Kyoto schools.[1]

This paper is a discrete study that aims to contribute to an overall aggregation of research and focuses on Kōzōin Nisshin (1508–1576). He was a Buddhist scholar and monk of the Nichizon School, which was a branch of the Nikko School, and engaged in a broad range of activities in the fields of ideology and history with Sengoku-period Kyoto as his stage Nisshin previously garnered much attention as a scholar-monk who brought the teachings of the Nichizon School into prominence; and it has been pointed out that his teachings contained many elements that distinguished him from other masters (Shigyō, 1952, pp. 145–149; Mochizuki, 1968, pp. 296–311; Inoue, 1979; Inoue, 1988; Tamura, 1996; Tamura, 1996; Tamura, 1997; Tamura, 1997; Daikoku, 2004; Kagami, 2006).

In this paper, I examine the process in which Nisshin brought Nichizon School's teachings with such unique feature into prominence, focusing on his far-reaching diligent studies. I also want to examine how scholarly ties cultivated through his activities resulted in the formation of his teachings and his awareness of the issues and intention as he established his school's teachings conveyed through his far-reaching diligent scholarship.

1. Noteworthy Achievements in Nisshin's Life

Nisshin's many achievements have been described in Nisshin Tomiya's *Restoration of Yōbōji Head Temple in the Imperial Capital: Biography of Venerable Nisshin* and Nichinin Hara's *Reviving the Light of Buddhism: Venerable Kōzōin Nisshin*. However, since the publication of these books, many sources on Nisshin and related fields have become available, so there is more to be added to the study of Nisshin. Furthermore, not enough work has been done to back up the intimate connection between historical facts in his lifetime and the intellectual aspects that make up the other side of the coin, so there is plenty of room for more research.

A work titled *Soshiden*, which summarized Nisshin's achievements when he was 53 years old on the seventh day of the eleventh month, Eiroku 3

(1560), has been passed down. It contains an autobiographical account of his life at the end (Gakurin, 1970a). According to the autobiography, Nisshin was born in Ayanokōji-Nishinotōin in Kyoto on the twenty-sixth day of the eighth month, Eishō 5 (1508), and entered the Jūhonji Temple of the Nichizon School when he was 7 years old during the Spring Higan in Eishō 11 (1514).

The Nichizon School based in Kyoto is a branch of the Nikkō School that was founded by Nichizon (1265–1345), a disciple of Nikkō (1246–1333) who was one of the Six Senior Disciples personally taught by Nichiren himself, and goes back to the building of the Jōgyōin Temple in Rokkakuaburanokōji, Kyoto by Nichizon on the thirteenth day of the fourth month, Ryakuō 2 (1339). The Jōgyōin Temple was passed on to the disciple Nichiin (?–1373), but with the construction of another Jōgyōin Temple (later Jūhonji Temple) in Ichijō Inokuma, Kyoto, by another disciple named Nichidai (1309–1369), two strands of the Nichizon School appeared in Kyoto.

Nisshin's tonsure and entry into monkhood was conducted by Nippō (?–1516), the eleventh Chief Abbot of the Jūhonji Temple. However, just two years later, on the twenty-eighth day of the first month, Eishō 13 (1516), the master Nippō died and the young Nisshin was entrusted to the twelfth Abbot Jōon'in Nichizai (1475–1555). Nichizai had the 15-year-old Nisshin study under the learned elder Jōrakuin Nichiji (years of birth and death unknown) at the Jūhonji Temple in Daiei 2 (1522). There, Nisshin familiarized himself with the tradition of the Nichizon School, cultivated his ability to take in Buddhist teachings, and fostered his awareness to belong to the Nichizon School. Subsequently, Nisshin had to engage in a wide range of activities that transcended the Jūhonji Temple and the framework of the Nichizon School. By discovering a consistent awareness of the issues through gaining such achievements and insights, we can clearly see the high position that the monk Nisshin held within the entirety of the Nichiren sect as well as the elements that made up the essential aspects of his teachings. I want to specifically bring attention to Nisshin's diligent scholarship as he engaged in academic exchanges and readings of the complete Buddhist scriptures with experts in other disciplines within and outside of his own sect, as examples of the noteworthy achievements in his life.

2. Nisshin's Diligent Scholarship

2.1 *Study under Jōfukyōin Nichishin.*

There is a section in Nisshin's autobiography that offers a detailed description of what he studied in his youth (Gakurin, 1970a, pp. 143–145). On the fourth day of the eighth month, Daiei 5 (1525), the 18-year-old Nisshin started seeking scholarship outside the Nichizon School and became a student of Jōfukyōin Nichishin (1444–1528), the founder of the Honryūji Temple in Shijō-Ōmiya, Kyoto, through the good offices of Jōenbō Nisshin (dates of birth and death unknown). The scope of his studies is described as the *Fahua xuanyi* of the Tiantai founder Zhiyi (538–597), the doctrines of the Ritsu and Zen schools, Nichiren's *Kanjin honzon shō*, and lectures on the Lotus Sutra.

Nichishin presented his *Tendai sandaibu kachū* to Emperor Go-Kashiwabara, was praised for his scholarship, and became widely known as one of the great scholars of that time. Nichishin originally belonged to the Myōhonji Temple (Myōkenji Temple, Shijō School) in Kyoto, but he withdrew because of disagreements on the teachings. Instead, he founded the Honryūji Temple and formed a connection with the Honnōji Temple, Kyoto, whose founder Keirinbō Nichiryū (1385–1464) was an old acquaintance, but subsequently became independent after a dispute over teachings, also with the Honnōji Temple (Risshō Daigaku Nichiren kyōgaku kenkyūjo, 1964, pp. 316–322).

Based on when Nisshin studied there, he must have come in contact with Nichishin's later-year matured teachings that had become more original, following the disputes with the Myōhonji and Honnōji Temples. Nichishin had an especially strong influence on the later teachings of Nisshin in the area of "manifestation theory" (*honji suijaku ron*), where he discussed ideas such as "the superiority of early chapters over later chapters" (*shōretsu*) and "the equivalence of chapters" (*itchi*) based on the division of the 28 chapters of the Lotus Sutra into the first 14 chapters (*shakumon*) and the last 14 chapters (*hommon*) (Shigyō, 1952, p. 297; Mochizuki 1968, p. 148). That is, one of the theories representative of Nisshin's teachings was his "theory of the superiority of one chapter over the others" (*ippon shōretsu ron*), which was an emphasis on "The Eternal Lifespan of the Tathagata," the 16th of the 28 chapters of the Lotus Sutra, for the sake of interpreting the other 27 chapters. Here, we can see a deep intellectual connection with the teachings of

Daiki Kanda

Nichishin.

Furthermore, although Nichishin died on the twenty-ninth day of the third month, Kyōroku 1 (1528), the connection between Nisshin and the Honryūji Temple was maintained well into his later years through the disciples of Nichishin, who had attended the same lectures. This takes us a bit later in time, but Kaden'in Nichietsu's (1651–1726) *Kemmon shusha shō*, which propagated Nisshin's teachings, includes a list of student monks that attended Nichishin's lectures together with Nisshin, excerpted by Nichietsu from one of Nisshin's works (the original has yet to be verified). People like Nichishin's personal disciples Keiryūin (Nittai, 1471–1558), Shōjōbō (Nichiō, ?–1571), Anjūbō, and Honshubō of the Honryūji Temple, Risshōbō Nichigaku and Jijū Jūshō of the Myōmanji Temple in Kyoto, and Jōjōbō of the Myōsenji Temple in Kyoto were included there. Both Myōmanji and Myōsenji Temples belong to the Nichijū School founded by Acharya Genmyō Nichijū (1314–1392). This means that Nichishin's lectures were attended by monks from three schools: his own disciples, student-monks of the Nichijū School, and Nisshin from the Nichizon School. Textual sources reveal that Nisshin's friendship with Shōjōbō Nichiō and Anjūbō of the Honryūji Temple continued into his later years (Gakurin, 1970b, p. 141).[2]

2.2 *Studying under Nishiyama Nisshin.*

Next, Nisshin visited Fuji, the source of the Nikkō School, when he was 23 years old in Kyōroku 3 (1530), and became a student of Nishiyama Nisshin (1497–1557), the eleventh abbot of the Nishiyama Honmonji Temple located there. In the works *Yo Hon'inbō sho* and *Fuji to tōke igi*, which he wrote when he was 58 years old in Eiroku 6 (1563), he reminisced about his studies under Nishiyama Nisshin and expressed that the teachings transmitted to him during that time were deeply meaningful for the formation of his own teachings. According to what he wrote there (Honzan Hōyōji Kangakuryō, 1929, p. 232; Gakurin, 1970b, p. 141) what Nishiyama Nisshin transmitted was the theory of the descent into the hell, Avīci by creating images of Buddha and reciting the whole Lotus Sutra to them (Zōbutsu Dokuju Dagoku No Hōmon), which had become mainstream in the Nikkō School at the time. Nisshin believed the teachings transmitted from Nishiyama Nisshin to be the highest precepts and endeavored to spread them until he turned 30 years old in the eighth month of Tembun 6 (1538). However, as Nisshin engaged in debate with scholar-monks from other schools based on these teachings, he ended up losing every argument. He wrote that this was when he had realized that the teachings of Nishiyama Nisshin were wicked and he repented before the Buddha. This is an important fact in understanding the formation process involved in Nisshin's teachings. In other words, we can point out that Nisshin's thought process underwent a major transition in the eighth month of Tembun 6, when Nisshin was 30 years old. This transition was an expression of clear skepticism toward the theory that had become mainstream in the school founded by Nikkō. It was on the foundation of the awareness of this problem that the teachings of Nisshin came to be shaped in contrast to the teachings that operated after Nisshin turned 30 years old. The teachings of Nishiyama Nisshin constituted a critical element in establishing the distinctness and originality of Nisshin's teachings, and it is from this perspective that we need to frame his teachings as they were established in his later years.

2.3 *Studying Non-Buddhist Writings under Kiyohara no Nobukata.*

The study activities we have examined so far were explorations of truth by coming in contact with the insights of many masters as a means to determine Nisshin's own standpoint as a follower of the Nichiren sect (the religious organization that adheres to Nichiren's teachings). The studies of young Nisshin cannot be considered peculiar for a Buddhist who is aware of his responsibility to enlighten others and to attain enlightenment himself. A Buddhist's learning activities reveal his universal and unchanging efforts and attitude as he investigates the doctrines that express the reality of the salvation he adheres to, from among the extensive range of doctrines in Buddhist sects and especially among the diverse interpretations of the Nichiren teachings. However, Nisshin's autobiography revealed that he aspired to study writings outside the lineage of Buddhist thought, and even studied under renowned scholars and experts in their respective fields. This appears to be a strikingly distinct aspect of Nisshin's attitude toward studies.

After finishing his studies under Nishiyama Nisshin and returning to Kyoto on the eighth day of the fifth month, Kyōroku 4 (1531), Nisshin became a student of Kiyohara no Nobukata (1475–1550). Nobukata was the third son of Yoshida Kanetomo (1435–1511) who brought Yoshida Shintō into prominence. He was adopted by the Kiyohara family, known as experts (*hakushi/hakase*; hereditary occupation of studying and teaching the

Confucian Classics) in Myōgyōdō, and inherited the Shintō studies of his biological father, Kanetomo in the field of Confucian Classics and other aspects of Kokugaku. He is one of the greatest scholars of Japanese history. In the Sengoku period, Nobukata's friendships developed rich personal connections based on his scholarship and social standing, allowing him to deliver lectures at the requests of nobles and monks of various sects in Kyoto and many other locations.

The autobiography shows that Nisshin heard Nobukata interpreting the *Nihon shoki* ("*Jindai no maki*"). The relationship between the Buddhas and Bodhisattvas of Buddhism and the gods native to Japan has been debated since ancient times, and since belief in the "30 gods" had come to occupy an important place in the Nichiren sect, a diligent study of Shintō was a type of education found necessary for subsuming and giving value to Japanese native religion within the Buddhist system without separating them.

Although unpublished, Nisshin's *Gosho kenmon*[3] mentioned in the commentary on "*Kiden hakase*" (Risshō Daigaku Nichiren kyōgaku kenkyūjo, 2000, p. 263) in Nichiren's *Ken Hōbōshō*, that he actually learned about the *Mengqiu*, compiled by the Tang scholar Li Han, from the expert Nobukata. The second case shows that the scope of Nisshin's studies was not limited to the *Nihon shoki*, but also included Chinese classics.

Another interesting fact is that we can see commonalities between the two groups of monks who attended Nobukata's and Nichishin's lectures, as named in the aforementioned *Kenmon shusha shō*. Chigusa Kobayashi, who researched Nobukata's *shōmono* writings[4] on the *Nihon shoki* extensively introduced the *Nihonkishō* (held by Jingū Library, 4 volumes), which comprises transcriptions made by a "certain person" in Tembun 4 (Kobayashi, 2003, p. 300). According to Kobayashi, the *Nihonkishō* contains transcripts of lectures on the *Nihon shoki* from Tembun 1 (1532) to Tembun 4 (Kobayashi, 2003, p. 301). The contents include Nobukata lectures transcribed by a "certain person" as well as later additions and references to the transcriptions ("*Jūshō kikigaki*") made by a monk called Jūshō, who is introduced as the friend of the "certain person".

We do not know the full contents of the unpublished *Nihonkishō*, but according to Kobayashi, the lectures were attended by the monks Myōjō, Nichigaku, Jōjō, and Nishihachijōbō Ryūken, who exchanged views with Nobukata (Kobayashi, 2003, pp. 300–302). Nichigaku and Jōjō correspond to Risshōbō Nichigaku of the Myōmanji Temple in Kyoto and Jōjōbō of

the Myōsenji Temple in Kyoto who were listed among the monks mentioned in Nichishin's lectures together with Nisshin in the *Kenmon shusha
shō*. Furthermore, Jūshō, the friend of the "certain person" who wrote the
Nihonkishō, also has bore the name Jijū Jūshō. The fact that the Nichijū
monks who listened to the lectures of Nichishin of the Honryūji Temple also
had a connection with the lectures of Nobukata suggests the existence of an
academic association within the Kyoto Nichiren community of the Sengoku
period. It is likely that the monks of the Honryūji Temple and those of the
Nichijū School, as well as Nisshin, and others at the Jūhonji Temple came
together in search of the scholarship of Nichishin, who had been recognized
by the emperor, and that the study association that was organized there came
to share a path of learning with the lectures of Nobukata, one of the greatest
scholars of the time.

2.4 *Studying under Kutaku (also Kyūtaku).*

Nisshin's autobiography stated that he studied "divination" under "Kyūtaku
of Hyūga Province" in the fourth month of Tembun 5 (1536). Here, "divination" refers to bamboo stick divination related to the Confucian Classic
Book of Changes. The *Book of Changes* explains the state of all phenomena relevant to the myriad things, including humanity and nature, based on
"commentary" (*guaci*) interpreting the combinations of symbols called *yao*,
which represent yin and yang. The Ashikaga School, which was an authority
in the study of divination using the *Book of Changes*, referred to the theoretical interpretation of the *Book of Changes* as "*seiden*" and its application in
bamboo stick divination as "*betsuden*" (Kawase, 1948, pp. 229). The "divination" studied by Nisshin was "*betsuden*" divination, which means that
he also learned about "*seiden*" for the sake of application and practice. At
the time, divination rose in importance as the demand from general society
grew. The Ashikaga School was at its peak in Nisshin's day, and people with
deep knowledge of divination had been appointed *shōshu* (principal) since
the school's beginnings. While the study of other Chinese classics was also
popular at the school, they were thought of as introductory steps before the
more abstruse *Book of Changes*, and divination was perceived as the teaching
objective of the Ashikaga School (Ashikaga, 1932, p. 611; Kawase, 1948, pp.
223, 228).[5] Bamboo stick divination was based on the yin–yang theory (later
combined with *wuxing* theory) and the theory of astronomical calendars in

the *Book of Changes*, and this thought was used in all kinds of decision-making in the daily lives of regular people. This was most striking in the warrior class as divinations were carried out on a daily basis for important ceremonies in the family and even strategic plans in battle. The nature of the Sengoku period demanded more practical education of the Ashikaga School. Thus, they combined the study of divination not only with Chinese classics but also with books on military strategy such as the Seven Military Classics. It was not uncommon for graduates to serve warrior families as military strategists (Kawase, 1948, pp. 242, 246).[6]

We must ask about the identity of this "Kyūtaku of Hyūga Province," whom Nisshin approached in order to study divination. Hara identified a scholar named Tentaku from Hyūga Province whose livelihood was bamboo stick divination during the Tembun era, suggesting that the Kyūtaku who taught Nisshin was actually Tentaku (Hara, 1975, p. 17). However, if we look for information on Tentaku, we find *Nampo bunshū*, the collection of literature of Bunshi Genshō (1555–1620), who studied under him. In volume 2 of *Nampo bunshū*, it is said that Tentaku studied at the Ashikaga School for five or six years starting in Daiei 7 (1527) when he was 19 years old. After that, he studied for over 10 years under Ippaku (dates of birth and death unknown) in Echizen Province, and then returned home to Hyūga Province in Kōji 2 (1556) when he was 49 years old. If this is so, Tentaku would have still been studying under Ippaku in Echizen Province in Tembun 5 when Nisshin was a student, so they could not have met in Hyūga Province. However, the autobiography noted "Kyūtaku of Hyūga Province," and this line does not necessarily mean that Nisshin went to Hyūga Province. It is quite possible to imagine that Tentaku may have had an opportunity to meet Nisshin in Kinai while he was still a student under Ippaku in Echizen Province. If Kyūtaku was Tentaku, then the relations with the authorities of the various learned circles whom Nisshin engaged with in his diligent studies comes into focus rather clearly. There were academic connections intersecting around the central point of Ippaku, under whom Tentaku studied.

Ippaku traveled to Ming to study medical texts and also studied at the Ashikaga School (Hiraizumi, 1960; Yonehara, 1976; Haga, 1981). After finishing his studies at the Ashikaga School, Ippaku settled in Kyoto, where he delivered lectures on medical texts and the Confucian classics. He later moved to Ichijōdani on the invitation of Takakage (1493–1548), the tenth head of the Asakura clan ruling over Echizen Province. There, he met Tentaku and taught other visiting scholars with a love for Ippaku's academic knowledge. In the ninth month of Tembun 5 (1536), he revised the *Butsuchōshi Zokkai Hachijūichi Nangyō* on Takakage's order and participated in the publication of the Echizen edition of the *Zokkai Hachijūichi Nangyō*, which was the second publication of a medical text in Japanese history. Ippaku is primarily known for his medical scholarship, but medicine as an academic discipline at that time required the knowledge of divination, so he was also well-versed in it. Ippaku is ascribed a *shōmono* titled *Ekigaku keimō tsūshaku kōgi* (held by Kyoto University Library, Important Cultural Property) that is a commentary on divination. It is noteworthy that it says, "Lecture by Ippaku; Transcript by Gesshū" below the title slip and at the center of the title page of the *Ekigaku keimō tsūshaku kōgi* (fascicle 1.2). It is also noteworthy that this book is a manuscript copy by Nobukata. A person called Gesshū wrote a transcript based on Ippaku's lecture on the *Ekigaku keimō tsūshaku* and this was copied by Nobukata. I have already discussed the relationship between Nobukata and Nisshin. Gesshū is the Zen monk Gesshū Jukei (1470–1533), an expert in the literature of the Five Mountains, and was also involved in Nisshin's diligent scholarship. Just as there was a transfer of texts between Nobukata and Jukei, they were also intimately connected in terms of academia. Jukei had previously attended Nobukata's biological father Kanetomo's lectures on the *Nihon shoki* and produced transcripts of those lectures. Jukei's transcripts praised the lecturer Kanetomo as "the person who most ought to be considered an example for posterity," and Kanetomo himself copied Jukei's transcripts as a written record of his own lectures. As Nobukata sought to propagate the Yoshida Shintō doctrine of his biological father Kanetomo, he must have referenced quite a few of Jukei's transcripts while writing the notes for his own lectures on the *Nihon shoki* (Kobayashi, 2003, pp. 236–239).

The friendship between Ippaku and Jukei was also close. The *Gen'un monjū*, a collection of Jukei's works, includes an afterword written by Jukei for one of Ippaku's works. That afterword praises him, saying, "As with Zen studies, it is not easy to learn divination at the deepest level, yet Ippaku is a great man who has mastered both" (Hokiichi, 1959; *Zoku gunsho ruijū*, vol. 13.1 (Zoku gunsho ruijū kansei kai), p. 413, p. 434). I believe that the presence of Ippaku, whom Tentaku studied under, in the scholarly connection between Nobukata and Jukei, which we know is relevant to Nisshin's diligent study, serves to back Hara's Tentaku theory up. It is quite possible that Nisshin may have first become aware of the divinatory authority Ippaku by attending Nobukata's lectures before approaching his disciple, Tentaku in search of that scholarship. Of course, Nobukata, whose livelihood centered on delivering lectures on the Confucian Classics, must have also had a deep knowledge of divination. However, it was pointed out in research in recent years that the establishment of a theory of divination in the Kiyohara house came later than other classics (Mizukami, 2010), which is supported by the fact that we actually have no records of him lecturing on divination despite the broad range of books he interpreted (Ashikaga, 1932, p. 472; Yamada, 1957). I mentioned that the Ashikaga School's approach was to study other books before introducing divination, so it might have been the case that Nisshin came to realize the need to study divination as the next step after hearing Nobukata's interpretations, and that he must have gone looking look for a scholar with specialized knowledge thereafter.

2.5 *Studying under Manase Dōsan.*

The next field of study described in Nisshin's autobiography is medicine. Nisshin mentioned "medical classics." It is likely that he referred to ancient Chinese medical texts such as the *Huangdi neijing* and the *Shennong bencao jing*. The basic medical theory expounded in the *Huangdi neijing* contains the aforementioned *wuxing* theory based on the *Book of Changes*, while the *Shennong bencao jing* adopted the same theory to explain medical efficacy. Here, we can get a glimpse of what drew Nisshin's attention to medical books after studying divination. Nisshin wrote in his autobiography that he studied this "after 32 or 33 years of age." This means that it was after Tembun 8 (1539) or Tembun 9 (1540), and his medical master was Manase Dōsan (1507–1594).

A glance at Dōsan's history shows that he also studied at the Ashikaga School in Kyōroku 1 (1528) when he was 22 years old. I mentioned that the Ashikaga School was an authority in the field of divination, but that was an area of study necessary for medicine, and the Ashikaga School also had a medical facility called the Shōgyōdō, so there were many students who came there to study medicine (Yūki, 1959, p. 159; Wajima, 1961). Dōsan and Tentaku were at the school during the same period. While traveling to Kantō for his studies, Dōsan became a student of Tashiro Sanki (1465–1544), who had previously traveled to Ming. Sanki was a doctor who was renowned for his achievement of bringing Li Zhu's brand of medicine,[7] which was the mainstream form in China at the time, to Japan, and it was this kind of state-of-the-art medicine that Dōsan sought from Sanki, who passed on a total of seven certificates of transmission to Dōsan before the second month of Tembun 5 (1536), and in those certificates he referred to his own medicine as *tōryū igaku*.[8] Dōsan's achievement was that he systematized this Tōryū Igaku that he received from Sanki (Yakazu, 1982, p. 133; Endō & Nakamura, 1999; Miyamoto, 2006a, Miyamoto, 2006b). Upon his return to Kyoto, Dōsan created a school called Keitekiin to spread the knowledge of Tōryū Igaku and in Tenshō 2 (1574), when he was 68 years old, he compiled his magnum opus, the *Keiteki-shū* (8 volumes). This book ushered in dramatic developments in Japanese medicine, which until then consisted mainly of mechanical medicine that determined prescription and usage based on the name and symptoms of a disease as instructed by medical texts, by incorporating the stance of "treatment based on observation" (*sasshō benchi*) (Yakazu, 1982, p. 148). This is why Dōsan is usually referred to as "the restorer of Japanese medicine" (Kyōto-fu ishikai igakushi hensashitsu, 1980, p. 232).[9]

Nisshin's autobiography indicated that he studied this when he was around 32 or 33 years old (Tembun 8 or 9). However, if we look up this time in the sources presenting Dōsan's personal history, we come across an inconsistency that makes their meeting decisively improbable. The problem is that Dōsan also has an autobiography and it says that he returned to Kyoto on the sixteenth day of the second month, Tembun 14 (1545) when he was 39 years old. If this is so, Dōsan had not founded the Keitekiin yet in the period in which Nisshin studied there; he had even been in Kantō in that period. As a result, we are forced to reconsider how the two may have met. Dōsan's autobiography was appended to a reference text titled *Tōryū igaku no gen'i* (Endō & Nakamura, 1999; Machi, 2012). The extant copy of this book contains an afterword by the late-Edo doctor Meguro Dōtaku (1724–1798), but no copy written by Dōsan's hand remains. However, the descriptions in Dōsan's autobiography are quite realistic, which makes them highly credible (Miyamoto, 2006), and his activities around the time of his return to Kyoto are described so concretely that it does appear to be a reliable account (Kinsei kindai Nihon Kanbun han, 2009, pp. 244-255). I suspect that Nisshin studied under him at some point after the sixteenth day of the second month, Tembun 14. Nisshin's autobiography was authored after the eleventh month of Eiroku 3 (1560). That is more than 20 years after Tembun 8–9. If we consider how long and far-reaching Nisshin's studies were, it would be strange if something as trivial as this is misremembered. Tomiya stated that a manuscript of the *Gikin honzō*, which was compiled by Dōsan and copied by Nisshin was available at the Yōbōji Temple (Tomiya, 1925, p. 24), so we have concrete proof of their scholarly connection.

2.6 Studying under Ikka of the Kenninji Temple.

Nisshin's autobiography states that he studied "non-Buddhist texts" under Ikka of the Kenninji Temple in the fall of Tembun 10 (1541) when he was 34 years old. As suggested by the term "non-Buddhist texts," what he learned from Ikka was likely not a specified field such as "the Confucian Classics," "divination," or "medical classics," but a wide range of books outside of Buddhism. Hara argued that Nisshin studied under the Five-Mountain Zen monk Gesshū Jukei (Hara, 1975, p. 17). He based this on the fact that Jukei went by the name Ikka Wajō while engaging in literary activities after founding the Ikkain on the premises of the Kenninji Temple in his later years (Ashikaga, 1932, p. 434).

Jukei served as the chief priest of famous temples such as the Kenninji Temple and the Nanzenji Temple in Kyoto and was well-known as a Zen monk with education in literature and related disciplines. Some of his major works are the *Gen'un bunshū* and the *Gesshū Wajō goroku*, which are sermons and Chinese poems compiled by his disciples for posterity, as well as the *Zoku kinshūdan*, which was a reorganization of his master Ten'in Ryūtaku's (1422–1500) Chinese poetry collection *Kinshūdan*, and the commentaries *Kinshūdan shō* and *Zoku kinshūdan shō*. Jukei was invited by the court to deliver several lectures on the Santaishi in the emperor's presence on in the Kyōroku era (Hanawa, ed., 1934, pp. 405–407; Ryūzō Takahashi, ed., 1958, pp. 141, 142, 144, and 145; Tōkyō daigaku shiryō hensan sho, ed., 1944, pp. 257–258), which resulted in the shōmono *Santaishi Gen'un shō*.

Jukei had an academic connection with both the aforementioned Nobukata and Tentaku's master Ippaku. Like the two, Jukei was also appointed chief priest at a temple in Echizen Province during the Eishō era on the invitation of Sadakage (1473–1512), the ninth head of the Asakura clan, and the tenth head of Tadakake. At the time, Echizen Province reached the peak of its own development under the rule of Takakage. The reason of the development was the invitation of some of the greatest educated men active in Kyoto at the same time. He, who loved learning, welcomed these intellectuals cordially,

making their academic activities much easier than when they had lived in
Kyoto which had become extremely chaotic. As a result, they could promote
the development of the province remarkably (Yonehara, 1976, p. 265). If we
consider Nisshin's diligent learning activities and focus on their relationship with the Honryūji Temple, we cannot avoid paying attention to Echizen
Province as a common sphere of activity.

However, if Nisshin studied under Jukei, then the period of study given as
"Tembun 10" in the autobiography makes any connection between the two
impossible. This is because Jukei had died already on the eighth day of the
twelfth month, Tembun 2 (1533), long before Tembun 10. Hara, who argued
that he studied under Jukei, also leaves this problem to be solved later (Hara,
1975, p. 20), but no alternative theory has appeared. Since then, there has
been no progression in this academic field. It was here that I took "Ikka of
the Kenninji Temple" as a clue and examined several sources. I came across
the existence of a monk called Keiten Jusen (1495–1549), who was a disciple of Jukei and served as the chief priest of the Kenninji Temple just like
his master. Jusen's signature appeared in the beginning of the *Gesshū Wajō
goroku* as its compiler (*Zoku gunsho ruijū*, vol. 13.1, p. 242). Jusen dissem-
inated the *Santaishi Gen'un shō* later on. He took the lead in publicizing his
master's achievements. In Echizen Province, he filled in for his master by
drafting a laudatory tribute for a portrait requested by the Asakura clan. He
also accompanied Jukei to *renga* meetings at the court in Kyoto. Jusen supported Jukei's academic activities as his aide (Hanawa, ed., 1959, p. 380;
Hanawa, ed.,1934, p. 315).

We have a source indicating a link between Jusen and the Ikkain founded
by Jukei. The entry from the twelfth day of the second month, Tembun 6
(1537) in the *Rokuon nichiroku*, which was held at the Rokuon'in of the
Shōkokuji Temple, recorded how Jusen gave the monk registrar (*sōrokushi*) a
hanging scroll stored at the Ikkain when the registrar visited (Tsuji, 1934, p.
278). He also visited the Ikkain together with the chief priest of the Kenninji
Temple on the twenty-fourth day of the twelfth month, and was entertained
by Jusen (Tsuji, 1934, p. 325). Entries concerning the Ikkain about three
years after Jukei's death reveal that Jusen inherited the Ikkain from Jukei
and served as its head. After Jukei's death and in Tembun 10 (1541), when
Nisshin was supposed to have studied under Ikka, the only person for which
that name would have made sense was Jusen.

What was Nisshin's goal in studying under Jusen? The autobiography uses

81

the ambiguous expression "non-Buddhist texts," so it is unclear what the contents were. If we guess based on Nisshin's path of learning, it is possible that he was tracing Jukei's footsteps in the Ikkain library and his disciple Jusen, since Jukei had contributed to the Shintō of Nobukata that Nisshin studied and had deep knowledge of divination and medicine as well (The second medical book to be published in Japan was Ippaku's Echizen edition of the *Zokkai Hachijūichi Nankei*, but the first one was the Sakai edition of the *Isho taizen* published by Asaino Sōzui (?–1531) in Daiei 8 (1528), the afterword to which was written by Jukei).

Yet, among the academic fields Jusen was skillful in, was not his literary technique which stands out in Chinese poetry, the most likely His master Jukei was part of the lineage inheriting the "*hoshitsuso* style" (four-six *pianwen* prose) of Zekkai Chūshin (1334–1405), extolled as the apex of Five-Mountain literature, and his disciple Bioku Sōkō (?–1545) was actually appointed by the Ōuchi clan of Suō Province to draft diplomatic documents (Sakurai, 1959; Itō, 2002, p. 194).[10] Jukei's expertise in literary style was likely also the main reason why he was asked to write afterwords for various learned circles and was invited by the Asakura clan. This culture was something that Jusen learned on the side. He made drafts in his master's place. Literary styles, of which Chinese poetry is emblematic, was an important element of the monk status. Even if one was able to pursue legitimate teachings and ideologies, one still needed to author books explaining those teachings to communicate their insights in a refined manner, and this was an important means of spreading this knowledge to others. If we look at Nisshin's intellectual debates with monks from other schools, there is a case in which he prides himself for making use of what he had learned from "men of letters" (persons whose livelihood is letters) in his own teaching,[11] so the scholarship he obtained from Jusen played an important role in the explication of his theories.

2.7 Perusing the Complete Buddhist Scriptures at Kitano-sya.

Be it the Confucian Classics or Shintō, the elucidation of all phenomena is a theme common to all religions. The Buddhist Nisshin needed to discuss those worldly theories by harmonizing them with the Buddhist system without separating them. Nisshin's far-reaching studies were not guided by his love for learning alone. We should consider them as being based on a consistent awareness of the issues that he had as a Buddhist (how to realize salvation).

At the end of the entries in the autobiography that inform us of his diligent studies that we have discussed so far, we are told that he perused the
entire set of Buddhist scriptures at the Kitano Miyatera. This means that he
had read all the sermons by Sakyamuni and all scriptures related to them.
He is supposed to have perused them when he was aged between 38 and 40
years, from the fifteenth day of the ninth month, Tembun 14 (1545) to the
second day of the seventh month, Tembun 16 (1547). Nisshin's chief literary
work *Kaishaku kenpon hokke nirongi tokui shō* mentioned "Kitano rotating
sutra shelves," so we can determine that they were the complete Buddhist
scriptures contained on rotating bookshelves in Kitano. These "Kitano rotating sutra shelves" are quite well-known in Japanese history and the books
contained there were copies of the complete Buddhist scriptures put together
in Ōei 19 (1412), which is now preserved as an Important Cultural Property
comprising 5,048 volumes in all at the Daihōonji Temple (Senbon Shakadō)
in Kyoto. Woodblock printing became the mainstream in the early-modern
period, so the Kitano books are lauded in cultural history as a final great effort
among the complete range of hand-copied Buddhist scriptures (Usui, 1959).

The Historiographical Institute of the University of Tokyo has photo
albums showing the postscripts of these books. I surveyed them and verified
the existence of 103 postscripts added by Nisshin (Kanda, 2015). Following
the period given in the autobiography, these additions suggest that some
of his perusals happened until the twenty-ninth day of the seventh month,
Tembun 16 (1547) as well as in Tembun 18 (1549). Moreover, a 15-year-
old disciple called Ukyō belonging to the Jūhonji Temple also participated
in Nisshin's perusal (I found 17 additions by Ukyō). This set of complete
Buddhist scriptures also contains many postscripts added by monks of other
schools, those of Nisshin and Ukyō are the most numerous and the duration
of their perusal is the longest.

The complete Buddhist scriptures are mentioned in Nisshin's writings,
rather frequently (Kanda, 2014). This is because perusing the complete scriptures, which is a model act of Buddhists, is a manifestation of the desire to
directly approach Sakyamuni. It is noteworthy that the period of perusal co-
incided with a time of major transition for Nisshin and the Nichizon School.
The study of various subjects and the perusal of the complete scriptures
become strikingly significant as a noteworthy life achievement first when
we take into consideration the historical background of the time. I want to
conclude by discussing the intention contained in the studies we have looked

at so far, while also paying attention to the then circumstances prevailing for Nisshin and the Nichizon School.

3. Diligent Study and the Aspiration to Establish a School's Teachings

When Nisshin was engaged in his far-reaching diligent studies, the Nichiren schools in Kyoto were involved in a major incident that threatened their very existence. On the twenty-third day of the seventh month, Tembun 5 (1537), the Kyoto community was attacked by the Enryakuji Temple of Mount Hiei, which completely burned down several head temples and destroyed them entirely. This was the so-called Tembun Hokke Riot, a well-known event in Japanese history. The Nichizon School also lost the Jōgyōin and Jūjonji Temples to the flames, and like other schools, they fled to Sakai in Izumi Province, and were forced to take refuge there (Imatani, 2009)[12] until they received imperial permission to return, in Tembun 11 (1542) (Fujii, Ueda, Hatano, & Yasukuni, 2006, p. 71).

After receiving imperial permission to return to Kyoto, the Nichiren schools gradually restored their presence in the city. The Nichizon School that took care of the Jōgyōin and Jūjonji Temples found it difficult to restore its two head temples. One ground-breaking suggestion was that they could merge the two Temples into one head temple. However, antagonism and discord had long existed between the two, so any promotion of this suggestion required careful coordination and a search for mutual compromise. Tomiya claimed that the merger took shape on the seventeenth day of the third month, Tembun 17 (1548) (Tomiya, 1994, p. 321), which was about six months after imperial permission was provided. Nisshin also stated that the Yōbōji Temple was founded as a new head temple in Kyoto and that they had completed this restoration on the nineteenth day of the third month, Tembun 19 (1550) (Gakurin, 1970a, p. 138).

In the eleventh month of Kōji 1 (1555), Nisshin was recommended as the first chief abbot of the Yōbōji Temple by the monks and almsgivers of the Nichizon School, and he admitted inheriting the chair of the temple. Even so, the new management of the Nichizon School was in no way unified, so cruel slander was also directed toward the new chief abbot, Nisshin from inside the school. Concerned about this situation, Nisshin authored a text titled the

Fushinki in the twelfth month of Eiroku 1 (1558), with the aim of providing new principles to guide the Nichizon School. *Fushinki* clarified Nisshin's own consistent position and principles as he identified the issues faced by the Nichizon School and the entire Nikkō School at that time, as well as on what awareness of the issues his long-time studies were based.

The *Fushinki* is in the format of questions and answers and lets the askers present slander such as that Nisshin is completely devoted to scholarship and displays the behavior of a wise man enlightened in wicked ways, or that he perused the complete Buddhist scriptures for the sake of fame and profit. Moreover, the askers are also presented as claiming that the immorality of the chief abbot Nisshin is causing monks at the Yōbōji Temple to flee, almsgivers to decrease in number by the day, and the temple to decline in various other ways, ridiculing the fact that their monastery building, which was smaller than other schools' monk's dwellings to begin with, had not expanded no matter how many years passed since their return to Kyoto (Gakurin, 1970b, pp. 25–32).

In response to these problems, Nisshin insisted on the importance of refining wisdom to align with the Buddha's true intentions, despite diligent study being a toil that cannot be perceived by others. That is, unless they struggled with the truth of their teachings and sought to establish legitimate school teachings, they would end up as a branch temple of another school, irrespective of how many temples they built or how big they made their monastery buildings. Suspicions about the right and wrong ways of their teachings persisted among the monks and almsgivers of the Nikkō School, and their questions could only be answered by a wise man. It becomes clear that it was based on this awareness of the issues that Nisshin prioritized refining his wisdom over expanding the temple or building new ones, aspiring to study a wide range of subjects in both Buddhist and non-Buddhist books and even perusing the complete scriptures (Gakurin, 1970b, pp. 32–40).

The transition that made this awareness of the issues of Nisshin's definite must have been the ideological shift that he made when he was 30 years old in the eighth month of Tembun 6 (1538). The Tembun Hokke Riot deprived the Nichizon School of their head temples, and in the year that followed, he recanted the theory of the descent into the hell Avīci by creating images of Buddha and reciting the whole Lotus Sutra to them, which Nishiyama Nisshin had transmitted to him. At their place of refuge in Sakai, Izumi Province, Nisshin urgently needed to come up with a strategy to ensure the school's survival and its restoration in Kyoto and explore new teachings that he could stand by. That is, he underwent a major transition in terms of both ideology and history.

Facing a threat to the school's survival and at a time when the plan to merge the Jōgyōin and Jūjonji Temples was being implemented, Nisshin aspired to study under Dōsan and Jusen, as discussed above, and he maintained study activities such as perusing the complete scriptures right until the year before the founding of the Yōbōji Temple in the third month of Tembun 19 (1550). What does this mean?

It probably means that Nisshin perceived that resolving the intellectual stagnation that the Nichizon School and the entire Nikkō School had suffered since a long time ago was directly relevant to passing on legitimate Nichizon and Nikkō teachings into the far future. It is true that the damages from the Tembun Hokke Riot caused the Nichizon School much adversity, but the antagonism between the Jōgyōin and Jūjonji Temples had been a considerable hindrance to the Nichizon community since earlier on (Shigyō, 1952, p. 145). Nisshin made use of the proposal to merge both temples to innovate the intellectual aspects of the Nichizon School, to play the role of a bridge that could bring about real unity under a new system, and to establish outwardly solid school teachings by using his own academic career.

Following the Tembun Hokke Riot and the ideological transition in the eighth month of Tembun 6 (1537), Nisshin's learning activities became even more colored by this awareness of the issues. In the twelfth month of Tembun 8 (1539), Nisshin copied Nichiryū's *Jūsan mondō shō* because of questions about the theory of the fundamental reason for becoming a Buddha (Hon-Immyō Shisō) (Kanda, 2017).[13] In the eleventh month of Tembun 9 (1540), he copied the *Shūyō Kashiwabara anryū* of Jōshun (1334–1422), a monk of the Japanese Tendai sect, because of questions about the medieval Tendai theory of inherent enlightenment (Chūko Tendai Hongaku Shisō) (Kanda, 2017).[14] In the first month of Tembun 11 (1542), he copied the *Sōshaku*, which is traditionally said to have been written by his teacher Nichishin (1444-1528),[15] and in the first month of Tembun 15 (1546), he also copied Nichishin's *Hokke ronryaku taikō* (*Hokke ron kachū*).[16]

In the *Fushinki*, Nisshin indicated that the theory of the fundamental reason for becoming a Buddha expounded in Nichiryū's *Jūsan mondō shō* had a major influence on the formation for the theory of the descent into the hell Avīci by creating images of Buddha, which he adhered to until he was 30 years old (Gakurin, 1970b, p. 43). Nisshin also took issue with the ideas in Jōshun's *Shūyō Kashiwabara anryū* while explaining the essence of the principal image of worship. These copies were by Nisshin's side when he wrote his texts and were important materials as Nisshin sought to establish school teachings that could overcome the ideas contained therein, which were highly influential at the time. Moreover, while the former two were negative, his copying of Nichishin's works seems to have been done in a largely receptive manner. Following his intellectual transition, Nisshin referenced the theories of his former teacher Nichishin as he sought to find a standpoint for new teachings.

These activities to promote the school's teachings, realized through adversity, were a mobilization of education and experiences nurtured through learning since Nisshin's youth, and if we examine the systematic teachings of Nisshin in his later years from this vantage point, we will possibly discover a new dimension as the awareness of the issues and intention contained in the uniqueness of those teachings become concrete.

4. Conclusion

I have discussed Nisshin's far-reaching study of various subjects as a noteworthy achievement in his life. This pursuit of wisdom by Nisshin was not conducted simply out of a love for learning, but was for the realization of salvation, which is the main purpose of Buddhism, and was thus a quest for truth.

Nichiren incidentally argued that the salvation of all living things in the age of decadence will be realized by chanting *Namu-myōho-renge-kyō*. This was also an "essential point" selected as a result of Nichiren's far-reaching studies and research. That essential point has been steadily passed on to this day and has become a tenet of the Nichiren sect. However, to determine whether something essential is truly essential, one must necessarily consider not only other Buddhist ideologies but also the entire of religion. It is only after that essential point has been compared and demonstrated in relation to others that it can finally be received and understood by adherents as something essential. Without criticism, that faith risks becoming blind faith. I believe that Nisshin's attitude of broad learning really came from such a critical mindset.

We can see that Nisshin's emphasis on learning remained a constant until his final years. One example is that a study facility named Kangakuryō was created at the Yōbōji Temple in his later years, and Nisshin drafted a code called *Gakutō Shiki* (Tomiya, 1994, p. 332). The code stipulated the conditions for becoming a Gakutō, which was an important position for the Yōbōji Temple's management, as well as their authority. According to the code, one condition is that one must learn a number of truths that Nisshin himself systematized into the core of the teachings of the Nichizon School and be able to lecture about them without faltering. The Gakutōs were entrusted not only with study matters, but also with the supervision of all ceremonial matters, starting with the annual and monthly events held by monks and almsgivers at the Yōbōji Temple. Moreover, it was decided that all divergent opinions at the temple finally required the approval of the Gakutōs. Nisshin's perception was that the most important thing for maintaining a school was not magnificent halls or many people, but the passing on of that school's original teachings, which justifies its existence.

Notes

1. Kankō Mochizuki (1968) and Kaishū Shigyō (1952) are examples of studies that have sought to paint a comprehensive picture of the diversification of teachings in the Nichiren sect. Both books systematically discuss not only the theories of the scholar-monks of the Kyoto Nichiren schools, but those of all masters who played central roles in the intellectual changes from Nichiren's death to the Meiji period. However, more than half a century has already passed since their publication, so it is now time to rewrite them.
2. Anjūbō had to do with the intellectual transition in the eighth month of Tembun 6 (1538) when Nisshin was 30 years old. In particular, it seems that he was close and on good terms with Nichiō, so when Nisshin copied Nichishin's lecture record *Sōshaku* in Tembun 11 (1543), the copy's postscript came to include a comment saying that Nichiō had provided information about Master Nichishin's year of birth (*Sōshaku*, copy held by Risshō University Library). A text written by Nichiō in Eiroku 6 (1563) also contains many mentions of Nisshin's name (*Nikkōryū shoha*, copy held by Risshō University Library).
3. Nisshin, *Gosho kenmon* (copy held by Risshō University Library).
4. Owing to Nobukata's active scholarship, a large number of sources called "*shōmono*" continue to exist today. They include notes used by Nobukata for lectures and transcripts by students at his lectures. Guiding marks for rendering the

Chinese text into Japanese, including those used for Kokugaku and Confucian texts, were added to these *shōmono*, and so they have played a crucial role in clarifying the history of the pronunciation of Chinese characters in Japan in the Sengoku period. Since *shōmono* contain a lot of colloquialisms and use a lot of *kana* writing, they are very valuable as sources for Japanese linguistics. Nobukata's mass-production of such helpful sources and the fact that they are still extant today is the reason why he is a popular topic of study in many fields.

5. Kawase's research also suggests that this was the Ashikaga School's approach as the school's library catalog listed an especially large number of texts relating to divination.

6. Kawase pointed out cases of Ashikaga School graduates serving warrior families and argued that, "Ashikaga School graduates can be said to have been learners who met such demands of warrior families in this period, and if we fully understand to what extent the Ashikaga School prepared all kinds of elements according with the demands of the Sengoku warlords, then we should understand how welcome its properties were in that warrior society. In other words, we can say that the Ashikaga School was created and continued to thrive in accordance with the inescapable demands of the warrior families of the Muromachi period."

7. Medicine that can be traced back to Li Dongyuan and Zhu Danxi in the Chinese Jin-Yuan periods (1115–1367).

8. Yoshimi Miyamoto (2006b). This paper contains reprints of all seven certificates of transmission.

9. Among the acquaintances of Dōsan, a well-known person in the medical world of that time, were Ashikaga Yoshiteru (1536–1565), the thirteenth shogun of the Muromachi shogunate, Hosokawa Harumoto (1514–1563), Miyoshi Nagayoshi (1522–1564), Matsunaga Hisahide (1510–1577), Mōri Motonari (1497–1571). Oda Nobunaga (1534–1582), Toyotomi Hideyoshi (1537–1598), and other people representative of the Sengoku period, suggesting academic exchanges via medicine and his medical activities as a doctor.

10. Itō pointed out that such literary techniques inherited by Zen monks were an indispensable form of learning as those in power would generally appoint such monks to draft diplomatic documents for the Ming and Korea.

11. *Honjaku ōrai shō* (copy held by Risshō University Library).

12. This contains a detailed examination of facts of the Tembun Hokke Riot based on contemporary sources.

13. Nisshin's copy is preserved in the Hōyōji Temple in Kyoto. It contains numerous notations reflecting his problem awareness at the time of copying.

14. Nisshin's copy is stored in the Hōyōji Temple in Kyoto.

15. *Sōshaku* (copy held by Risshō University Library).

16. *Hokke ronryaku taikō* (copy held by Risshō University Library).

References

Ashikaga, E. (1932). *Kamakura Muromachi jidai no jukyō* (Confucianism of the Kamakura Muromachi Periods). Tokyo: Nihon koten zenshū kankōkai.

Daikoku, K. (2004). "Nikkō monryū ni okeru hon'inmyō shisō keisei ni kansuru oboekaki (3)" (Memoranda on the Formation of the Theory of the Fundamental Reason for Becoming a Buddha in the Nikkō School). *Kōfu*, vol. 16, 369-422.

Endō, J. & Nakamura, T. (1999). "Manase Dōsan no zenhanki no igaku (1): tōryū no igi" (The Early Medicine of Manase Dōsan (1): The Significance of the Contemporary Medicine). *Nihon ishigaku zasshi*, vol. 45, no. 3, 323-337.

Gakurin, F ed. (1970a). *Fuji Gakurin Textbook: Research and Learning*, vol.2. Tokyo: Fuji Gakurin

Gakurin, F ed. (1970b). *Fuji Gakurin Textbook: Research and Learning*, vol.5. Tokyo: Fuji Gakurin

Hanawa Hokichi ed. (1934). Zoku gunsho ruiju hoi 3. Tokyo: Zoku gunsho ruiju kansei kai.

Hara, N. (1975). *Hōtō yomigaeru: Kōzōin Nisshin jōjin* (Reviving the Light of Buddhism: Venerable Kōzōin Nisshin). Kyoto: Honzan Yōbōji.

Hiraizumi, A. (1960). "Echizen no kuni Ichijōdani ban no isho to Ippaku rōjin" (The Echizen Ichijōdani Edition of Medical Texts and Old Ippaku). *Geirin*, vol. 11, no. 2, 53-58.

Imatani, A. (2009). *Tembun Hokke no ran: busō suru machishū* (The Tembun Hokke Riot: Local Businessmen Armed). Tokyo: Yōsensha.

Inoue, H. (1979). "Kinsei shotō Kyōto Nikkō monryū kyōgaku no tenkai: Kōzōin Nisshin no zōbutsu ron to dokuju ron o megutte" (The Development of the Teachings of the Nikkō School in the Early Early-Modern Period: Kōzōin Nisshin's Theories on Buddha Images and Sutra Chanting). *Kenkyū nenpō: Nichiren to sono kyōdan*, vol. 4, 84-126.

Itō, K. (2002). *Chūsei Nihon no gaikō to zenshū* (Medieval Japanese Diplomacy and Zen Buddhism). Tokyo: Yoshikawa kōbunkan.

Kagami, K. (2006). "Kōzōin Nisshin no happin kyōgaku hihan ni tsuite" (On Kōzōin Nisshin's Criticism of the Eight-Chapter Teachings). *Kōryū gakurin kiyō*, vol. 12, 31-68.

Kanda, D. (2014). "Kōzōin Nisshin kyōgaku no ichi kōsatsu: Nisshin no Kitano is-saikyō hiken no jiseki o chūshin ni" (A Study on the Teachings of Kōzōin Nisshin: Centering on Nisshin's Achievement of Perusing the Kitano Complete Buddhist Scriptures). *Nichiren kyōgaku kenkyūjo kiyō*, vol. 41, 44-65.

Kanda, D. (2015). "Kōzōin Nisshin no Kitano issaikyō hiken no jiseki: Kitanosha issaikyō ni mirareru Nisshin no shikigo o chūshin ni" (Kōzōin Nisshin's Achievement of Perusing the Kitano Complete Buddhist Scriptures: Centering on Nisshin's Added Postscripts in the Kitano Complete Buddhist Scriptures). *Daigakuin nenpō*, vol. 32, 1-34.

Kanda, D. (2017). "Kōzōin Nisshin kyōgaku ni okeru geshu ron no ichi kōsatsu: Keirinbō Nichiryū cho *Jusan mondō shō* no in'yō o megutte" (A Study on the Lower-Seeds Theory in the Teachings of Kōzōin Nisshin: Citing Keirinbō Nichiryū's *Jusan mondō shō*). *Nichiren kyōgaku kenkyūjo kiyō*, vol. 44, 75-111.

Kanda, D. (2018). "Kōzōin Nisshin no juryō hombutsu kan" (Kōzōin Nisshin's View on the Life Span of the Original Buddha). Master Zenchō Kitagawa koki kinen rombun shū *Nichren kyōgaku o meguru shomondai*, Tokyo: Sankibō busshorin

Kangakuryō, Y. (1929). *Summer Course Record (4)*. Kyoto: Kyoto Yōbōji Temple.

Kawase, K. (1948). *Ashikaga gakkō no kenkyū* (Ashikaga School Research). Tokyo: Dai-Nihon yūbenkai Kōdansha.

Kinsei, K. N. K. H. (2009). *Kenkyū seika hōkoku kai, wākushoppu, Manase Dōsan: koisho no Kanbun o yomu* (Research Findings Report Meeting and Workshop on Manase Dōsan: Reading Chinese in Old Medical Texts). Tokyo: Nishō gakusha daigaku 21-seiki COE puroguramu jimukyoku.

Kobayashi, C. (2003). *Kiyohara no Nobukata kō "Nihon shoki shō" honbun to kenkyū* (The Main Text and a Study of the "*Nihon shoki shō*," Lectures by Kiyohara no Nobukata). Tokyo: Bensei shuppan.

Kōshirō, H. (1981). *Chūsei zenrin no gakumon oyobi bungaku ni kansuru kenkyū* (Research on the Learning and Literature of Medieval Zen Temples). Kyoto: Shibunkaku shuppan.

Kyōto-fu, I. I. H. (1980). *Kyōto no igakushi* (Medical History of Kyoto). Kyoto: Shibunkaku shuppan.

Machi, S. (2012). "Kinsei Nihon no igaku ni miru 'manabi' no tenkai" (The Development of "Learning" in Early-Modern Japanese Medicine). *Nihon Kambungaku kenkyū*, vol. 7, 53-78.

Miyamoto, Y. (2006a). "'Tōryū igaku' genryū kō: Dōsan–Sanki–Sanki ron no saikentō" (Study of the Origin of "Contemporary Medicine": Reconsidering the Dōsan–Sanki–Sanki Theory). *Shichō*, vol. 59, 4-29.

Miyamoto, Y. (2006b). "Manase Dōsan no 'tōryū igaku' sōden" (The Inheritance of Manase Dōsan's "Contemporary Medicine"). *Sengoku Shokuhōki no shakai to girei*, Tokyo: Yoshikawa kōbunkan.

Mizukami, M. (2010). "Kiyahara no Nobukata no keigaku: kochū no goji to shinchū no juyō" (The Confucianism of Kiyohara no Nobukata: Protecting Old Commentaries and Receiving New Commentaries). *Ryūkyū Daigaku kyōiku gakubu kiyō*, vol. 76, 51-65.

Mochizuki, K. (1968). *Nichiren-shū gakusetsu shi* (History of the Theories of the Nichiren Sect). Kyoto: Heirakuji shoten.

Risshō Daigaku Nichiren kyōgaku kenkyūjo, ed. (1964). *Nichiren kyōdan zenshi, jō* (Complete History of the Nichiren Sect I). Kyoto: Heirakuji shoten.

Sakurai, K. (1959). "Baioku Sōkō to Jōfukuji Hon'ōan ikō tō ni tsuite" (Baioku Sōkō and the Posthumous Manuscripts of Hon'ōan of Jōfukuji Temple). *Kokushi ronshū*, vol. 1, 933-948.

Shigyō, K. (1952). *Nichiren-shū kyōgaku shi* (History of the Teachings of the Nichiren Sect). Kyoto: Heirakuji shoten.

Takahashi, R ed. (1958). Sanetaka kōki kan-8. Tokyo: Zoku gunsho ruijū kansei kai.

Tamura, K. (1996a). "Kōzōin Nisshin no hon'u rokkai ron o megutte" (On Kōzōin Nisshin's Innate Six-World Theory). *Nichiren kyōgaku kenkyūjo kiyō*, vol. 23, 50-65.

Tamura, K. (1996b). "Kōzōin Nisshin no senshi hihan nit suite: Keirinbō Nichiryū hihan o chūshin ni" (On Kōzōin Nisshin's Criticism of Former Teachers: Centering on his Criticism of Keirinbō Nichiryū). *Daigakuin nenpō*, vol. 14, 1-13.

Tamura, K. (1997a). "*Hokke gengi* rokujū honjaku to Kōzōin Nisshin no hombutsu ron" (The Six Interpretations of Manifestation in the *Fahua xuanyi* and Kōzōin Nisshin's View on the Original Buddha). *Nichiren kyōgaku kenkyūjo kiyō*, vol. 24, 42-54.

Tamura, K. (1997b). "Kōzōin Nisshin no hombutsu ron to daimoku ron" (Kōzōin Nisshin's Original Buddha Theory and Sutra Chanting Theory). *Bukkyōgaku ronshū*, vol. 21, 48-71.

Tomiya, N. (1925). *Ōjō honzan Yōbōji chūkō: Nisshin shōnin den* (Restoration of Yōbōji Head Temple in the Imperial Capital: Biography of Venerable Nisshin). Kyoto: Nisshin jōjin go-onki kinen hōe shuppan jigyōbu.

Tomiya, N. (1994). *Honshū shikō* (General History of This School). Kyoto: Honzan Yōbōji.

Tōkyō Daigaku shiryō hensan sho ed. (1944). Old Records of Japan: Nisuiki 3. Tokyo: Iwanami shoten.

Usui, N. (1959). "Kitanosha issaikyō to Kyōh-dō" (The Kitano Shrine Complete Buddhist Scriptures and the Kyōh-dō). *Nihon bukkyō*, vol. 3, 37-53.

Wajima, Y. (1961). "Ashikaga gakkō shinron (jō)" (New Theory on the Ashikaga School I). *Ronshū*, vol. 8, no. 1, 1-22.

Yakazu, D. (1982). *Kinsei Kanpō igaku shi: Manase Dōsan to sono gakukei* (Early-Modern History of Traditional Chinese Medicine: Manase Dōsan and His Academic Lineage). Osaka: Meicho shippan.

Yamada, H. (1957). "Kiyohara no Nobukata ni tsuite" (About Kiyohara no Nobukata). *Kokugo to kokubungaku*, *34*(10), 118-126.

Yamagami, K. (1988). "Kōzōin Nisshin kyōgaku no kenkyū (jō)" (Research on the Teachings of Kōzōin Nisshin I). *Kōfu*, vol. 6, 1-62.

Yonehara, M. (1976). *Sengoku bushi to bungei no kenkyū* (Research on Warriors and the Arts in the Sengoku Period). Tokyo: Ōfūsha.

Yūki, R. (1959). *Kanazawa Bunko to Ashikaga Gakkō* (Kanazawa Bunko and the Ashikaga School). Tokyo: Shibundō.

An Examination of the Complementary Currencies Past and Present

Yasushi Hayashi
Tetsuya Utashiro

Abstract

So-called complementary currencies are broadly divided into community currencies, whose main purpose is to deepen and restructure relationships between constituents within a community, and "market transaction" type complementary currencies, whose main aim is to activate transactions within a given market. Complementary currencies flourished in various countries in the 1980s, during which time community currencies were the dominant form. Stamp scrip, which is viewed as the original form of a "market transaction" type complementary currency, was used in the US and Europe in the 1930s. Actual stamp scrips partially complement the functions of legal tender by finely adjusting the legal tender system. Free money, a method of affixing the stamps to a certificate, conceived by Gesell and others, is a substitute for legal tender, i.e. an alternative currency. The difference between alternative currency and complementary currency needs to be considered distinctly. Moreover, stamp scrip is frequently talked about in terms of negative interest rates, but it is a mistake to consider the depreciation of stamp currency as a negative interest rate. Confusion can be seen in interpretations of Gresham's Law. In this paper, while examining these misperceptions and misunderstandings, we investigate the mechanisms and roles of stamp scrip and market transaction type complementary currencies, and consider the use of complementary currencies.

Acknowledgments

We graciously accept a 2018 grant from the Rissho University Economic Research Institute.

Introduction

Regular money (currency) is a tool used to smoothly conduct market transactions, regardless of industrial or financial circulation, and the market is composed of that money. In that sense, there is today both a market economy and a monetary economy. The unification of currency is effective for the strong promotion of growth in market transactions. For example, advancing unification with legal tender, introducing a common currency, dollarization or alignment with the euro or renminbi, and so on. On the other hand, there is money that also exists as an antithesis to the market and monetary economies. These are the so-called complementary currencies, which connote a departure from a unified currency or the act of unbundling.

Money is diverse; however, that is not to say that diversity is acquired automatically or voluntarily. Markets and money can be described as organic things, but naturally this is only rhetoric. Money is diverse because the community has given it the roles it expects for the money it uses, and so its role is a definition given by the community. This dynamic is termed "ambiguity."

Although complementary currencies have frequently been used in Japan as communication tools, our academic interest is in complementary currency as money that is used to activate transactions within a market or a "market-transaction" type of complementary currency. A market-transaction type complementary currency is one that can be exchanged for goods as legal tender in transactions between people in their daily lives. Of course, because a market-transaction type complementary currency is used by a community, it may also play a role as a communication tool.

This paper recognizes and examines the mechanisms of depreciation, circulation and the pattern of users' value changes in stamp scrip in Europe and the US since the 1920s, as well as the stamp scrip conceived by Irving Fisher in 1933. We investigate the role of complementary currency, motives for storing money, and negative interest, as well as the possibility of use as a fiscal easing policy in designated regions. We further consider topics involving Gresham's Laws of complementary currency, and the use of complementary currency with the aim of stimulating disaster recovery.

This paper is a short summary that focuses on chapters 3 and 4 of *The Contemporary Interpretation and Significance of Irving Fisher's 'Stamp Scrip' (Complementary Currencies)* (Utashiro & Hayashi, 2019), with additional adjustments.

1. Historical Development of Market-transaction Type Complementary Currencies

1.1 Silvio Gesell's Free-Money

Gesell proposed free money in 1916 in *Die Natürliche Wirtschaftsordnung* to reduce and eliminate the predominance of coin.[1] Put simply, Gesell's idea was as follows (Gesell, 1916, pp. 179-183): The value of all goods besides money decreases over time due to deterioration, wear, destruction, rot, etc. Money, by contrast, does not deteriorate or wear out. Money is superior to other goods in terms of carrying costs, and it is easy to postpone its use; in other words, money tends to be a method of savings. Money was originally simply a medium used to facilitate the transaction of goods, but differences in carrying costs hinder smooth exchange. Gesell therefore proposed the introduction of free money, the value of which decreases with time, as follows.

- Issue 6 types of bills in denominations of 1, 5, 10, 50, 100, and 1,000 marks.
- The 6 types of marked bills would lose 0.1% of their face value each week. A supplementary bill equivalent to 0.1% must be affixed to the back of the bill, which the holder bears the cost.

Gesell's proposal was a reform of legal tender itself. The government issues free money according to demand for bills (an alternative currency applying the stamp system) and collects any surplus (Gesell, 1916, pp. 184-185). The existing currency, the mark, would initially be continued, and individuals would be free to exchange free money for the currency; the two currencies would circulate simultaneously during an exchange period several months long. At the end of the exchange period, the conventional mark would lose its status as legal tender and only free money would be distributed.

1.2 Stamp Scrip from the 1930s

Since around 1930, local governments and citizens' groups in Europe have issued complementary currencies with the aim of aiding local employment and reviving stagnant economic activity. The Wara (Wära) was issued in Germany in 1929, the JAK in Denmark in 1931, the Woergl Certified Compensation Bill (Arbeitswertscheinen) in Austria in 1932, and the WIR in Switzerland in 1934.[2,3,4,5]

In the US, states, local governments, and chambers of commerce had also issued many such bills as measures to counter a recession. Stamp scrip was frequently issued in the city of Anaheim in California between late 1932 and early 1933. The US was comprised of 48 states at the time, since Hawaii and Alaska had yet to achieve statehood, but according to depressionscrip. com, in the 48 states, 319 municipalities in 45 states, and one municipality in the Alaskan territory, a total of 320 municipalities, were issuing complementary currencies.[6] Of these, around 50 municipalities were issuing stamp scrip, chiefly in Iowa and California.[7]

The stamp scrip found at that time in various regions in Europe and in the US were directly born from Gesell's idea of free money. However, the stamp scrip actually issued then, as well as the stamp scrip devised by Fisher, was not the alternative currency that Gesell seems to have contemplated; rather, it temporarily and partially complemented the function and/or role of legal tender, as a means of fine-tuning the conventional legal tender system.[8]

1.3 Evaluation of Stamp Scrip by Keynes and Fisher

Complementary currency circulates simultaneously with legal tender in a society where legal tender are in circulation (this is called a parallel currency system). Alternative currency is used in a single currency system and intended to be circulated in place of the existing currency. The difference between alternative currency and complementary currency needs to be considered distinctly. What role stamp scrip should play, and, moreover, the mechanism that should be adopted differ depending on whether the stamp scrip is to be an alternative currency or a complementary currency.

In the quantity theory of money, the amount of money in circulation in society and the velocity of its circulation determine the price level, expressed by Fisher's Equation of Exchange. Fisher thought that the circulation rate of money (velocity of circulation) ought to be increased to lift the economy.

Fisher published "Stamp Scrip" in 1933. In the 1930s, Fisher, who was interested in the use of stamp scrip in various parts of the US to lessen the pain being caused by the Great Depression, sought to find a path out of the recession by positioning stamp scrip as a means of raising money's velocity of circulation to promote consumption. Only the part about reducing value was adopted from Gesell's idea of free money, to be a tool to cause reflation and overcome deflation.

Keynes also refers to Gesell's stamp scrip in his 1936 *General Theory* (Keynes, 1936, p. 358). However, Keynes' criticism was of Gesell's free money, which had never been realized, and not of Fisher's idea or stamp scrip in practice.

1.4 The Stamp Scrip Family Tree

Complementary currencies have spread in various countries since the 1980s. LETS and the Time Dollar are said to be the pioneers of complementary currencies, and, as of 2013, there are thousands of examples of their implementation around the world (Seyfang & Longhurst, 2013, pp. 69-70). These complementary currencies are largely found in Europe and the US, and spread primarily in developed economies. The LETS and Time Dollar types, as well as the eco-money type in Japan, are complementary currencies generally referred to as community currencies.[9]

Conversely, there are over 200 types of market-transaction (market-economy) type complementary currencies, with a few examples of their implementation (Seyfang & Longhurst, 2013, pp. 70-71). The principle aim of "market-transaction" type complementary currency is its use for exchange with market-transactable goods that are transacted using legal tender. Rather than circulate within a specific group, it can be obtained and used by anyone in the region, and its main use is to pay for general merchandise in the same way as legal tender. Fisher's stamp scrip was also intended to stimulate market transactions, and market-transaction type complementary currencies are descended from stamp scrip (however, some adopt a stamp system).[10]

Stamp scrip and market transaction-type complementary currency, similar to legal tender, basically do not lose purchasing power through the provision of that currency, and purchasing power is transferred to the person receiving it. Moreover, it is intended to be distributed, unlike gift cards, which are in-tended for a single use. The transferred purchasing power circulates through its subsequent use in goods transactions, and continues to function as a medium for exchange.

2. The Stamp Scrip Mechanism

2.1 Overview of the Issuance and Distribution of Stamp Scrip

Here, rather than describe individual stamp scrip, we instead explain the stamp scrip Fisher sought to adopt. Fisher states the characteristics of stamp scrip as being similar to money in that it "can be deposited, invested and consumed," and different in that it "cannot be hoarded" (Fisher, 1933, p. 8).

There are frames on the rear side of the stamp scrip on which stamps can be attached, and the date is printed in each frame. When stamps are affixed each month, 12 frames are printed, and 52 frames are printed when stamps are affixed each week. The first user after a set date and time (for example, each Wednesday at midnight) is required to purchase and affix a stamp in the form of a postage stamp or frank to the designated frame on the stamp scrip. This system of affixing stamps prompts people to use stamp scrip promptly, and as a result increases its velocity of circulation (Fisher, 1933, p. 13).

To obtain acceptance as currency, the exchange of issued stamp scrip for cash was guaranteed. If a stamp is two cents, over 52 weeks this would have a sales price of $1.04, of which one dollar could be redeemed and the four cents would be used to print stamps and manage the plan.

The major point of difference between Europe and the US is that in Europe the timing for affixing stamps was regular (for example, every Wednesday), while in the US this was generally done for each transaction.[11] In addition, in Europe, where stamps were affixed on a regular basis, annualized stamp costs were 12% of face value for the Wara and the Woergl Certified Compensation Bills and 24% for WIR bills, while in America these costs exceeded 100%.

2.2 The Shape of Stamp Scrip Value

For stamp scrip to be circulated efficiently, the movement of change in value is important in the system design. This consists of: 1) the price of stamps, or the ratio of stamps to face value, and 2) the frequency of affixing stamps (the interval between the date to affix a stamp, t_n, and the subsequent date to affix a stamp, t_{n+1}). Here, we consider a European-style stamp scrip in which the first user must affix a stamp after the date to affix a stamp t_n.

The value of stamp scrip without the newly affixed stamp declines from face value to zero at the moment the date changes from the day before the date to affix a stamp, t_{n-1}, to the date to affix the stamp, t_n. However, in practice, the stamp scrip is returned to face value by paying the additional cost of the stamp, since its actual value does not become zero, and depreciates only by the value of the stamp (see Fig. 1).

However, assuming that it is highly likely that others will not accept this, at the extreme, even when received immediately after affixing a stamp the value of the stamp scrip to the recipient is its face value less the value of the stamp. In other words, its actual shape is as shown in Figure 1, but exactly when the decrease in value occurs is an individual issue. Furthermore, if it is thought that it (the scrip) has no acceptance at all, its value will not be the face value less the value of the stamps, but almost zero. Even if Figure 1 has a logical shape, the value differs between individuals.

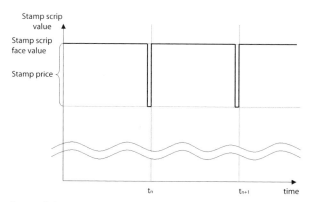

Fig. 1 The shape of changes in stamp scrip value. (Created by the author)

Next, we consider a case that did not exist in the 1930s, one of paying for stamps on a daily basis. If done electronically, it would not be difficult today to require stamps on a daily basis. Although different from actual stamp scrip, we consider a situation where the cost of stamps must be paid on a daily basis.

From the date a stamp is to be affixed, t_n, to the next date on which a stamp is to be affixed, t_{n+1}, the value of the stamp scrip decreases linearly from its face value at t_n to the time t_{n+1}, and affixing a stamp increases the value vertically back to its face value. At this time, the shape of its value is regarded as a sawtooth shape, repeating this motion (Fig. 2).

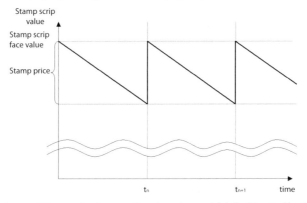

Fig. 2 The shape of changes in stamp scrip value when paid daily. (Created by the author)

However, in this case it is possible that different shapes are drawn in the minds of different people.

Although Figures 1 and 2 above show the actual value per unit of time for the stamp scrip, this may be different for different people. Next, we consider how people generally perceive changes in value, and the general shape of value that people internalize.

The stamp price is paid only by the first person to use it after the date a stamp is affixed. Although it is unclear whether a specific individual will bear that cost, the probability increases as time goes by. When someone believes an individual will bear the cost, the shape of the change in value people perceive will be such that the linear sections that descend diagonally as the sawtooth edges will be convex in the top right direction in the daily-rate case described above (Fig. 3). People act on the premise that these are approximately worth face value for a certain period of time and begin to lose value as the stamp date approaches, and they act on the assumption that the value will fall sharply at some point. How to think about the acceptability of stamp scrip differs depending on the individual and the situation; some people may believe value begins to diminish at a different point in time than that in Figure 3, and the point when value begins to drop sharply will also differ between people and depending on the situation at the time.

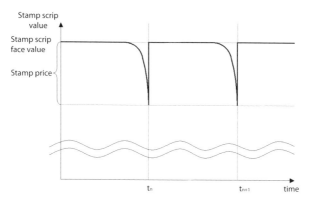

Fig. 3 The shape of people's perception of changes in stamp scrip value. (Created by the author)

3. Problems with Complementary Currencies

3.1 The Function and Role of Complementary Currency, and Motives for Storing Money

3.1.1 The function and role of money

What we often call the "function of money" should strictly speaking be called the "role of money."[12] While we do not discuss this in detail here due to space constraints, we describe it briefly.

How economists have expressed and handled this issue is deeply interesting. William Stanley Jevons is thought to have first compiled economists' views on the functions of money up to that point, and cites them as (1) a medium of exchange, (2) a common measure of value, (3) a standard of value, and (4) a store of value (Jevons, 1875, pp. 20-22).[13]

Financial theory textbooks today often cite (1), (2), and (4) as the three functions and/or roles.[14] Here there is also a notion separating exchange and settlement. Note that there are also some that regard (4) as not being unique to money.

Hayek was also skeptical about the expression "function," and did not use the term "function" in the *Denationalization of Money*; instead, he presented the uses of money.[15] Moreover, he comments,

I have always found it useful to explain to students that it has been rather a misfortune that we describe money by a noun, and that it would be more helpful for the explanation of monetary phenomena if "money" were an adjective describing a property which different things could possess to varying degrees. "Currency" is, for this reason, more appropriate, since objects can "have currency" to varying degrees and through different regions or sectors of the population (Hayek, 1976, p. 56).

The difference between "noun" and "adjective" appears to be consistent with an awareness of the issue we are considering between "function" and "role" (Nishibe, 2014, p. 94, pp. 148-154).[16] For example, Goodhart describes "money's initial role" and seems to consciously use the term "role" (Goodhart, 1998, p. 413).

It is often pointed out that money is diverse, but considering that its expected role is conferred by society, it is more than diverse; it is ambiguous in the sense that it can be defined by others.

3.1.2 The functions and roles of complementary currencies

So-called complementary currencies can be viewed as not being fully-fledged currencies in that they are not given the three roles. Yet when we consider currency as ambiguous, the role of complementary currency re-emerges.

Speaking in terms of so-called hard and soft classifications, hard money will satisfy some of its expected roles more strongly, while soft money has fewer expected roles and satisfies these less strongly or more sparsely.[17]

Role	Hard money (legal tender)	Soft money (complementary currency)
Settlement (Exchangeability)	○	△
Storability	○	△?
Scale	○	△✕

Fig. 4 The Role of Money (Legal Tender and Complementary Currency). (Created by the author)

With respect to legal tender and complementary currency, legal tender is hard, while complementary currency is soft. This difference arises from the scope and strength of their expected roles. For example, if its expected role can no longer be fulfilled, the currency will soften, even for legal tender. The order in which these can be expected to not be satisfied is storage, settlement, and then measurability. Legal tender has the strength of having to be accepted; however, it is not necessarily hard money. Where there is a discrepancy between general acceptability and compulsory acceptance, compulsory acceptance may not be exerted (in that sense, the term "compulsory acceptance" may be more appropriately called "legal acceptance"). Even if it is legal tender, if the state or government lacks credibility, it will lose compulsory acceptance.

For example, in Ecuador in 2000, immediately prior to dollarization, the softening of the Sucre was accompanied by the loss of its storability, a sharp decline in its use for settlement, and at the same time, the loss of its measurability, and so was replaced by the US dollar (see Hayashi & Kinoshita, 2014).

Storability, the third role of money, which is characteristically lost in complementary currency, is the ability to bring today's purchasing power into the future. There are few complementary currencies that play the role of storage. From the outset, complementary currencies lacked compulsory acceptance and had less credibility than legal tender, and so have been more oriented towards promoting consumption in the present rather than for carrying purchasing power over into the future.

3.1.3 Motives for storing complementary currency
Next, let us look at the differences between hard and soft money from the perspective of motives for storing money.

Motive	Hard money (legal tender)	Soft money (complementary currency)
Transaction	○	△
Precautionary	○	△
Speculative	○	×

Fig. 5 Motives for Holding Currency (Legal Tender and Complementary Currency). (Created by the author)
※The motivation to hold cash upon understanding that opportunity costs have occurred.

Comparing the two, as with their roles, hard money is superior to soft money for each motive.

Rather than comparing them, let us assume there is only one currency and consider the three motives. Where no money is held, the order of priorities for the receiving side is generally thought to be the transaction motive, precautionary motive, and finally, the speculative motive. In other words, money is first received to satisfy the transaction motive, and when that is satisfied, or is "expected to be satisfied," the subsequent precautionary motive begins to act to receive money. Last, money is received through the speculative motive.

These three motives are often thought of as similar to the process by which water fills in a cascade from upstream of a triple dam; in reality, however, the transaction motive is not fully satisfied before the subsequent precautionary motive acts. The three motives are arbitrarily selected according to the combination of expectations about the future receipt of money and payment.

The same holds where hard and soft money coexist. The three motives are arbitrarily selected according to the combination of expectations about the future receipt of the two currencies and payment. For example, let us consider a case where a person is in the following financial position.

Target of possession	⟨1⟩	⟨2⟩	⟨3⟩	⟨4⟩	⟨5⟩	⟨6⟩	⟨7⟩	⟨8⟩
Transaction motive	+	−	+	+	−	−	+	−
Precautionary motive	+	+	−	+	−	+	−	−
Speculative motive	+	+	+	−	+	−	−	−

Fig. 6-1 The State of Hard Money Holding [Assumption] (Created by the author)
※The + symbol indicates that it is fully satisfied, and the - symbol indicates that it is insufficiently satisfied.

At this time, the room for that person to accept soft money is thought to be as follows.

Target of possession	⟨1⟩	⟨2⟩	⟨3⟩	⟨4⟩	⟨5⟩	⟨6⟩	⟨7⟩	⟨8⟩
Transaction motive	−	+	−	−	+	+	−	+
Precautionary motive	−	−	+	−	+	−	+	+
Speculative motive	−	−	−	+	−	+	+	+

Fig. 6-2 Room for Accepting Soft Money (Created by the author)
※The + symbol indicates that it is fully accepted, and the - symbol indicates that it is not fully accepted.

These include combinations that are thought to be virtually non-existent in practice. For example, in case <1>, there is no room to accept soft money for any motive. In case <2>, there is scope to accept soft money under the transaction motive, and in case <3>, there is scope to accept soft money under the precautionary motive. The situation in case <3> must be transferred to case <2> for the purpose of circulating soft money throughout a city. This also depends on the state of that individual's holding of hard money; however, this may be possible by devising a plan with soft money. For example, if soft money depreciates at fixed intervals, the precautionary and speculative motivations for soft money are reduced.

Regardless of the manner in which hard money is held, case <2> is desirable as room for accepting soft money. Cases <5> and <8> show the excessive issuance of soft money.

3.2 The Significance of Stamps and Monetary Easing

3.2.1 Stamps as demurrage
The notion of a depreciating complementary currency is Gesell's starting point, but Gesell did not position the depreciation of free money as a negative interest rate. Not limited to agricultural products, Gesell believed that goods deteriorate and wear, and he thought the only issue was that money does not deteriorate; thus, the tool by which to cause money to deteriorate was stamps.[18]

Stamp scrip depreciates at regular intervals, and stamps are affixed not to restore depreciated value; rather stamp scrip is forcibly stopped at fixed intervals, and a stamp is affixed to lift this cancellation. Strictly speaking, stamp scrip does not "depreciate," but rather demurrage (carrying costs) must be paid at regular intervals.[19] In that respect, it is "subordinated" to currency with regular circulatory power.

Gesell explains that for money to travel on the roads of the market, tolls must be paid. Stamps are the tolls to lift the barriers (Gesell, 1916, pp. 141-142).[20]

Fisher terms stamps as an ambulatory tax or a tax on hoarding, and described stamp scrip thus: "I think, to liken the scrip to a pre-dated check" (Fisher, 1933, pp. 4-5). "The stamp is more like a tax on hoarding than a sales tax. Hoard, and the tax is heavy; spend (or invest or deposit), and the tax is light" (Fisher 1933, p. 15). He states that if it is not paid on each transaction but instead apportioned based on the number of times used, then it cannot be considered a consumption tax. In pursuit of demurrage, stamps can be considered a public fee for the public stamp scrip system, used to promote the circulation of stamp scrip. However, there is a lack of fairness to its burden. This is, however, by design.

3.2.2 Misunderstanding interest rates

Recently, in the debate surrounding so-called negative interest rates, depreciation and negative interest rates are often confused, and complementary currency is mentioned. Focusing on the decrease in value over time is a mistake. Strong opposition may not be warranted if we treat the "depreciation" of stamp scrip and complementary currency as "negative interest" because its actual social effects are similar. However, discussions based solely on an analogy as a phenomenon is erroneous, and must be discussed with the proper understanding. Usually, where money lacks a lending relationship, no interest occurs. For example, even if it appears at a glance that there is no lending relationship, as with net present value, if we receive and deposit (use) it today, this means calculating the value of interest, and can be said to be a pseudo-loan relationship because it imitates a loan relationship.[21]

Fisher never considered this system of depreciation to be a negative interest rate. It is subordinated to legal tender using the mechanism of demurrage.

Keynes states:

According to my theory it should be roughly equal to the excess of the money-rate of interest (apart from the stamps) over the marginal efficiency of capital corresponding to a rate of new investment compatible with full employment. The actual charge suggested by Gesell was 1 per mil. per week, equivalent to 5.2 per cent per annum. This would be too high in existing conditions, but the correct figure, which would have to be changed from time to time, could only be reached by trial and error (Keynes, 1936, p. 358).[22]

We cannot say directly from this sentence that Keynes considered the cost of the stamp as interest, and do not know whether he dared to do so, but Keynes treats it as a kind of interest.

3.2.3 The issuance of complementary currency as a monetary easing measure

Currency other than legal tender circulates in areas where stamp scrip is used. If legal tender is not used for the amount of stamp scrip issued, the base shared by the two currencies, legal tender and stamp scrip, will not change. However, if the rotation velocity in the process of circulation differs, the multiplier effect will be greater for the stamp scrip, which is expected to circulate more. The same also applies for systems where stamps are not affixed.

Even within a limited scope of distribution, the total amount of money issued and the volume of circulation are likely to increase, which is equivalent to performing quantitative easing (see Nishibe, 2018, p. 13 et al.). As described later, complementary currency used for disaster recovery can be expected to play a role as a regional monetary easing measure. Of course, this can be implemented not only for special purposes such as recovery, but also during normal periods. The issuance of complementary currency can be considered a measure for lifting the economy in regions suffering prolonged economic stagnation. For example, development in the American region of Appalachia began under government leadership in 1965, but has been said to be the poorest region in the entire US.[23] Besides governmental fiscal spending, monetary easing can be considered to ease the economy; however, it is almost impossible to reduce the interest rate of the US dollar, which is legal tender only in limited regions.[24] Monetary easing effects can be expected by issuing complementary currency.[25]

3.3 Gresham's Law and Complementary Currency

Gresham's Law is an ideology, and the definition varies from person to person. In addition, Gresham himself did not claim it to be a "law," and the fact that it has not been defined has created confusion.

3.3.1 The validity of Gresham's Law
Gresham's Law immediately comes to mind when there is competition between two types of currency, or the withdrawal of currency. Let us investigate Gresham's Law.

The law's name appears to have been derived from Thomas Gresham, who in the mid-16th century suggested that the cause of the outflow of good money (or that English sovereign debt was trusted) from England overseas was due to its low unit value, and that the unit value should be increased.

The general understanding of Gresham's Law is that "bad money drives out good," which can be summarized as "for precious-metal currency, a phenomenon that occurs in which high unit value currency is hoarded or used for foreign trade, and only low unit value currency features in the process of circulation."[26] Currency with a high unit value is good money and currency with a low unit value is bad money. Note that the process of circulation refers to a narrowly-defined circulation market, and Gresham's Law does not describe society as a whole. Jevons states that the reason the phenomenon occurs where good money is withdrawn and only bad money remains in the circulation process is that the side purchasing goods tries to purchase the best goods with inferior money, but this is thought to be a misunderstanding (Jevons, 1875, p. 74). For such a phenomenon to occur, it must be assumed that good and bad money with the same face value are traded at face value rather than at unit value. Hayek points out that this is only the case where a fixed exchange rate between good and bad money is enforced. Because the exchange rate is fixed, the goods purchaser pays in bad money; if the exchange rate is variable, the value of bad money declines, and people may choose not to accept it (Hayek, 1976, pp. 42-43).[27]

Fisher regarded Gresham's Law as concerning precious-metal currency, and moreover, that it depended on transactors' power relationships. He states that if the buy-side is dominant they will pay with bad money and the bad money will drive out the good, while if the sell-side is dominant they will receive good money and so good money will drive out bad money.[28]

Gresham's Law must be relative because the relationship between the two types of currency is not substitutional but rather complementary.

3.3.2 Fiduciary currency and Gresham's Law

Here, whether Gresham's Law also holds for bills becomes an issue. Being literally made of paper, there is no difference in the unit value of materials between bills, and the strength of its credibility determines whether to hold it or use it quickly. In short, bills with high creditworthiness (generally legal tender) are usually considered good money. Again, if Hayek's idea is expanded to the story of bills, banknotes will be selected based on differences in creditworthiness because the unit value has no relevance to paper bills. If currency can be freely chosen, there should not be anyone who chooses the one whose value will deteriorate.

For example, if a certain country's foreign exchange is a floating exchange rate system, foreign exchange is established as a market. However, if a fixed exchange rate is assumed, Gresham's Law is likely to be observed because a currency whose purchasing power is likely to be maintained will be retained.

Foreign currency with high creditworthiness drives out foreign currency with low creditworthiness. This is considered the driving force for transition to a floating exchange rate system. Ecuador's dollarization can be regarded as having been a forced dollarization because the superior purchasing power of the dollar over the Sucre had grown to a point that became intolerable (see Hayashi & Kinoshita, 2014).

However, it should be noted that the meaning of "drive out" here differs from that used by Gresham. According to Gresham's Law, the reason only bad money features in the circulation process is that good money is withdrawn, but that does not mean good money is driven out of society as a whole. In Hayek's case, he states that bad coins are driven out of the circulation process as well as from society at large.

Moreover, in the relationship between legal tender and stamp scrip, bad money will circulate during recessions because goods buyers have the initiative. In other words, Fisher dared to create "bad money" called stamp scrip to circulate it in parallel with the legal tender.

4. Use of Complementary Currency

4.1 Community Regeneration Type and Market Transaction Type Complementary Currencies

Since the 1980s, so-called complementary currencies have been implemented in various parts of the world. These complementary currencies have two main purposes: community revitalization and revitalization of a local economy. There are many examples of the implementation of community-revitalization type complementary currencies in developed economies such as those in Europe, the US, and Japan. The significance of a complementary currency as a medium for promoting volunteerism, mutual assistance, and connections is stronger than its significance as a medium for the exchange of currency or goods. There are, of course, also cases where community regeneration or revitalization of the local economy is an intermediate goal, and the final goal is something else. In any case, these two goals are nearly inseparable.

The discussion thus far has focused on stamp scrip and market transaction type complementary currencies, but let us mention the possibility of complementary currencies, including community currency, while considering the relationship between community regeneration type and market transaction type complementary currencies. Considering complementary currency can contribute socially and economically as a medium for exchange, we consider what type of uses it is suitable for.

Take so-called *genkai shūraku* (depopulated villages) as an example of the relationship between a community currency and market transaction type complementary currencies. In some depopulated villages, the community is so extremely small that a community currency is unnecessary. Half a century ago, there were five shops in the village, but today there is a single general store, which is also a place for the village community. As residents of the village, it may be possible to maintain the store through donations or charity, for example, but this may differ from the residents' original intentions; from the viewpoint of sustainability, it may lead to the future collapse of the village as a community. What this village could do is issue and circulate a complementary currency that can only be used at the general store. It may be necessary for the municipal office to accept a public charge from residents as a special case. This complementary currency is an extreme market transaction type that incidentally becomes a community currency. Regional economic development effects would generally be expected concomitantly from a community currency, but it is highly interesting that in this case the opposite is true. While that is not to say any new concept is introduced here, it can be seen that the current economic system has been modified. This example of a depopulated village clearly shows the relationship between community regeneration type and market transaction type complementary currencies, and moreover, implies the possibility of complementary currency.

4.2 Reconstruction and Development Currency

The use of the stamp scrip mechanism is not limited to overcoming recessions that occur during normal business cycles. Let us consider expanding complementary currency to maintain the general store in the depopulated village described previously. For example, we consider it meaningful to apply it as one measure for reconstruction support in areas damaged by earthquakes, heavy rainfall, and so on. A great many disasters have occurred in Japan recently. There may also be cases where there are short reconstruction goals; however, in many cases it is extremely prolonged. Recovery from disasters such as earthquakes and heavy rain carried out using conventional macroeconomic policy does not always proceed smoothly. Reconstruction budgets such as emergency disaster response measure budgets are spent in legal tender. In this reconstruction work, the restoration of infrastructure essential to the livelihoods of local residents in the affected areas and rapid response to new disasters is emphasized. The businesses that undertake this are not only from the affected area but also from outside the area. Although infrastructure will recover, the funds invested in the recovery will flow out of the stricken area. These conventional methods inevitably restrict the return of reconstruction-related funds to local residents who have suffered damage to their homes and loss of their employment and livelihoods.

Thus, a complementary currency (reconstruction and development currency) for reconstruction projects can be considered a method of contributing not only to the disaster recovery but also to the local economy.[29] For example, suppose the government provides ¥100bn to the local government (or joint business group) as special financial support for disaster recovery. This financial support also may incorporate private sector donations.The local government could create a reconstruction fund with this ¥100bn, and issue a volume of reconstruction and development currency that can continue to circulate in the area backed by those funds as an asset.[30] Taking that ratio to be 70%, for example, ¥70bn of reconstruction and development currency will be issued. The remaining ¥30bn will be spent as yen on projects that must be paid in yen, such as those performed by businesses from outside the region with the aim of carrying out emergency recovery work. The ¥70bn of reconstruction and development currency will be paid to local businesses for reconstruction projects and spent as financial support for rebuilding and supporting the lives of poor households. The remainder of the ¥70bn yen can be used outside of the stricken area where legal tender (yen) is particularly necessary, for example scholarships for disaster victims, as well as interest-free loans for companies and individuals.

If, for example, this reconstruction and development currency is accepted for payment of taxes in the municipality, payment of public utility fees, and repayment of loans, circulation is unlikely to be impeded.[31] To promote the use of reconstruction and development currency, it may be desirable to provide a premium, such that ¥95 in legal tender can be exchanged for 100 units of the reconstruction and development currency, or a discount (by including a commission) such that 100 units of the reconstruction and development currency can be exchanged for ¥90.[32] Moreover, in light of the objective of disaster recovery, it may also be desirable not to exchange it for yen, or to have a mechanism whereby it can only be exchanged for yen after a period of time has elapsed.

It is good for the scope of circulation of the reconstruction and development currency to be large. While it may also depend on the scale of the disaster, it is desirable to have one or more prefectures or, at a minimum several municipalities, in the scope of circulation, and it may be better to design the system such that circulation includes not only the stricken area but also neighboring prefectures or parts thereof. The wider the scope of circulation, the more balanced the supply and demand of goods, making the use of the complementary currency easier, and increasing the opportunity for transactions. The circulation of currency centered on the stricken area and its partial acceptance in the surrounding region can increase opportunities to use the reconstruction and development currency for transactions for goods that cannot be procured from within the region and for special reconstruction skills. The issuance and circulation of these currencies also provides an incentive for volunteer activities.

Besides reconstruction and development currency, complementary currency can also be used. For example, it is possible to issue event support currency or volunteer support currency during events such as the Olympics or World Expo.

5. Conclusion

There are several creation and characteristic systems for money, and these are difficult to understand comprehensively and exhaustively. Because of ambiguity, it is natural that there are differences in what we wish to newly conceptualize and introduce into society. It is necessary to fully understand not only the mechanism and form, but also what it is we wish to conceptualize.

It is impossible to avoid discussions of propositions about the enigmas of human history and the nature, use, and role of money when considering the new currencies that have been gathering recent attention, such as cryptocurrencies and electronic money, so-called negative interest rates, and present or near-future monetary economic systems like cashless economies. Complementary currency is one clue in considering these kinds of new currency systems.

Notes

1 Besides Gesell, C.H. Douglas, Heinrich Rittershausen, and Henry Meulen argued for free money.

2 Stamp scrip was issued by the Wara-Exchanges (Wära-Tauschgesellschaft), founded in Germany in 1929. Offices for the exchanges were opened in 14 cities in Germany where the Wara could be purchased. Issuance was halted in 1931 because the German government banned emergency currency, including the Wara.

3 This was a complementary currency issued in Denmark by the Land, Labor and Capital Cooperative (JAK) in 1931. Bills were issued; however, a stamp mechanism was not adopted. This attempt was banned and ended based on a High Court decision in 1933.

4 Stamp scrip was issued and operated by the Austrian town of Woergl in 1932. It was circulated and used for paying an unemployment relief allowance within the town. It was banned and ended in 1933 for violating money sovereignty (Hoheit) set out in Article 122 of the National Banking Law.

5 This was a complementary currency operated by the Economic Circle Cooperative (Wirtschaftsring-Genossenschaft), established in Zurich in 1934. Rather than issuing bills, the Cooperative used a method of exchanging balances using books it managed collectively. Stamp scrip was issued and circulated between 1938 and 1948.

6 Collected and published images of the bills issued during the period of The Great Depression can be found at http://www.depressionscrip.com/index.html

7 Some documents indicate that Roosevelt prohibited stamp scrip. However, there is no such fact. They seem to be confused with the bank's prohibition of handling stamp scrip. (see Elvins, 2005 & Miyazaki, 2009 & Gatch, 2012)

8 Alternative currency is a single currency system that circulates in place of the currency already in circulation, while complementary currency is a parallel currency system in which multiple currencies circulate.

9 Community currency is a complementary currency that circulates within communities; local residents gather and exchange the currency with one another based on a particular purpose or interest, such as production, consumption, education, cultural activities, sports, etc. The LETS type is a system that records contents and value in a bankbook where transactions are recorded. The Time Dollar type is a unit-of-time type complementary currency that adopts the time spent for activities, such as volunteering (or labor), as the currency's scale of value. The eco-money type is a currency specializing in activating volunteer services that are not usually used in market-type transactions and are not measured in yen.

10 Market transaction type complementary currencies were specifically the stamp scrip and WIR in the 1930s. The Ithaca Hour is said to be a pioneer of complementary currencies after the 1980s, and since the 2000s, there have been the

Bristol Pound and Brixton Pound in the UK, the Italian Sardex, the German Chiemgauer, which uses stamps, and UDIS in Latin American countries.

11　Fisher opposes the method of affixing a stamp for each transaction (Fisher, 1933, p. 31). If stamps are affixed for each transaction, it can be called a consumption tax.

12　The word "function" is the inherent ability or property of the thing itself, whether it is an ability that is provided or fulfilled from the outset. "Function" is the kind of item described in specifications, and it is relatively clear whether the "function" is fulfilled. The term "role" refers to a position within an organization as a whole, and is a function that is expected to be fulfilled. "Role" is a crude standard that does not involve details, and has the characteristics described in articles of incorporation. For example, in the case of bills, "function" and "role" are often confused in discussions, but in the case of engines, it is easy to understand that these are different concepts.

13　Note that the 1870s was a period during which European countries were shifting from the double standard system to the gold standard.

14　In many books on complementary currency, growth is a fourth. This point is discussed in the next section.

15　There are four uses; use as cash for the purchase of goods and services, use to prepare for future needs, use for deferment payment, and use as a unit of account (Hayek, 1976, pp. 66-67). Exchange is its basic function, and as a result, its other uses are secondary.

16　Nishibe states that money is not just a "physical object" but a "matter."

17　Hard/soft is relative, not absolute.

18　Gold and silver do not deteriorate, but incur storage fees.

19　This refers to excess storage fees in the logistics industry. Excess storage fees are incurred where a container is not picked up during the free storage period and is kept in the container yard. Lietaer explains this as "demurrage fees." Gesell revived this concept, but historically, demurrage was introduced into the monetary systems in Europe between the 10th and 13th centuries and ancient Egyptian dynasties from about 3000 BC to 332 BC (from the Early Dynastic Period through to the Old Kingdom, Middle Kingdom, New Kingdom, through to the end of the Late Period) (Lietaer, 2000).

20　However, Gesell also describes "depreciation."

21　When talking of real values that take into account the rate of price increase, even if there is no lending relationship, in practice, the purchasing power of money will increase or decrease.

22　As already described, stamp prices in the US were a source of redemption, which when converted to an annual rate often exceeded 100%, resulting in an unfairly high rate of interest. At least in the US, it is unlikely this was considered by converting it to an interest rate. Moreover, with regard to the method of affixing a stamp for each transaction, stamps are independent of the time axis, and can be said to be completely separate from the interest rate.

23　According to the Appalachian Regional Commission, a vast region spanning 13 eastern states.

24　Countries can use fiscal, monetary, and exchange rate policies as macroeconomic stabilization policies. In general, under the system where only legal tender is distributed, only fiscal policy can be considered to conduct macroeconomic stabilization in a particular region within a country, however, monetary policy using complementary currency may offer region-specific effects.

25　In the International financial trilemma, the three policy goals of stable exchange rates, free movement of capital, and independent monetary policy cannot be achieved simultaneously. Following dollarization, Ecuador performed monetary policy by regulating banks and capital. Hayashi and Kinoshita (2014, pp. 52-58). The Ecuador example is not a tale of complementary currency; however, complementary currencies have a limited circulation area, which is to say there is no movement of capital, but the issuance of complementary currency may contribute to regional monetary easing.

26　This is a case where two or more types of currency with different ratios between face value and unit value exist in parallel.

27　Hayek points out that Jevons is not valid, excluding the part that describes how everyone chooses the better one and rejects the worse, conversely, in currency, it seems bad money is left and good money is removed.

28　"Bad money drives out good. When anyone has the choice of paying his debts in either of two moneys, motives of economy will prompt him to use the cheaper. If the initiative and choice lay principally with the person who receives, instead of the person who pays the money, the opposite would hold true. The dearer or 'good' money would then drive out the cheaper or 'bad' money" (Fisher, 1911, p. 69).

29　Reconstruction and development currency is a temporary currency partially circulated within a region, with legal tender supplied by the national or local government as a deposit. Its purpose is to increase the velocity of circulation of money in disaster recovery areas. For reconstruction and development currency, the difference is that rather than the price of stamps, legal tender supplied at the outset is used as a deposit; either way, it does not impose a burden on local government finances.

30　Reconstruction and development currency does not prevent the inflow of capital or labor from external sources nor does it aim to restrict the outflow of funds. The funds invested in reconstruction in cases of large-scale disasters are also large, a very small part of which might be used for a reconstruction and development currency.

31　Nishibe cites (1) the premium rate when exchanging yen for the complementary currency, (2) the commission fee when converting the complementary currency to yen, (3) the rate of depreciation or negative interest rate of the complementary currency, and (4) the relative strength of the complementary currency (against the legal tender) as factors that determine the circulation of complementary currency (Nishibe, 2018, p. 13).

32   The value used is ¥1=1 unit (of complementary currency), however the conversion rate with the yen, when expressed in yen, is 100 units (of complementary currency) = 90-95 yen.

References

Depressionscrip.com. (n.d.) Retrieved from http://www.depressionscrip.com/index. html

Elvins, S. (2005). Scrip money and slump cures: Iowa's experiments with alternative currency during the Great Depression. *The Annals of Iowa, 64*(3), 221-245.

Fisher, I. (1911). *The purchasing power of money, its determination and relation to credit, interest and crises.* Macmillan (The Online Library of Liberty 2011)

Fisher, I. (1933). *Stamp Scrip.* Adelphi.

Gatch, L. (2012). Tax anticipation scrip as a form of local currency in the USA during the 1930s. *International Journal of Community Currency Research, 16*(1), 22-35.

Gesell, S. (1916). *Natürliche Wirtschaftsordnung durch Freiland und Freigeld* (1949 edition, Herausgeber: Karl Walker).

Goodhart, C. A. (1998). The two concepts of money: Implications for the analysis of optimal currency areas. *European Journal of Political Economy, 14*(3), 407-432.

Hayashi, Y. & Kinoshita, N. (2014). Monetary policy in countries implementing dollarization policy: Case studies from Ecuador, El Salvador and Panama. *The Quarterly Report of Economics, 64*(1), 35-65.

Hayek, F. A. (1976). *Denationalization of money: The argument refined: An analysis of the theory and practice of concurrent currencies.* Institute for Economic Affairs.

Jevons, W. S. (1875). *Money and the mechanism of exchange.* D. Appleton and Co. (The Online Library of Liberty 2010)

Keynes, J. M. (1936). *The general theory of employment, investment, and money.* Macmillan.

Lietaer, B. A. (2000). *Mysterium geld: Emotionale eedeutung und wirkungsweise eines tabus.* Riemann I. Bertelsmann Vlg.

Nishibe, M. (2014). *The mystery of money: Gold, Bank of Japan notes and Bitcoin.* NHK Publishing.

Nishibe, M. (2018). Hokkaido's virtual complementary currency: Aiming for an autonomous and decentralized local economic society. *Center for Regional Economic and Business Networks Annual Report, 7,* 3-18.

Seyfang, G. & Longhurst, N, (2013). Growing green money? Mapping community currencies for sustainable development. *Ecological Economics, 86,* 65-77.

Utashiro, T. & Hayashi, Y. (2019). The contemporary interpretation and significance of Irving Fisher's "Stamp Scrip" (Complementary Currency). *The Quarterly Report of Economics*, 68(2-3,), 39-119.

Warner, J. (2012). Iowa stamp scrip: Economic experimentation in Iowa communities during the Great Depression. *The Annals of Iowa*, *71*(1), 1-38.

A Historical Sketch of the National Institute of Genetics in Japan

Hazime Mizoguchi

Abstract
The National Institute of Genetics was established on June 1, 1949 under the jurisdiction of the Ministry of Education. In 1939, there was an argument for the establishment of a special facility for specific genetic research in Japan by members of the Genetics Society of Japan. In 1994, the National Institute of Genetics was reorganized as an inter-university institute for joint use by universities. I will present a historical sketch of the National Institute of Genetics from 1939 to 1984. First, I will give a brief history of genetics in Japan. Second, I will discuss the idea of the establishment of an institute of genetics. Third, I will introduce the Goldschmidt Collection in the National Institute of Genetics. Finally, I will discuss the careers and personalities of the previous directors of the National Institute of Genetics. In the 1950s, the staff members of the National Institute of Genetics were against Michurin-Lysenko genetics. Conversely, it seems that the National Institute of Genetics gathered the Mendel-Morgan line's researchers. However, the most famous National Institute of Genetics' researcher, Motoo Kimura, was not part of the eugenic movement, though his thoughts on eugenics are found in his essay.

Introduction

In this study, I will describe the history of the National Institute of Genetics in Mishima, Japan. The National Institute of Genetics was established on June 1, 1949, under the jurisdiction of the Ministry of Education, Japan (National Institute of Genetics, 1989). Fig.1 shows the main entrance of the institute.

Fig. 1 Main entrance of the National Institute of Genetics (Photo by the author)

I will discuss three topics in this article. First, I will provide a brief history of genetics in Japan. Second, I will introduce how the National Institute of Genetics was established. Third, I will show the results of the research for the Goldschmidt Collection in the institute. Finally, I will discuss the careers and personalities of the previous directors of the National Institute of Genetics.

Genetics began in Europe after 1900 (Shinoto, 1946; Sturtevant, 1965). It is well known that, at that time, three European scientists, Hugo Marie de Vries (1848–1935, the Netherlands), Carl Franz Joseph Erich Correns (1864–1933, Germany), and Erich Tschermak von Seysenegg (1871–1962, Austria) rediscovered Mendel's laws of heredity. The term "genetics" became popular after the 1909 publication of *Mendel's Principles of Heredity* (Bateson, 1913), by British biologist, William Bateson (1861–1926) (Shinoto, 1946; Sturtevant, 1965; The Publication Committee of Mendel Centennial Anniversary in Japan, 1967; Allen, 1978).

1. A Brief History of Genetics in Japan

In Japan, the first description of Mendel's laws of heredity was written by botanist Seiichiro Ikeno (1866–1943). He was known for discovering the gingko sperm. In addition, he studied a hybrid of red pepper plants. In 1906, Ikeno wrote a voluminous book entitled *Plant Phylogeny* (Ikeno, 1906; Shinoto, 1946), in which he introduced Mendel's laws of heredity in section five of chapter four.

Kametaro Toyama (1867–1918) wrote a paper entitled "Mendel's laws of heredity as applied to the silk-worm crosses," which was published in a German journal in 1906 (Toyama, 1906). This paper was famous for approving Mendel's laws of heredity in animals and was received highly by European biologists (Matsubara, 2004).

Early genetics research in Japan focused on hybrid experiments in silk-worms, goldfish, and variegated Japanese morning glories. The focus of early genetics research may be one of the backgrounds of earlier inheritance research in Japan.

Next, I focus on the establishment of societies of genetics and their journals. The Japan Society of Breeding was established in November 1915, but it changed its name to the Genetics Society of Japan in June 1920. The society had 135 members when it began.

The American Genetics Association began as the American Breeder's Association in 1914. William Bateson established the Genetics Society in the United Kingdom in 1919. The *Journal of Genetics*, a British journal, was first published in 1910. In the United States, the *Journal of Heredity* published its first issue in 1910. Another journal, *Genetics*, was first published in the United States in 1916.

In Japan, the *Proceedings of the Japan Breeding Society* published its first issue in 1916. The *Japanese Journal of Genetics* by the Genetics Society of Japan began in 1916. Fig. 2 shows the title page of the first issue of the *Japanese Journal of Genetics*.

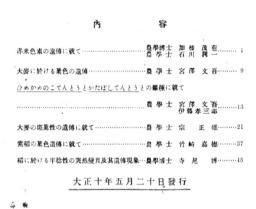

Fig. 2 Title page of the first issue of *Idengaku Zasshi* (*Japanese Journal of Genetics*) (Photo by the author)

The first genetics lecture at a Japanese university was presented by Yoshimaro Tanaka at Hokkaido Imperial University in 1913. The first genetics course, which was sponsored by an enterprise, was taught at the Botanical Institute of Tokyo Imperial University in 1918. Kenjiro Fujii was the first chair of the Botanical Institute of Tokyo Imperial University (Shinoto, 1946).

Four years before Yoshimaro Tanaka's lecture in Japan, William Bateson gave a lecture titled "Genetics" at Cambridge University in the United Kingdom in 1909 (Sturtevant, 1965; Allen, 1978), which is believed to be the first lecture on genetics in the world. Hence, by the early 20th century, Japan had caught up with the United States and the United Kingdom in terms of genetics organizations and research.

2. Historical Background of the Establishment of the National Institute of Genetics

The eugenics movement and the enactment of a eugenics law have been discussed since the mid-1930s in Japan. Mamoru Oguma, a professor at Hokkaido Imperial University, promoted genetics to adapt to the human race. Simultaneously, he also emphasized the need for an institute of genetics and the importance of geneticists. In 1939, he drafted a mission statement for the establishment of an institute of genetics (Oguma, 1939). In 1940, the eugenics law entitled "People's Eugenics Law" was enacted (Suzuki, 1975). At that time, a minister of state also noted the need to establish an institute of genetics.

At the 12th annual meeting in Tokyo in October 1939, Committees of the Genetics Society of Japan discussed the establishment of an institute of genetics. At the next meeting in Seoul, Korea in 1940, the society unanimously approved the establishment of the institute. In 1941, Mamoru Oguma wrote a booklet entitled *Toward a Promotion of Genetics*, in which he explained that there were many unknown fields in genetics. In addition, he explained that the promotion of genetics led to increased food production and a decrease in superstitions, such as those related to prenatal care (Suzuki, 1975). In the same year, the Special Committee of the Japanese Association for the Promotion of Science supported the decision of the Genetics Society of Japan to establish an institute of genetics. However, the institute was not established until after World War II.

There were three departments in the original vision for the Institute of Genetics:

Racial Genetics (population issues, blood types, fingerprints, twins)

Experimental Genetics (hybridization experiment, pedigree method of breeding)

Cytological Genetics (numbers of chromosomes) (National Institute of Genetics, 1989).

Geneticists insisted that the institute should be an independent organization and should be separate from the Ministry of Health, Ministry of Education, and Ministry of Agriculture.

3. Establishment of the National Institute of Genetics in 1947

Shortly following the end of World War II, two geneticists, Mamoru Oguma and Hitoshi Kihara, appealed to the Japanese Government and General Headquarters (GHQ) to establish the Institute of Genetics. They believed this institute would play a part in reconstructing Japanese culture. The following is a chronology of the events leading up to the institute's establishment:

June 1946   The Ministry of Education provided a budget for the Institute of Genetics to the Ministry of Finance.
February 1946   Mamoru Oguma explained the institute to Dr. Henshow of GHQ.
April 1947   The Special Committee of Japanese Association for the Promotion of Science approved the establishment of the Institute of Genetics as a foundational juristic person.
May 1947   The Institute of Genetics was established. The institute was housed in a room rented from the Yamashina Institute for Ornithology. There were twenty-six staff members. Kiyoshi Masuda was the chairperson of the board, and Mamoru Oguma was the director of the institute. The staff intended to change the institute from a foundation to a national institute. The institute had five departments.

These were the five departments of the Institute of Genetics in 1947:
Department of Genetics (Director: Yoshimaro Tanaka)
Department of Physiological Genetics (Director: Taku Komai)
Department of Cytology (Director: Kihito Shinohara)
Department of Breeding (Director: Hitoshi Kihara)
Department of Human Genetics (Director: Tanemoto Furuhata)

Finally, after many twists and turns, the National Institute of Genetics was established in Mishima in central Japan on June 1, 1949. However, because new construction was not allowed, the National Institute of Genetics was housed in the buildings of another company. The institute had sixteen staff members and was composed of three departments in 1949. The departments are as follows:

First Research Department (Morphological Genetics) (Director: Yoshimaro Tanaka)
Second Research Department (Cytological Genetics) (Director: Mamoru Ogura)
Third Research Department (Physiological Genetics) (Director: Taku Komai)

These departments were reorganized into the Department of Morphological Genetics, Cytological Genetics, and Physiological Genetics on January 1, 1953. Before the National Institute of Genetics was reorganized as an inter-university research institute on October 1, 1976, the National Institute of Genetics had one facility and eleven departments: Department of Morphological Genetics, Cytological Genetics, Physiological Genetics, Biochemical Genetics, Applied Genetics, Induced Mutation, Human Genetics, Microbial Genetics, Population Genetics, Molecular Biology, and the Gene Stock Center.

4. Research for the Goldschmidt Collection

The National Institute of Genetics used a quarter of its budget in 1951 (20.98 million yen) to purchase approximately 50,000 copies of reprints that the Jewish German geneticist, Richard Goldschmidt (1878-1958), had owned. The Goldschmidt Collection in the building of the institute was opened in February 1951 (Fig. 3).

Fig. 3 Goldschmidt Collection in the National Institute of Genetics (Photo by the author)

I checked the actual situation of the remnants of the reprints with the collection cards of the collection. There are twenty-one foreign researchers with over one hundred academic papers and articles in the Goldschmidt Collection. I list five of the foreign researchers in the order of the number of academic papers and articles in the collection:

1. Lipschütz, Alexander (1883-1980) Latvia, endocrinology, 273 in total
2. Muller, Hermann Joseph (1890-1967) USA, genetics, 178 in total
3. Parker, George Howard (1864-1955) USA, comparative physiology, 161 in total
4. Blakeslee, Albert Francis (1874-1954) USA, botany, 156 in total
5. Dobzhansky, Theodosius (1900-1975) Russia Raw USA, genetics, 156 in total

There are only fourteen Japanese researchers with twenty or more reprints whose reprints have been saved. The top three are the fifty-eight reprints of Akira Kihara (1893-1986, major in genetics), the fifty reprints of Sajiro Makino (1906-1989, major in cyto-genetics), and the forty-three reprints of Hiroshi Oshima (1885-1971, major in zoology). In addition, Goldschmidt became acquainted with many researchers before he started his genetic research, and he knew many American biologists since he lived in Germany.

Some Japanese researchers became acquainted with Goldschmidt during their stay in Germany, and some Japanese researchers became acquainted with him here in Japan before the establishment of the National Institute of Genetics. Many of these Japanese researchers continued to communicate with him.

The Goldschmidt Collection was extremely attractive as well as supportive to researchers after World War II, when it was difficult to access the latest foreign literature. From today's viewpoint, although it may seem like the Goldschmidt Collection has actually completed its mission, the material value and educational significance of the collection have not diminished at all.

5. Former Directors of the National Institute of Genetics

Below is a list showing the first five directors of the National Institute of Genetics.

	Name	Period	Graduated from
First	Mamoru Oguma	1948-1955	Hokkaido, Agriculture
Second	Hitoshi Kihara	1955-1969	Hokkaido, Agriculture
Third	Daigoro Moriwaki	1969-1975	Tokyo, Zoology
Fourth	Yataro Tajima	1975-1983	Kyushu, Agriculture
Fifth	Ei Matsunaga	1983-1989	Tokyo, Medicine

This study will discuss the first three directors. Mamoru Oguma (1885–1971) was the first director (Fig.4). He was born in Tokyo and graduated from the Department of Agriculture at Hokkaido Imperial University in 1911. He was a pupil of entomologist Shonen Matsumura (1872–1960). From his childhood, insects fascinated Oguma. Matsumura's book, *Japanese Entolomological Souvenirs* (1898), impressed him to a great extent. Matsumura also wrote a book, *Evolution and Idea* (1925), in which he described the necessity of the struggle for existence between human races. In 1919, Oguma received a doctorate degree in agriculture. His thesis was a histological study of insect organs.

Fig. 4 Mamoru OGUMA
(From the 25th anniversary book published by the National Institute of Genetics)

Thereafter, Oguma studied the number of chromosomes in humans. He had assumed that there were many places to teach in Japan. However, few places allowed researchers to study as freely as he had wished. Thus, he established two institutes related to Hokkaido Imperial University in 1943: the Institute of Low Temperature and the Institute of Catalysis. These, I believe, served as a background for the establishment of the National Institute of Genetics.

Fig. 5 Hitoshi KIHARA
(From the 25ᵗʰ anniversary book published by the National Institute of Genetics)

Hitoshi Kihara (1893–1986) was the second director (Fig. 5). He was born in Tokyo and graduated from the Department of Agriculture at Hokkaido Imperial University in 1917. He studied plant physiology under the direction of Kan Koriba (1882–1957). Koriba moved to the Faculty of Science at Kyoto Imperial University in 1920, and Kihara accompanied him. Thereafter, Kihara studied the genome analysis of wheat. He studied abroad from 1924 to 1927 and then studied under C. Correns, one of the rediscoverers of Mendelian inheritance, at the Kaiser Wilhelm Institute. He attended the 8th International Congress of Genetics in Stockholm in 1948. Kihara was the first Japanese scientist to move abroad after World War II.

Fig. 6 Daigoro MORIWAKI
(From the 25th anniversary book published by the National Institute of Genetics)

Daigoro Moriwaki (1906–2000) was the third director of the National Institute of Genetics. He was born in Osaka and graduated from the Zoological Institute at Tokyo Imperial University in 1929. He was a pupil of Naohide Yatsu (1877–1947). Yatsu studied at Columbia University and was acquainted with Thomas Hunt Morgan. Yoshitaka Imai, who was a pupil of Morgan, was a teacher at Tokyo Metropolitan High School. At that time, Moriwaki was a teacher at the same high school as Imai. Thus, Yatsu recommended Moriwaki to study genetics under the direction of Imai. Imai studied the genetics of morning glories, and just like Morgan, Moriwaki studied the genetics of Drosophila. Fig. 6 shows a photograph of Daigoro Moriwaki.

Fig. 7 Motoo KIMURA and the title page of his most famous paper
(https://www.nig/ac/jp/museum/ accessed April 16, 2019)

Clearly, Motoo Kimura (1924–1994) was the most famous researcher in the National Institute of Genetics (Fig. 7). He was born in Okazaki, in central Japan, and he graduated from the Department of Botany in the Faculty of Science at Kyoto University. Just after graduation, he accepted the post of research associate under Hitoshi Kihara in the Faculty of Agriculture at Kyoto University.

Kimura moved to the National Institute of Genetics from Kyoto University in 1949.

First, he belonged to the Department of Cytological Genetics, where he initially studied mathematical models of population genetics. Then, he conducted research with James F. Crow at Wisconsin University from 1954 to 1955. Kimura moved to the Department of Human Genetics in 1961 and to the Department of Population Genetics in 1964. It is often said that in the 1960s and 1970s, Kimura was peerless in the field of population genetics models. His most renowned paper, "Evolutionary rate at the molecular level," was published in *Nature* (Volume 217) in 1968. The Royal Society of London awarded him the Darwin Medal in 1992.

5.1 Discussion

To conclude this study, I will make a few observations. Genetics began at the beginning of the 20th century, and since then, genetics has been closely related to political ideas. During World War II, genetics was connected to the eugenics movement and food production. Some geneticists claimed the need to establish the National Institute of Genetics as a research center.

After World War II, the Michurin-Lysenko vs. Mendel-Morgan controversy confronted genetics. Taku Komai, a staff member of the National Institute of Genetics, was a pupil of Morgan. Daigoro Moriwaki, the third director of the National Institute of Genetics, also studied Morgan's line of Drosophila Genetics. Staff members of the National Institute of Genetics were against Michurin-Lysenko genetics, and the National Institute of Genetics seemed to attract Mendel-Morgan's line of researchers.

However, the most famous researcher of the National Institute of Genetics, Motoo Kimura, was not part of the eugenics movement, although his beliefs on eugenics were included in his essay. The promotion of human genetics inaugurated by Taku Komai is likely the most notable contribution of the National Institute of Genetics.

A part of this study was presented at the XXIII International Congress of History of Science and Technology in Budapest, Hungary, in 2009.

References

Allen, Garland. 1978 *Life Science in the Twentieth Century*, Cambridge University Press, Cambridge, UK.
Bateson, William. *1913 Mendel's Principles of Heredity*, University of Cambridge Press, Cambridge, UK.
Ikeno, Seiichiro. 1906 *Shokubutsu Keitogaku (Plant Phylogeny)*, Shokabo Co. (in Japanese).
Matubara, Yoko. 2004 The Reception of Mendelism in Japan, 1900-1920, *Historia Scientarum* 13(3), 233-236.
National Institute of Genetics. 1989 *Soritsu 40 Shunen Kinenshi, (Commemoration Issue of 40th Anniversary, the National Institute of Genetics)*, The National Institute of Genetics, Mishima, Japan.

Oguma Mamoru. 1939 *Kokuritu Idengaku Kennnkyusho Setsuritsu No Kyumu (Urgent Project of Establishment of National Institute of Genetics)* Self-Publication

Shinoto Yoshito. 1946 *Idengakushi Ko (Lectures on History of Genetics: revised version)* Chikara Shobo, (in Japanese).

Sturtevant Alfred Henry. 1965 *A History of Genetics,* Harper & Row Publishers, New York, USA.

Suzuki, Zenji. 1975 Geneticists and the Eugenics Movement in Japan, *Japanese Studies in the History of Science* (14), 157-164.

The Publication Committee of Mendel Centennial Anniversary in Japan 1967 *Idengaku No Ayumi: Mendel Idenhosoku 100 Nen Kinen (Upon the Steps From Mendel in Commemoration of Mendel Centennial Anniversary)*, Shokabo Co. (in Japanese).

Toyama, Kametato 1906 Mendel's laws of heredity as applied to the silk-worm crosses, *Biologisches Centralblatt*, Band 26, 321-334.

Lineage of Western Social Enterprise Theory and Japan's State of Introduction

Kentaro Kawamoto

Abstract
Social Enterprise is a concept resulting from the conflict and intermingling of two ideologies: the ideology of public interest/non-commerciality (which pursues social aims) and the ideology of commerciality (which seeks to maximize capital). One reason for the recent global attention that social enterprises have been receiving can be attributed to the growing nebulousness of the lines between a for-profit company and a not-for-profit company (Tsukamoto, 2008).With social contribution strategies such as philanthropy and corporate social responsibility, participation by for-profit enterprises in the public interest and non-profit sectors has been growing stronger in the efforts of the for-profit enterprises to tackle social problems and create social value (Tsukamoto, 2008). New marketing strategies are being introduced to the repertoire of those already used by for-profit enterprises. These strategies differ from the previous customer-oriented marketing strategies. These strategies are social marketing and cause-related marketing (CRM).[1] However, Non-profit organizations that wish to escape their reliance on grants and public subsidies have been emerging. These organizations wish to "commercialize" with the aim to obtain revenue in the market. In advanced countries with growing non-profit sectors, this blurring of the lines between commercial gain and non-commercial gain that has resulted in active research into social enterprise and the rise of social enterprise is evident. However, the definition of social enterprises varies depending on the country and the region. It is well known that the definition differs from the British/American concept and how it is viewed in Europe. In Britain/America, the idea is based on the commercialization of non-profit organizations. However, in Europe, the social enterprise can

be given as an example in the context of the welfare state and restructuring of the third sector. As Fujii (2013) states, "it is a political word," and Japan is no exception. As the government moves to restructure the third sector, the concept changes depending on one's stance on enterprise and administration, and the concept has not been unified into one established theory. Thus, in this paper, I would like to outline the historical matters and conceptual framework of the brand of American social enterprise centered on America, where marketization is key, and the restructuring of the third sector in Europe. My aim is to define the Japanese Social Enterprise as it relates to these two contexts.

1. The Research Approach of Social Enterprise in America

1.1 Context of the Emergence of American Social Welfare Theory

Social Enterprises in America is considered to fit on a spectrum. Organizations on this spectrum, be they for profit or not-for-profit, conduct socially valuable projects and activities. Research in this area has been lively since the 1980s.[2] The background factors are the change in the social economic climate surrounding non-profit organizations and the resulting organizational changes. The post-Reagan administration's promotion of privatization is also to blame. Reagan strived for a "small government" and aimed to cut social welfare spending through the aggressive introduction of market principles. More than anything, budget cuts to social services, including welfare because of budgetary austerities, had a great impact on the fiscal structure of non-profit organizations (NPOs). Cost cutting measures by the federal government exacerbated conflicts among NPOs vying for donations and grants as substitutionary finances. This pressure compelled the commercialization of NPOs. To continue their existing projects, more and more of them began to participate in profit-making ventures such as selling goods and services.

Skloot (1988) gives the following reasons for the commercialization of non-profit organizations:
- Strict finances/reduction in capital given to them by the government
- The exacerbation of conflicts surrounding donation money
- A national propensity to support enterprises
- Response of the NPO to a change in environment which can be characterized by tendencies to accept a stable coexistence between commercial exploits and charity among NPOs

1.2 Social Enterprise Theory

The commercialization of NPOs is not deemed as simply a change to a for-profit organization; it can bring about changes in management also (Weisbrod, 1998). For example, some are also of the opinion that there is no need to find value in business activities for the sole purpose of profit. Rather, special attention should be paid to the fact that some business actions can decrease the necessity of income from donations and lead to more stable, diversified financial foundations, in addition to the fact that saturation of market discipline increases the quality of enterprise and an organization's efficiency and efficacy (Dees, 1999). Utilizing the concept of "non-profit enterprise," Skloot (1988) finds that profit-making ventures for non-profit organizations can be beneficial; not only do they increase revenue, but they also contribute to the longevity of the organization through diversification of sources of capital, improve administrative capability, and improve fiscal discipline. Dees et al. (2001) present social enterprise as a strategic response on behalf of the non-profit organization in an environment of commercial tendencies and ever-blurring lines between sectors.

According to Dees et al. (2001), social enterprises behave akin to commercial entities; however, most organizations go about production while taking discretionary measures in their incorporation of commercial elements. Purely philanthropic or commercial organizations are not included. A specific example of this is DC Central Kitchen. DC Central Kitchen does not give food to the poor. The employment support program collects and prepares food that is to be disposed and sells it (the safety of the food is guaranteed). Based on the axiom of teaching a man to fish, they achieve monetization of their service by collecting and preparing food ingredients that were to be discarded, and by teaching people how to prepare these foods, they create opportunities for people to find employment in other organizations. Sales are important in funding covering these administrative costs.

Dees (2001) sought this kind of entrepreneurial leadership in NPOs, the kind that spurs the usage of sales for the administration of business and ties the goal to job opportunities in corporations. In other words, Dees asserts that "entrepreneurs in the social sector are people who link sources of capital to business performance, not only additional sources of funds" and that "not only should social entrepreneurs emphasize commercial approaches but they should also develop strategic methods based on the spectrum of social enterprise" (Table 1). By shining a positive light on commercialization, social enterprise research has presented new approaches in the study of NPO research.

Table 1—The Spectrum of American Social Enterprise

Purely philanthropic◄────────────────────►Purely commercial

Motives, Methods, Goals		Philanthropic Appeal Mission oriented Social Value	Combined Motivations Mission and Market-orientations Social and Economic Value	Appeal to Private Interests
Principal stake-holders	Benefic iaries	No payment	Combination of cheapness or payers nonprayers	Price at market rates
	Capital	Donations and grants	Combination of capital not exceeding market rates	Capital at market rates
	Labor force	Volunteer	Combination of wages below market rates or volunteers and paid staff	Salary at market rates
	Suppliers	Payment in kind	Combinations of sepcial discounts or commodities/donations that cover all cost	Price at market rates

source: Dees 1998: 60

1.3 Tasks for Commerciality-oriented Social Enterprise Theory

Some researchers have also presented negative viewpoints of American Social Enterprise. Kerlin (2009) states that increasing commercialization of an NPO can lead to actions that deviate from their original goals, for example, the danger of eliminating many of their latent beneficiaries in the underclasses. Over long periods, there is also the danger of severing ties with the locals and private donors with whom they have established a rapport in addition to the NPO being unable to build the social capital that they originally had and finding it harder to contribute to civil society.

It is the exclusion of the poor, more than the other phenomena, which calls the *raison d'être* of the NPO into question. Spending is of great concern when discussing enterprise via market trade. Those who do not have assets do not have purchasing powers. Such is the limit of the beneficiary. In addition, the principle of competition is at play in the market. The producer is often evaluated on merit. A person who does not have the necessary skills for a job does not find employment. The NPOs' existence of being for the public good is null if such exclusivity cannot be overcome (Fujii, 2013). Actually, such deficits in aid to the poor by NPOs are considered losses of public benefit and are used as logic in arguments that call for the revocation of preferential tax treatment for NPOs.

A marked tendency toward the systemic homogenization of non-profit organizations affects the trend of social enterprise in America. Looking back, this brands the NPO with the insignia of "market failure," much like with enterprises, which destroys the basis of its validity (Fujii, 2013). How American Social Enterprise will surmount this negative aspect is a problem to be solved in the future.

2. European Social Enterprise Approach to Research

2.1 Historical Background of Social Enterprise Theory in Europe

For Europe, Social Enterprise emerged from the trend of solidarity economies. To be precise, the solidarity economy incorporates collective relationship dynamics such as mutual aid and democratic participation. In a political sense, it strengthens ties among the people and supports democracy. Economically, it has been understood as an alternative form of economy that would overcome the bottleneck of formerly predominant forms of economic systems through a hybridization with pluralistic economies (Kitajima, 2004).

It began as a social economic idea in the 19th century; however, it only began to be truly regarded in Europe since the oil crisis in 1973. Due to the social insufficiencies that follow economic slumps such as long-term unemployment, increasing social exclusion, and inadequacies in child-care and caring for a post-advanced age civilization, several small-scale business endeavors started by the citizens began to emerge, for example, youth employment support organizations and mom-and-pop associations. Movements in the solidarity economy include various grassroots economic activities that were put into place for solidarity and not profit, such as regional currencies, fair trade, and microcredit.

In the midst of a competitive market, social economy centered on cooperative mutual-benefit associations expanded and began to shift gradually to ventures that were more commercial. In comparison, these solidarity economies were characterized by the way they eschewed this practice and breathed new life into the definitions of solidarity and democratic participation. In an endeavor to solve the problem of social exclusion while at the same time starting to undertake interpersonal social services, the people began to create organizations that incorporated multi-stockholder ownership systems, avoiding systems where only union members who can participate glean any profit (mutual aid) for a system of public profit.

2.2 Restructuring of the Welfare State and Social Enterprise Affinity

While the European Social Enterprise did use solidarity economies as a springboard, how can we understand its political background? Of course, the definition of social enterprises differs from country to country; however, social policies, social security systems, and traditional third sectors affect all of them.

However, in broad terms, it is possible to assume that the foundation of the establishment and development of European Social Enterprise lies in the restructuring of the welfare state and the subsequent reorganization process of the third sector (Fujii, 2013). The countries of the European Union have faced a common pressure: global competition and a decreasing birthrate coupled with an aging population. However, this did not immediately lead to the dismantling of the welfare state. The conventional policies of the welfare state form an unwavering blueprint because of the welfare state's certain steadfastness (Fujii, 2013).

Even so, the welfare state was compelled to change. This change highlighted a responsibility to rights and equal opportunities to equal results. Consequently, the stimulation of the workforce emerged as an important political undertaking by the welfare state that meant a shift to an active welfare state centered on active labor market policies.

In addition, the prediction that a declining birthrate and aging population would lead to a financial crisis due to budget cuts and rationalization caused the spread of new public management, which introduced market principles to public services. In addition, this prediction also led to the permeation of the contract culture in administrative organizations. This restructuring of the welfare state caused the public to expect the provision of services and job creation under the contract culture. One can assume that the government served to underpin the development of the social enterprise during this process of third-sector reorganization.

Thus, European Social Enterprise differs from American Social Enterprise in that the government invested much public capital into it mainly through consignment contracts. Support from the European Union also plays an important role. Not only has the European Union supported research relating to European Social Enterprise, but the European Union's social funding has also played a role in financially supporting European Social Enterprise.

It must be noted that, in Europe, the legal framework has been outfitted for Social Enterprise when compared to America, where one has not. The corporate makeup of European Social Enterprise comprises mainly cooperatives and non-profit organizations. For example, in France and Belgium, the social enterprises are established as NPOs and, in Sweden, Finland, Italy, and Spain, associations do not conform to how businesses develop. Further, they tend to be established as cooperatives in countries where the establishment of associations are not difficult (Fujii, 2013). With the enactment of the Italian Social Cooperative Law in 1991, new legal systems had cemented the social enterprise in law. Following this, the Belgian Socially Oriented Company, the Portuguese Social Solidarity Cooperative, the Grecian Limited Social Cooperative, the French Social Association, and the United Kingdom's Community Interest Company were established in 1995, 1998, 1999, 2001, and 2004, respectively.

2.3 The Concept of Social Enterprise in the EMES Network

Much research has been done on European Social Enterprise, with the Emergence Des Entreprises Sociales (EMES) at the heart of such research. The EMES is an interdisciplinary network of researchers formed in 1996 in the wake of an international comparative research project on European Social Enterprise that started with the help of the European Union.

Their concept of social enterprise explicitly excludes for-profit enterprises unlike that of America. It is understood as a modern expansion of the third sector that is composed of NPOs and associations. Rather than calling it a concept radically different from the third sector, this type of social enterprise is perceived as a subset while also being a new driving force behind the third sector.

According to Defourni, social enterprise is understood as a kind of organization at the intersection of an NPO and an association (Fig. 1). This is related to the manner in which European Social Enterprises find their basis in solidarity economies. In other words, associations that were driven previously by common profit became driven by the public interests of their local community while less enterprising NPOs became even more focused on enterprising and, as the two drew closer together, the word Social Enterprise began to be used.

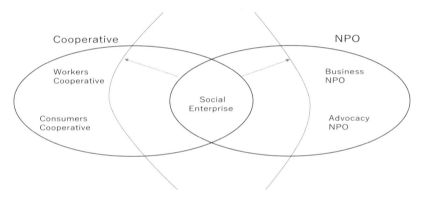

Source : Defourny,J.2001「Introduction:From third sector to social enterprise .Cborzaga snd J.Defourny」
The Emergece of Social Enterprise,Routledge.p22

Fig. 1 Positioning of European Social Enterprise

3. The Sociality of Social Enterprise

3.1 Commonalities between American and European Social Enterprise

The above has discussed the differences in the concepts of social enterprise in Britain/America and Europe. Yonezawa (2012) characterizes social enterprise with a focus on three different criteria—source of income, outcome, and governance—and outlines three different albeit similar British/American schools of thought: revenue acquisition, social innovation, and social economics, which come from European Social Enterprise research. These are outlined below.

① Revenue acquisition: This was developed around American business administration studies. It deems the expansion of income from the NPO market and the application of business administration significant in the achievement of the NPO's mission.

② Social innovation: This focuses on the effects of social enterprise. It highlights the significance and expects creative solutions from social entrepreneurs in solving the societal problem of social innovation. The focus is on how social change is brought about.

③ Social economics: This targets European Social Enterprise. Using traditional research on associations, social economics focuses on the governance of social enterprise and stresses the significance of resource diversity as it depends on social enterprise and the democratic decision-making-process in organizations.

While they are classified in this way, there is one similarity: the link between social aims and economic activity. Researchers of the social economics school emphasize the social aims embedded in social activities, much like the other three schools. In addition, the social enterprise is a hybrid entity that acts across multiple organizational styles and principles. Social enterprises are hybrids in a sense and are considered hybrid organizations.

In the schools of revenue acquisition and social innovation, it bridges both social sectors and we can see properties of both at play in a social context. According to Dees (2001), who adheres to the school of revenue acquisition, "many social enterprises cannot become purely philanthropic or purely commercial, nor should they. Most social enterprises should incorporate a productive balance of both commercial and philanthropic elements." In addition, Nicholls (2006), of the school of social innovation, finds that social entrepreneurs who launch and manage social enterprises are entities that "eclectically incorporate business, charity, as well as social movement models and reconsider solutions to community problems while providing sustainable, new value." Furthermore, according to the social economics school, the social enterprise lies at an intermediate location, at the intersection of public policy and civil society, and stresses the hybrid-ness of the social enterprise's dependence on resources and its goals.

Based on such arguments, Fujii (2013) states that the essence of social enterprise lies in its "structure and strategies that aim to innovate solutions to new problems and guarantee sustainable and autonomous administration as it makes expert use of the powers of the community, the market (business), and systems (government) to solve social problems and change society." In other words, it is a hybrid organization that borrows from different areas to solve problems.

3.2 The Sociality of Social Enterprise

The above has been an outline of the background context of the concept of social enterprise in America and Europe as well as a look at the conceptualization of the social enterprise. While the flow of events differs between America and Europe, it is evident that they share a link in their being hybrid organizations and linkages between social aims and economic activities. The sociality in social enterprise is what is most important here. Overlooking that point makes one unable to see the difference between the social enterprise, NPOs, and average enterprise theory, calling the significance of even discussing social enterprise into question.

The American Social Enterprise can be split into four types: the enterprising NPO, the socially oriented enterprise, the intermediate social enterprise, and the average social enterprise (Tanimoto et al., 2006). Tanimoto explains that the enterprising NPO, socially oriented enterprise, and the intermediate social enterprise are social enterprises because their goods and services are social. In other words, the social contributions of commercially oriented social enterprises can be roughly divided into three types: provision of social goods and services, involvement in social issues through economic activities, and social contribution aside from the social enterprise's principal projects. Focusing on such a diverse social-ness and the social enterprise's state of being for-profit but not limited to being a third-sector organization are two sides of the same coin (Hashimoto, 2012). For example, such an explanation would lead one to conclude that using enterprising efforts and technological innovation to create environmentally friendly electric cars that do not produce exhaust fumes is in the same vein. Since such production of cars in this manner is treated as a social matter on the whole, it would be desirable to study all kinds of enterprising organizations be they for-profit or not-for-profit (Hashimoto, 2015).

The social-ness of the European Social Enterprise would come from the fact that it deals with social exclusion, if we were to depend on the other kind of social enterprise. The actions of the EMES are to combat social exclusion. Its main fields are interpersonal social services and work integration. Interpersonal social services mean providing services that are social, such as welfare, to people who find themselves excluded from society. In other words, social-ness is found in the nature of the provided services. Work integration means reintegration into society by providing opportunities for people to work, specifically people who are socially excluded and have difficulties finding employment.

In work integration social enterprise (WISE), the consumer is also given a good or service while the socially excluded individual receives support in finding employment or job training. Examples of these would be a bread shop that provides work opportunities for persons with disabilities or the Big Issue (a magazine marketer) that provides work opportunities for the homeless. The goods provided are bread and magazines, not social goods. The goods provided here are not vastly different from those provided by the average social enterprise. Therefore, the social aspect is the fact that they provide a place for people to work (Hashimoto, 2015).

In this regard, there are enterprises that not only hire persons with disabilities, but also ones that go beyond the call of duty to actively hire persons with disabilities. In this case, the good or service they provide to the consumer is another matter entirely; they are displaying their social activism by increasing opportunities for persons with disabilities to find employment. What divides the two kinds of social enterprises is the matter to which they give precedence. In other words, do they aim to provide work opportunities to the socially excluded or do they aim to provide goods and services? In the case of dependence on the European social enterprise, the difference between it and the average enterprise lies in the organizational aim or mission to which it gives precedence. For enterprising organizations that deal with work integration, the launching point of their enterprise is how they create opportunities for work.

4. Coordinates of Social Enterprise Theory in Japan

4.1 The State of Social Enterprise Adoption in Japan

The two trends in Europe intermingle in Japan, and since the end of the 1990s, they have been introduced gradually. It can be said that these imported types of social enterprise have created a complex slew of discourse regarding social enterprise in Japan and have affected public policy as well, with their inter-mingling with arguments regarding concepts overlapping that of the social enterprise, such as civic organizations, community business, enterprising NPOs, workers cooperatives, and workers collectives.

Traditional civic organizations and associations are exploring a develop-ment of Japanese Social Enterprise by incorporating the trends of European Social Enterprise. For example, they are establishing unique social enterprise institutions that are based on Italian social cooperatives regarding finding work for persons with disabilities. The enterprising development of associ-ations can be seen as the source for such actions (Kawamoto, 2015). The institutions for social enterprise are characterized by their encouragement of financial independence through employment contracts between persons with disabilities and the company and their equal wage structure that pays no at-tention to individual able-ness. This system is in effect in Shiga Prefecture and the prefecture and its cities are giving grants for its operation. The work-ers cooperatives aim to reincorporate socially those who have been excluded from society through democratic organizational processes and governance and to make reincorporation through labor opportunities their primary goal.

Other than these conventional enterprise entities that aim to follow Europe's path, some other social enterprises can be said to follow the American trend.

4.2 Social Enterprises as Important Players in the New Public Commons

The New Public Commons is a concept mentioned in the Hatoyama Cabinet's general address to the public and is a new value system in which not only indi-viduals in the bureaucracy bear the role of supporting people, but also people from every facet of society, be it education, childcare, crime and disaster pre-vention, medical care, or welfare, work together. Since 2010, the New Public Commons Roundtable has been held to spread the idea of the New Public Commons and its prospects to the people, enterprises, and administrations as well as discuss the course Japan is to take and the systems and policies therein. Much discussion has been held. The following year, the Cabinet Office an-nounced the "Guidelines on the Implementation of Supporting Enterprises for the New Public Commons." The document outlines specific measures and policies regarding the application and the institution of the funds gleaned from the various administrative regions of Japan. Under this, the Cabinet Office defines the New Public Commons and its key players.[3]

The key players in the New Public Commons are citizens, NPOs, and businesses that act spontaneously and independently to work with administrations that have supported the public in the past to solve the various problems in the local community and will support the public in the future. The main targets of this support are spontaneous and independent organizations, that is, personal entities, specified non-profit corporations with vulnerable financial infrastructure, volunteer groups, public service corporations, social welfare service corporations, incorporated educational institutions, territorial organizations, and private cooperative non-profit organizations.

The government has designated the citizens, NPs, and enterprises as actors who will act to solve various local problems, but has given social work companies, Japanese-style social enterprise cooperatives, and social offices as corporate institutions in the new system in which the New Public Commons is to provide support to victims. New corporate systems related to social enterprises have been broached and debated.

4.3 Background on the introduction of the social enterprise theory

It is implied that the political intention of the New Public Commons is based on the statement "with a declining birthrate and aging population, the Japanese government cannot continue to throw money and things at problems as it has before, nor will we choose that path." It has also been seen that their policy is "if the New Public Commons can birth a bustling society of support, it will lead to a community of high social capital, civic happiness, and trust with low social cost."

In other words, much like the West, Japan is facing a financial crisis. The concept of social enterprise is arising through the government's spurring of marketization and localization (where expectations are thrust on civic society) through the participation of various agents. The government fails to attempt to draft a breakthrough solution in the restructuring of social security while trying to become a welfare state.

This can also be seen in the current administration. The concept of the social enterprise is in full force with discussions on the promotion of decentralization of power, social welfare policies, aggressive labor market policies, local inclusion support systems, and payment through welfare and collective participation. Social enterprises are defined as an extension of the debates about the Social welfare service corporations and NPOs that have been dependent on public funds increasing their financial independence and the state of the NPO and civic organizations that are supposed to achieve economic goals. In practice, the traditional Japanese Social Enterprise and the social enterprise that has grasped attention due to the New Public Commons intermingle. However, on the government side, the American model of social enterprise is being emphasized. As can be seen above, Japan's concept of social enterprise straddles the fence as the two sides fight over whether to follow the European concept of social enterprise or the American concept of social enterprise (Fig. 2).

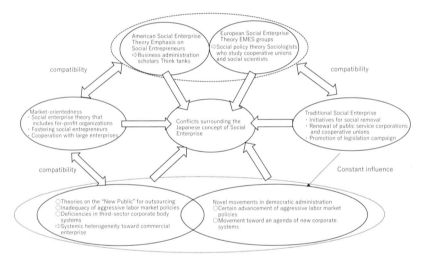

Based on Atsushi Fujii et al. (ed.) (2013) "Fighting Social Enterprises" Keiso Shobo. Revised by author.

Fig. 2 Flowchart of Two Different Concepts of Social Enterprise

5. Conclusion

This paper discussed where Japanese Social Enterprise lies after having outlined how its origins, the contexts therein, and the issues with both of the Western theories. The social enterprise is a business entity that achieves both social and economic goals and is a concept that is political, civic, and economic.

In the midst of such conflict, how is modern Japan's development significant? Since the Social Welfare Basic Structural Reform and Community Welfare, the line that demarcates a for-profit and non-profit business is becoming vague. Reform of social welfare corporations has been underway recently as they are dependent on public funds and receive preferential tax treatment. With reconsideration of governance and reinvesting in public enterprises on the docket for discussion, the idea of even abolishing preferential tax treatment completely is being discussed. A passive intermingling is occurring; to increase longevity, businesses have dabbled in acquiring funds from the market and from donations.

Marketization and localization (a form of care system based upon civic participation) is being accelerated by the government, as can be seen with active labor policies centered on independence support, local inclusion systems, and the Ministry of Health, Labour and Welfare's all for one, one for all policy. It compels one to say that the incorporation of the social enterprise in this sort of discussion is negative.

It is difficult to assess the true nature of the social enterprise in Japan due to its lack of related legislative systems; however, in practice, the two concepts are at work. A typical example in the case of Japanese work integration social enterprise are the exploits of the NPO Heart in Heart Nangun Ichiba in Ainan in Ehime Prefecture (please refer to What is Needed by All Social Enterprises Chapter 3, Minerva Shobo), where a large population outflow has made it akin to a remote region and Yosanoumi Social Welfare Service Cooperation that lies in Yosano, Kyoto Prefecture (Kawamoto (ed.), 2015).

What these have in common is that the people cannot live as citizens in their own regions, and the systemization of professional and local citizens (the source) who have stood up, unable to overlook the needs of the individuals that have been isolated. Apart from the fruits of labor, one other guiding post for Japanese Social Enterprise will be the recovery of the right to live as citizens by previous beneficiaries of welfare services while receiving the care they need and giving back to the community through work. Still another is the adoption of the business entity that fulfills the needs of the local community as a social enterprise.

Such business entities lead to better development of support, while garnering community involvement and lead to the natural intermingling of goods through market activity and calls to administrative responsibility. Makisato (2015) stated the following regarding the systemization of social enterprise: "[it] is a reformation movement via enterprise that not only gives opportunities and public support to those who are prone to societal exclusion to contribute to society, but also combines the contributions of civic society, including nongovernment associations, enterprises."

Social enterprise is not an option meant to be taken to increase the sustainability of policies or organizations; rather, it should be thought of as an integral way of systemization to assist people who have had their rights to live as citizens suppressed.

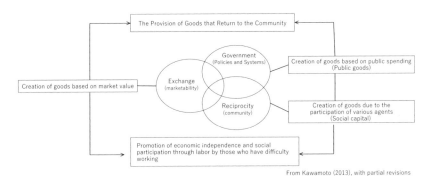

From Kawamoto (2013), with partial revisions

Notes

1. The Volvic company's sales campaign/ or /PR campaign slogan "1ℓ for 10ℓ" stands out among cause-related marketing strategies. It is a sales strategy that they have widely promoted where the purchase of 1ℓ of soft drinks at regular price secures 10ℓ of fresh water for developing countries. Such cause-related marketing goes beyond philanthropic initiatives where the proceeds are donated. Elevation of profits is incorporated into the strategy. In fact, Volvic increased its overall sales due to this campaign.

2. In 1980s America, Yang and Skloot created the basis for the development of social enterprise and began to utilize the concept explicitly from the 1990s onward as the world focused on entrepreneurs, the entrepreneurial spirit, and the concept of leadership as it related to the non-profit organization.

3. Examples of this are the ETIC, an intermediate support organization that fosters social entrepreneurship and Florence that develops childcare in business entities. Florence is an innovative business entity that develops childcare facilities for sick children, which has been difficult for average childcare businesses, and has applied this method to other areas. ETIC is a representative that works in conjunction with major communications company Nihon Electric Communication to open classes on starting businesses and entrepreneurship.

References

(English References)

Defourny, J. & Nyssens, M. (2006). Defining Social Enterprise. In M. Nyssen (Ed.), *Social Enterprise at the Crossroads of Market, Public Policies and Civil Society* (pp. 3-26). Routledge.

Defourny, J. & Nyssens, M. (2012). The EMES Approach of Social Enterprise in a Comparative Perspective, EMES Working Paper.

DiMaggio P. J. & Anheier, H. K. (1990). The Sociology of Nonprofit Organization and Sectors. *Annual Review of Sociology, 16*, 137-59.

EMES Research network (n.d.) International Comparative Social Enterprise Models, (ICSEM) Project.

Evers, A. & Laville, J. L. (2004). Social Services by Social Enterprises: on the Possible Contributions of Hybrid Organizations and a Civil Society A. Evers and J. L. Laville wds. Third Sector in Europe (=Uchiyama, T., Yanagisawa, T. [translation] *Third Sector in Europe - History, Theory, and Policy,* Nihon Keizai Hyoronsha Ltd, 15-58).

Nicholls, A. (Ed.). (2006). *Social Entrepreneurship: New Models of Sustainable Social Change.* Oxford, UK: Oxford University Press.

Nicholls, A. & Cho, A. (2006). Social Entrepreneurship: The Structuration of a Field. In A. Nicholls (Ed.), *Social Entrepreneurship: New Paradigms of Sustainable Social Change* (pp 99-118). Oxford, UK: Oxford University Press.

Skloot, E. (ed.). (1988). The Nonprofit Entrepreneur : Creating Ventures to Earned Income. New York: The Foundation Center.

Weisbrod, B.A. (1974). Toward a Theory of the Voluntary Non-profit Sector in a Three Sector Economy. In S.P. Edmund (Ed.), *Altruism, Morality, and Economic Theory.* New York: Rusel Sage.

Weisbrod, B.A. (Ed.). (1988). *To Profit or not to Profit: The Commercial Transformation of the Nonprofit Sector.* Cambridge: Cambridge University Press.

(Japanese References)

Fujii, A. (2010). What is social enterprise – two of the theoretical trends. In K. Harada, A Fujii, & M. Matsui (Eds.), *The Road to NPO Reconstruction – a Mechanism for Supporting the Partnership* (pp. 103-23). Keiso Shobo.

Hashimoto, S. (2009). Current State and Issues in Social Enterprise Theory. *Municipal Research, 162,* 130-159.

Ito, N. (2013). *The Protection and Possibility in Japan for Employment and Social Welfare for the Handicapped.* Kamogawa Publishing.

Kawamoto, K. (2015). Social Enterprise which Promotes Social Participation. In A. Kawamura, J. Takeda, K. Kawamoto, & M. Shibata (Eds.), *From Social Startup to Social Enterprise: Casting off Charismatic Idols and Clarification of Partnerships* (pp 46-63). Minerva Shobo.

Laville, J.-L. & Nyssens, M. (2004). From Third Sector to Social Enterprise. In C. Borzaga, J. Defourny (Eds.), Uchiyama, T., et al. (translated), *Social Enterprise – EU Third Sector Employment and Welfare* (pp 420-427). Nihon Keizai Hyoronsha Ltd.

Sakurai, M. (2013). Supporting Community Outreach. In Fujii, A., Harada, K. & Otaka, K. (Eds.), *The Fighting Social Enterprise.* Keiso Shobo.

Tanimoto, K. (Ed.). (2006). *Social Enterprise: the Rise of Social Enterprise.* Chuokeizai-sha, Inc. Tanimoto, K., Karaki, K., SIJ, (Eds.), (2007) *Social Entrepreneurship - Ideas Change Society.* NTT Publishing.

Tsukamoto, I. & Yamagishi, H. (Eds.). (2008). *Social Enterprise: Making a Business out of Social Contribution.* Maruzen Co., Ltd.

Work-Joy Design Office, Co., Ltd. (2013). What do A-type offices think and do? – *Kotonone, 6,* 33-41.

Yonezawa, A. (2009). Mixing of Resources in Work-Integrated Social Enterprise – A case study of associations. *Sociologos, 33,* 101-122.

Yonezawa, A. (2013). Social Enterprise as Hybrid Organizations: Reconsidering Problems and Solutions in Target Identification. *Ohara Institute for Social Research, 662,* 48-63.

Attention-seeking Behavior Acquisition from Others' Speech in Children with Autism Spectrum Disorders

Takatsugu Watanabe

Abstract

The subject of this study was a child with autism spectrum disorder (ASD). The subject had difficulty in recognizing the orientation of auditory information from others. Thus, the subject sometimes failed to interact with others as he communicated unilaterally even when others expressed spoken language. It was speculated that if these characteristics were left untreated, the child would have reduced opportunities to interact with others, leading to a greater risk of school refusal, social withdrawal, and mental illness such as schizophrenia. The child was given instructions to understand others' visual information in the past. Therefore, the aim of this study was to enable the child to communicate by recognizing the orientation of others' auditory information. Prior to training, the child with ASD communicated unilaterally without paying attention to others. Subsequently, training was provided by using a video image to show a sample action, which was a video that evoked attention by saying "Hey, please listen to me." At the end of the training, it was possible for the child to be attentive when others were talking and to communicate when they were listening carefully. These results suggest that it may be possible to acquire the ability to recognize the orientation of others' auditory information.

Introduction

The diagnostic criteria published by the American Psychiatric Association (APA) was revised in DSM-5 in 2013. Subsequently, in 2018, ICD-11 was announced by the World Health Organization. In DSM-5, diagnosis of autism spectrum disorders (ASD), which had been traditionally characterized as "class 3 disorders," is evaluated using 2 criteria: 1) deficits in social communication and social interactions; and 2) restricted, repetitive patterns of interest and behaviors. Children with ASD have difficulties in handling communication with others smoothly due to deficits in social communication. Therefore, children with ASD are more likely to fail to interact with others and may avoid communication. In such cases, there is concern that children with ASD may suffer from school refusal, social withdrawal, and mental illness such as schizophrenia (Inoue and Kuboshima, 2008; Sumi, 2011).

One of the causes of social communication deficits in children with ASD is a lack of joint attention which emerges during an early stage of development in typically developing children (e.g. Baron-Cohen, 1989; Beppu, 1994; Leekam, Lopez, and Moore, 2000; Franchini, Glaser, Wood de Wilde, Gentaz, Eliez, and Schaer, 2017; Uchiyama, 2013). Children with ASD do not pay attention to socially relevant cues such as facial expressions and visual orientation (Fukumoto and Hashimoto, 2008; Kikuchi, 2017). Therefore, children with ASD have difficulty in joint attention, which requires the ternary relation to pay attention to the common subject (Uchiyama, 2013; Okada, 2010). The lack of joint attention with others may prevent children with ASD from understanding the concept of "standing in others' shoes" or imagining "how others see" and "how others listen" (Gutstein, 2000 translated by Sugiyama and Ono, 2006). Furthermore, it is also possible that due to this, they cannot choose appropriate behavior, increasing maladaptive behaviors (Nagai, Hinobayashi and Tadahiro, 2017).

In order to address this problem, studies have investigated the specificity of joint attention in children with ASD (Hatanaka and Yamamoto, 2000; Kakutani and Yamamoto, 1997; Konno, 2015; Watanabe, Suto, Oishi, 2014; Yoshii, Nakano, Nagasaki, 2015). In particular, studies such as Hatanaka and Yamamoto (2000) and Watanabe, Suto, and Oishi (2014) used applied behavioral analysis. Hatanaka and Yamamoto (2000) and Kakutani and Yamamoto (1997) pointed out the importance of acquiring referent fixation behaviors where children with ASD see what others are looking at. Watanabe et al. (2014) also demonstrated the importance of acquiring behaviors triggered by others' visual orientation in children with ASD. The studies mentioned above focused on visual attention to enable children with ASD to understand others' visual orientation.

Other studies have also examined auditory attention, and tested if children with ASD listen to others. Taniguchi (2007) suggested that since spoken language is the primary means of communication in humans, difficulties in auditory information processing may underlie communication deficits in children with ASD. Similarly, Watanabe (2016) also demonstrated the difficulties in auditory attention in children with ASD. Watanabe (2016) suggested that attention may not be distributed to sounds properly due to a hypersensitivity to auditory stimuli in adults with ASD. However, there are few studies which provide evidence for these characteristics of auditory attention in children with ASD. Studies, such as Kawaminami and Noro (2014; 2015) and Watanabe, Suto and Oishi (2015), investigated the support for failure of exchanging auditory information with others. Kawaminami and Noro (2014) examined training procedures for functional tact using 3 words, in a child with ASD. As a result of behavioral training, to report the content of a video to a child with ASD, the child was able to call attention to a condition where the listener was not aware of the child's report. Furthermore, Kawaminami and Noro (2015) conducted behavioral training to report the name of a picture in a child with ASD. As a result, they could trigger a behavior which called the listener's attention to the condition when the listener was not aware of the child's report. Watanabe et al. (2015) examined the ability to select appropriate perceptions among visual, auditory and haptic perceptions which can be conveyed to others. As a result of procedures to call others' attention and review, the child was able to select visual communication (writing and showing letters) when auditory communication was not appropriate (listener was wearing headphones). Studies by Kawaminami and Noro (2014) and Watanabe et al. (2015) showed that children with ASD could switch their behaviors when the listeners were wearing headphones as they understood they could not be heard. However, it should be noted that in addition to the condition where the "listener cannot hear as they are listening to something else" as studied by Watanabe et al. (2015), there are many other conditions where "listeners cannot hear", such as "they cannot hear as they are concentrating on their work" as studied by Kawaminami and Noro (2014; 2015).

Therefore, for others' auditory attention, it was suggested that in addition to the conditions where "listeners cannot hear as they are concentrating on their works" as studied by Kawaminami and Noro (2014) and "they cannot hear as they are listening to something else" as studied by Watanabe et al. (2015), other conditions (e.g., others cannot hear while they are speaking) should also be investigated.

1. Objective

In order to promote an understanding of others' auditory orientation ("others cannot hear when they are speaking") in a child with ASD, it was necessary to let the child acquire attention-seeking behaviors triggered by others' speech. Therefore, the objective of this study was (a) to enable the child to discriminate the necessity of attention-seeking triggered by others' speech behavior; and (b) to enable the child to communicate the message to others.

2. Methods

2.1 Studied Child

A child (called *studied child* hereafter in the paper) who visited a counseling facility at University A participated in this study. The studied child was an 8-year old male at the beginning of this study. He was diagnosed with autism in a medical institution and the primary goals were improvement of communication and social skills. The studied child did not receive any special support until he participated in a clinical development session provided by university A from year X, and he was enrolled in a regular class at an elementary school. Behavioral characteristics obtained during the interview with the parents and behavioral observation conducted in year X were 1) enjoying communication with adults; and 2) difficulties in both language and non-language based communications, limited imagination and interest. The desires of the parents were for the child to be able to smoothly communicate with others in various situations. By the start of this study, the studied child had been instructed to express attention-seeking behaviors triggered by the visual orientation of others in a clinical development session at University A. However, he had never voluntarily instigated attention-seeking behavior triggered by the speech behaviors of others, often resulting in unilateral communication. For example, when he was talking to others, even when the other person spoke at the same time as the studied child, he continued his speech without considering the speech of the other person. Furthermore, he was able to verbalize simple causal relationships about changes in things and human behaviors presented in front of him. He was also able to read hiragana and katakana aloud.

2.2 Ethical Considerations and Consent for Research Participation

We obtained written consent for this research including for publishing the results in a journal from the parents of the studied child upon commencement of the clinical development session at University A, using a questionnaire. Explanation of the study, including scene settings and tasks, was provided both orally and in writing. The study protocol was reviewed and its implementation approved by the Research Ethics Committee of University A.

2.3 Study Period

The study was conducted as a part of behavioral training sessions in a counseling facility at University A, which the studied child regularly (about 20 min in a 60 min session). The study period was from September to December, year X. In total, 6 sessions were completed, with each session consisting of six to twelve trials.

2.4 Scene Settings and Task Contents

As shown in Fig. 1, the scene-setting in this study consisted of 3 people: 1) experimenter; 2) the staff who received a message (called "experimental co-operator 1" hereafter in this paper); and 3) studied child. In this study, spoken language was used when the message was delivered (called "message game scene" hereafter in this paper). A baseline period, intervention period, and test period in this study were carried out in the message game scene described above.

The content of the task was to deliver the message presented visually by the experimenter to the experiment cooperator 1 using spoken language.

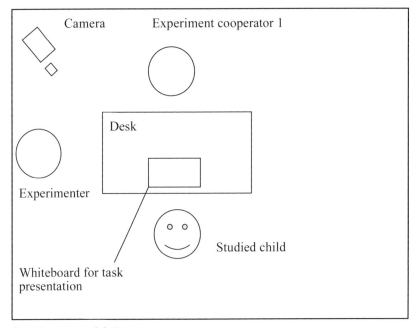

Fig.1 Experimental design

2.5 Stimulus Used in this Study

In this study, we used two B4 sized whiteboards, two A4 pieces of paper with a message which experiment cooperator 1 held, two magnets, and a plastic card. The A4 paper was attached to one of the whiteboards with a magnet. There was nothing attached to the other whiteboard. The messages consisted of between two to four words which the studied child was familiar with. The plastic card was a rectangle of 5 cm vertically and 15 cm horizontally, in which the words "Do you understand?", "Once again", and "I understand" were written in hiragana.

The video stimulus consisted of three people: 1) experimenter, 2) experiment cooperator 1, and 3) staff who played the studied child simulating him receiving the message (called "experiment cooperator 2" hereafter in this paper). The content of the video stimulus was in the same setting as the message game scene, experiment cooperator 2 voluntarily demonstrated the attention-seeking behavior triggered by the verbal behavior of experiment

cooperator 1. Specifically, the scene included behaviors of experiment cooperator 1 and 2 that were consistent with the experimental condition and target
behaviors. When experiment cooperator 1 presented verbal behaviors that
were not relevant to the message text, the experiment cooperator 2 expressed
attention-seeking behaviors such as by saying "Hey, listen to me." It also
included a scene where the experiment cooperator 2 continued delivering the
message while the experiment cooperator 1 remained silent.

2.6 Experiment Condition and Target Behavior

Experimental condition and target behavior are shown in Table 1. In this
study, we had two conditions: an attention-seeking condition and a control
condition. The attention-seeking condition was set to simulate a scene in
which the auditory attention of others deviated. The control condition was set
as a comparison to the attention-seeking condition. In the attention-seeking
condition, while the studied child was delivering the message to experiment
cooperator 1, experiment cooperator 1 demonstrated spoken behaviors that
were not related to the message, and this was continued until one second after
the child finished delivering the message. In the attention-seeking condition,
in order to confirm whether or not the target behavior triggered by speech
behavior of experiment cooperator 1 was voluntary in the studied child, two
types of trials were randomly presented: 1) speech behavior of experiment
cooperator was presented immediately before the studied child expressed
spoken language related to the message; and 2) speech behavior of experiment cooperator 1 was started one second after the studied child started to
express spoken language related to the message. In the control condition,
experiment cooperator 1 listened to the spoken language expressed by the
studied child quietly during the same period where experiment cooperator 1
was demonstrating speech behaviors in the attention-seeking condition.

There were two types of target behaviors: 1) attention-seeking behaviors
such as "Hey, listen to me", when experiment cooperator 1 used speech behaviors that were not related to the message in the attention-seeking condition
(Target behavior a); and 2) behaviors to deliver the message (Target behavior
b). The target behavior used in the control condition was only the behavior to
deliver the message (Target behavior b).

The target behavior was assessed by the occurrence of whether the target
behavior occurred or not during one trial.

Table 1—*Procedures for experimental conditions and definition of target behaviors*

Condition	Experimental conditions	Target behavior
Attention-seeking condition	Experimental cooperator 1 uses speech behavior which is not related to the message. This occurs from immediately after the studied child starts to deliver the message to experiment cooperator 1.	The studied child says "Hey, listen to me" or demonstrates similar attention-seeking behaviors (Target behavior a) during or after experiment cooperator 1 uses speech behaviors which are not related to the message, in addition to the behavior to deliver a message (Target behavior b). <Not applicable> Although there is an attention-behavior to experiment cooperator 1, attention-seeking behavior is not demonstrated.
Control condition	Experiment cooperator 1 keeps listening to the spoken language expressed by the studied child quietly during the period where experiment cooperator 1 uses speech behavior in the attention-seeking condition.	Using behaviors to deliver the message (Target behavior b). <Not applicable> Attention-seeking behaviors to experiment cooperator 1.

2.7 The Achievement Rate of Target Behaviors

In the attention-seeking condition, successful demonstration of the target be-havior was 0% when both the attention-seeking behavior and the behavior to deliver the message did not occur. Successful demonstration of the target behaviors was 50% when either the attention-seeking behavior or the behav-ior to deliver the message occurred. Successful demonstration of the target behaviors was 100% when both behaviors occurred. In the control condition, the desired behavior was shown 0% of the time, when behavior to deliver the message did not occur. The successful demonstration of the target behavior was 100% when behavior to deliver the message occurred.

2.8 Procedures

In this study, one trial was conducted in which the studied child delivered the message presented by the experimenter to the experiment cooperator and the experimenter provided feedback regardless of the result. During the intervention period, one trial consisted of observing the video stimulus which captured the procedures described above to reenact the target behavior.

During the baseline period, the message was delivered as described above. The specific procedures were as follows. Initially, the experimenter presented a message to studied child. Subsequently, the studied child delivered the message to experiment cooperator 1 after the experimenter's cue sign to start the game. Then, experiment cooperator 1 acted according to the experimental conditions described above. The studied child presented a plastic card saying, "Do you understand?" to experiment cooperator 1 after he finished delivering the message. In response, experiment cooperator 1 presented a plastic card saying "I understand" to the studied child. When experiment cooperator 1 presented the plastic card saying, "I understand", the experimenter presented a cue sign signaling the end of the communication and experiment cooperator 1 wrote the message on the whiteboard. After that, the correctness of the message written by experiment cooperator 1 was fed back, and the message game was finished. There was a total of 8 trials in the baseline period (3 trials for the attention-seeking condition and 5 trials for the control condition).

The intervention period included (a) verbalizing the presence/absence of speech behaviors of experiment cooperator 2 while he was delivering the message; and (b) correctly answering the necessity of attention-seeking triggered by the speech behaviors of experiment cooperator 1. Interventions (a) and (b) were implemented using the video stimulus described in the section "Stimulus." During the intervention period, (a) and (b) were substituted for the target actions (a) and (b), respectively.

During the intervention period, while the studied child was watching the video stimulus described above, he was required to demonstrate (a) and (b). Video stimulus for the attention-seeking and control conditions were presented for 6 and 5 trials, respectively. The success criteria were that (a) was demonstrated in 5 or more trials of the attention-seeking condition and that (b) was demonstrated in 4 or more trials of the control condition.

The test period was implemented in the same setting as the baseline period, where a total of 6 trials were completed, 3 trials for each condition.

The maintenance period was implemented at 1 week after the test period, which included 3 trials of the attention-seeking condition and 2 trials of the control condition.

During the generalization period, an interpersonal generalization probe and a task generalization probe were implemented. For the interpersonal generalization probe, it was examined whether the target behavior was demonstrated toward a member of staff who had never participated in this study. The interpersonal generalization probe protocol was the same as the test period, except for the change of staff. This probe included 10 trials (6 trials for the attention-seeking condition and 4 trials for the control condition).

The task generalization probe was used to examine whether the attention-seeking behavior could be generalized to other aspects of daily life. The settings of the task generalization probe were similar to those of the baseline, intervention and test periods. In this scene, the studied child was asked to observe what experiment cooperator 1 was doing on the other side of the partition and to report it with spoken language to the experimenter. Next, we examined whether he could judge the presence of speech behavior in the experimenter, when they were demonstrating the attention-seeking behaviors. The experimental condition was the same as the baseline. Since we previously had information that the studied child unilaterally communicated regardless of his mother's speech behavior in daily life, the reporting scene was set in the task generalization probe. In this probe, a total of 10 trials were implemented (6 trials for the attention-seeking condition and 4 trials for the control condition).

2.9 Study Design

This study used an experimental design of a single case. The study consisted of 5 phases: baseline period; intervention period; test period; maintenance period; and generalization period, where the ABAA' design was adopted.

2.10 Organization of the Results and Analysis Methods

The changes in the achievement rate of the target behaviors were expressed as a percentage, and they are shown in graphs to visually examine the correspondence between phases and behavioral changes. Furthermore, we used an analysis method which compared the achievement rate of the target behaviors between conditions.

2.11 Examination of Reliability

Two adults (1 male and 1 female) who did not know the purpose of this study observed 50% of the videos in each phase to judge whether or not the speech behaviors of experiment cooperator 1 during the baseline, intervention, and test periods and whether the experimenter in the task generalization probe obstructed speech behaviors of the studied child related to delivering the message. Next, a concordance rate was calculated between the three people and the first author. The concordance rate was calculated with the following formula: (the number of concordances / the number of concordances + the number of discrepancies) × 100; the concordance rate was 98% (in total of 25 trials).

2.12 Results

The results of the attention-seeking condition and the control condition are shown in Fig. 2. During the baseline period, target behavior b, which was to deliver the message, was demonstrated in all 3 trials during the attention-seeking condition, while target behavior a, which was the attention-seeking behavior, was not demonstrated, resulting in a 50% achievement rate of the target behavior in all 5 trials. However, target behavior b was demonstrated in all 5 trials in the control condition, resulting in an achievement rate of 100%. During the intervention period, both target behaviors were demonstrated in all 6 trials of the attention-seeking condition, resulting in an achievement rate of 100%. Target behavior b was demonstrated in all 5 trials of the control condition, resulting in an achievement rate of 100%.

During the test period, the studied child was able to demonstrate attention-seeking behavior when delivering the message to experiment cooperator 1 during the attention-seeking condition. Target behaviors were demonstrated in all 3 trials in both attention-seeking and control conditions, resulting in an achievement rate of 100% during both conditions.

During the maintenance period, target behaviors were demonstrated in all 3 trials of the attention-seeking condition and in both trials of the control condition, resulting in an achievement rate of 100% in both conditions.

During the interpersonal generalization probe of the generalization period, target behaviors were demonstrated in all 6 trials during the attention-seeking condition and in all 4 trials of the control conditions, resulting in an achievement rate of 100% in both conditions.

During the task generalization probe of the generalization period, target behaviors were demonstrated in all 6 trials of the attention-seeking condition and in all 4 trials of the control conditions, resulting in an achievement rate of 100% in both conditions.

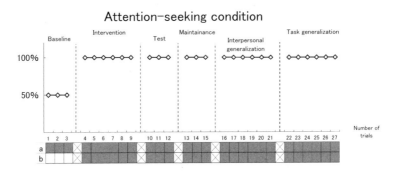

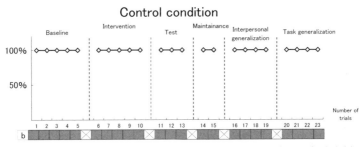

Fig.2 Changes in the achievement rate of the target behaviors in the studied child

The gray cells and white cells in the table indicate whether the target behavior occurred or did not occur, respectively, and × shows that it was not implemented. a and b in the table correspond to the target behaviors of the studied child.

3. Discussion

3.1 Experimental Significance of this Study

In this study, when others expressed speech behavior while the child with ASD was delivering the message, he demonstrated the attention-seeking behavior by saying "Hey, please listen," and was able to continue to deliver the message when others did not express spoken language. Studies by

Kawaminami and Noro (2014; 2015) and Watanabe et al. (2015) reported that children with ASD were able to understand that "listeners cannot hear what they are saying" when listeners did not show any responses or when they were wearing headphones. In addition to these points, our study showed that the child with ASD was able to understand a part of auditory attention function of others, i.e. "listeners cannot hear what they are saying whilst they are speaking."

Furthermore, in this study, we implemented an intervention to observe whether 1) the child with ASD needed to demonstrate attention-seeking behaviors by saying "Hey, please listen" when others expressed speech behaviors while the child was delivering his message through spoken language; and 2) the child needed to continue to deliver the message when others did not demonstrate spoken language. As a result, the child with ASD was able to voluntarily demonstrate the attention-seeking behavior. These results suggest that it is effective to conduct training for environmental impact on children with ASD's spoken language. This result is supported by the findings of the Koida, Sonoyama, and Takeuchi (2004) study which dealt with stimulus visualization.

3.2 Clinical Significance of this Study

In this study, the child formed an attention-seeking behavior when others were speaking while he was delivering the message using spoken language. These results suggest that the child understood that "he needed to call others' auditory attention as they could not hear what he was saying while they were speaking." Therefore, it was inferred that children with ASD may be able to act while being aware of the auditory attention of others. These results are supported by the findings of Kawaminami and Noro (2014; 2015) and Watanabe, Suto, and Oishi (2015), which showed that children with ASD can pay attention to others and share attention. It can be said that children with ASD are able to "stand in others' shoes" as they can understand the auditory attention focus of others. If children with ASD understand the auditory attention focus of others, communication may be facilitated, increasing the chances of establishing relationships. If possible, it may help to prevent school refusal, social withdrawal, and mental illness such as schizophrenia through the accumulation of positive experiences during communication with others.

3.3 Study Limitations

A limitation of this study was that as we dealt with tact in social behavior, it was difficult for the child behavior with ASD to reinforce. Children with ASD have difficulty in social reinforcement, such as having conversations and making others smile. Therefore, for children with ASD to acquire these behaviors it may be necessary to be accompanied by direct reinforcement such as winning a game.

Acknowledgments

We sincerely thank the studied child and his parents, as well as Professor Kouji Oishi of the College of Contemporary Psychology, Rikkyo University, who inspired this study and provided helpful advice and instructions.

References

American Psychiatric Association. (2013). Diagnostic and Statistical Manual of Mental Disorders: DSM-5. *American psychiatric publishing.*

Baron-Cohen S. (1989). Perceptual role-taking and protodeclarative pointing in autism. *British Journal of Developmental Psychology*, 7, 112–127.

Beppu S. (1994). Development of the making of relationships with specific others in an autistic non-speaking child. *Japanese Journal of Educational Psychology*, 42, 156–166.

Franchini M, Glaser B, Wood de Wilde H, Gentaz E, Eliez S, Schaer M. (2017). Social orienting and joint attention in preschoolers with autism spectrum disorders. *PLOS ONE*, 12.e0178859. doi: 10.1371/journal.pone.0178859.

Fukumoto R, Hashimoto T. (2008). Chapter 5 Practice of brain function tests. In: Hashimoto T (ed.) Understanding autism spectrum with brain morphology and function (pp. 60–125). *Diagnosis and Treatment.*

Guestein SE. (2000). Autism Aspergers: Solving the Relationship Puzzle. *Future Horizons.* (Guestein SE, Sugiyama T, Ono J (Translated from) (2006). Autism Asperger syndrome RDI "Instruction methods to develop interpersonal relationship" – Development support program to solve the relationship puzzle)

Hatanaka M and Yamamoto J. (2000). Investigation on listener's conditions that influences on the referential looking behaviors in autistic non-speaking children.

Meisei University Annual Report on Psychological Research, 18, 41–601.

Ikehata M. (2002). Development process of visual perception that supports the relationship of children with autism in the perception standard—Examination of developmental process and quality of viewing power, memorial gaze, and joint attention. *Clinical Studies in Child Development*, 20, 61–70.

Inoue Y and Kuboshima T. (2008). A study on the school-refusal students with developmental disorders: Review of the articles on the non-attendance at school. *Memoirs of Faculty of Education, Shiga University. I, Pedagogic science*, 58, 53–61.)

Kakutani A and Yamamoto J. (1997). Conditions for establishing descriptive communication behaviors in autistic non-speaking children—Analysis of referential looking behaviors and pointing behaviors. *Meisei University Annual Report on Psychological Research*, 15, 49–71.

Kawaminami S and Noro F. (2014). Evaluation for "reporting" with three-word utterances in a student with autism spectrum disorder. *Japanese Journal of Disability Sciences*, 38, 163–174.

Kawaminami S and Noro F. (2015). A case study on teaching reporting behaviors to a child with autism spectrum disorder: Focusing on establishing behavioral chains. *Japanese Journal of Disability Sciences*, 39, 141–150.

Kikuchi T. (2017). Imitation of facial expression sand gaze tracking in children with autism spectrum disorder. *Bulletin of the Faculty of Education, Kumamoto University*, 66, 127–132.

Koita H, Sonoyama S, and Takeuchi K. (2004). Communication training with the picture exchange communication system (PECS) for children with autistic disorder: Training program and current and future research. *Japanese Journal of Behavior Analysis*, 18, 120–130.

Konno Y. (2015). Effects of dohsa-method intervention for developing attachment and joint attentional behavior in a boy diagnosed with reactive attachment disorder and autism spectrum disorder. *Japanese Journal of Autistic Spectrum*, 13, 21–28.

Leekam SR, Lopez B, Moore C. (2000). Attention and joint attention in preschool children with autism. *Developmental Psychology*, 36, 261–273.

Nagai Y, Hinobayashi T, Kanazawa T. (2017). Influence of early social-communication behaviors on maladaptive behaviors in children with autism spectrum disorders and intellectual disability. *Journal of Special Education Research*, 6, 1–9.

Okada T. (2010). Validity of the diagnostic concept of pervasive developmental disorders: from a neuropsychological perspective. *Japanese Journal of Biological Psychiatry*, 21, 61–67.

Sumi Y. (2011). Developmental disorders and secondary comorbidity, related to school refusal and withdrawal. *Journal of clinical pediatrics, Sapporo*, 59, 15–19.

Taniguchi K. (2007). Auditory perception and social disturbance in autism spectrum disorder. *Japanese Psychological Review*, 50, 64–77.

Uchiyama C. (2013). Joint attention and language acquisition in the children with autistic spectrum disorder. *Higher Brain Function Research*,33,175–181.

Watanabe H. (2016). A study on auditory processing in autism spectrum disorder with magnetoencephalography. *Bulletin of the Faculty of Education Hokkaido University*, 124, 81–91.

Watanabe T, Suto K, Oishi K. (2014). Study on the discrimination of others' visual orientation in autistic children with intellectual disorders—Application of the prompt-fading method in a card classification task. *Japanese Journal on Support System for Developmental Disabilities*, 13, 51–59.

Watanabe T, Suto K, Oishi K. (2015). Modality selection based on the possibility of information processing in the visual and auditory perceptions in children with pervasive developmental disorders—Through three types of communications means: visual, auditory and tactile sense. *Clinical Developmental Psychology Research*, 10, 59–67.

Yoshii S, Nakano M, Nagasaki T. (2015). Use of joint action routines to develop spontaneous requests for clarification: Case study of a boy with autism. *Journal of special education*, 53, 1–13.

World Health Organization. (2018). International Classification of Diseases 11th Revision: ICD-11. *World Health Organization.*

Changes in the Remarks on Nanbyō (Intractable Diseases) in the National Diet

Miwa Sakai

Abstract

The Japanese word *nanbyō* (literally, "problem-disease") was formally de-fined in October 1972 with the publication of the Guidelines on Measures to Address Nanbyō by the Ministry of Health and Welfare. In this study, I analyzed how the word nanbyō was used in discussions in the National Diet in the years leading up to this publication. I specifically focused on three things: the diseases to which the term referred, all those who used the term, and the contexts in which the term was used. The analysis was pro-cessed on a computer using Higuchi's (2004) KH Coder, an open source program for quantitative analysis. Statements containing the term nanbyō were inputted into the KH Coder and yielded data such as frequency of references to nanbyō and the speakers of the statements. This analysis yielded two conclusions: first, nanbyō referred primarily to tuberculosis in the first phase of the discussions, and primarily to subacute myelo-optic neuropathy or Behçet's disease in the latter; second, the contexts in which legislators used the term differed from that of executive speakers.

Introduction

The Japanese word nanbyō (literally, "problem-disease[s]") is typically a catchall term for "intractable disease." However, the usage of the term has varied, with the referents and definitions depending on the person and time. Examples of such variations are found in the statements made in sessions of Japan's National Diet. On June 23, 1959, a Diet member described nanbyō as a disease "for which medical science currently offers no established therapy"

(32nd Diet Session, plenary meeting no. 2, June 23, 1959, Legislator Soma). Around a decade later, however, another member equated the term with "pollution-related disease" (55th Diet Session, special committee on indus- trial pollution countermeasures, no. 9, June 14, 1967, committee member Sakagawa).

According to Serizawa (1973), nanbyō entered the popular lexicon in 1963, in association with a campaign by patients with subacute myelo-optic neuropathy (SMON):

The term nanbyō had not been precisely defined by medical scientists or by healthcare professionals. Following an outbreak of SMON in the Warabi district of Toda, Saitama Prefecture, the treatment and rehabilitation of pa- tients became a major public concern. In the autumn of 1963, SMON patients organized a civic group to put their concerns to national and local author- ities. It was thanks to this campaign that the term entered widespread use (Serizawa, 1973, p.261).

Nanbyō received its first formal definition in October 1972, when the Ministry of Health and Welfare published the Guidelines on Measures to Address Nanbyō. This publication reflected the change in the usage of nanbyō. Originally, nanbyō was a generic illness-related term used in a number of contexts, but in the 1960s, it came to be associated in particular with the campaign to get government subsidies for SMON patients. Following this shift in usage, Diet members and civil servants began discussing the issue, using the word nanbyō to describe SMON. In response to the Diet discourse, the government announced a program to fund research on SMON and other nanbyō, as well as a program of welfare assistance for nanbyō patients. With the aim of funding such research and assistance, the ministry published the above-mentioned guidelines, thus providing the first formal definition of nanbyō. The guidelines specified eight nanbyō diseases that would receive government-funded research. The publication also specified that patients with one of four of the eight specified nanbyō diseases would be eligible to receive government assistance for medical costs.

Thus, following the above developments, the government formally rec- ognized some of the referents of nanbyō that were in popular usage at the time. However, there is no literature on how people interpreted, described, and used the term in the national discourse in the above-mentioned period. A study by Eto (2005) offered a political analysis into how measures to ad- dress nanbyō came to take effect. Another study by Horiuchi (2006) provided insights on the formation of welfare policies for nanbyō patients. However, no study has clarified the diseases to which nanbyō referred, or examined how legislators and civil servants used the term. It is essential to understand who used the term and how they used it in the national discourse leading up to the 1972 definition. This information can help us understand how the discourse culminated in the government finally recognizing nanbyō diseases as being eligible for publicly-funded research and medical subsidies.

1. Purpose

The purpose of this study is to analyze the usage of the term nanbyō (the diseases it referred to, who used the term, and in what contexts) before it was formally defined in the 1972 Guidelines on Measures to Address Nanbyō. To this end, I performed an analysis on the nanbyō-related oral and written statements that legislators, government officials, and others made in Diet sessions.

2. Method

To obtain data from the Diet record, nanbyō-related statements from among all the statements made between the Diet's first session (May 1947) and its 69th session (September 1972) were collected using the publicly accessible National Diet Library's online search service. After extracting the statements, I eliminated the orthographic variations among the words that occurred frequently. Examples of these words include *kaze* (common cold), rendered as 風邪 or カゼ, and *gan* (cancer), rendered as 癌 or ガン.

To gauge the contexts in which the statements featuring the word nanbyō were made, entire statements as recorded in the archives were used, instead of extracting only the sentences or phrases in which the word appeared. The documents that were analyzed encompassed the plenary sessions and committee meetings of both houses of the Diet.

In the analysis, each speaker was classified into one of three categories: legislative, executive, or other. "Legislative speaker" denotes a speaker who was a member of the upper or lower house of the Diet, but who was not a member of the executive category. "Executive speaker" denotes a speaker who was a member of the cabinet, a member of a government ministry or agency, or another official tasked with explaining government policy. The term "other speakers" refers to an unsworn witness or other individual speaking before a Diet hearing.

I processed the analysis on a computer using Higuchi's (2004) KH Coder, an open source program for quantitative analysis. Statements containing the term nanbyō were inputted into the KH Coder and extracted data such as frequency of references to nanbyō and the speakers of the statements.

After calculating the trends in the frequencies of nanbyō statements, I broke this data down by legislative and executive speakers. There were minimal nanbyō statements among other speakers, so the frequency of these speakers were broken down collectively, rather than individually. In analyzing the contexts for the nanbyō statements, only those statements made by legislative and executive speakers in the second phase (1970–1972) were considered. As there were a large number of statements in this phase, the other two phases will be taken up later.

3. Results

3.1 Nanbyō Reference Frequency

As Figure 1 shows, the first reference in the Diet archives to nanbyō was made in 1948. The word appeared once that year. In subsequent years up to and including 1969, the frequency remained low, with the word appearing only one to six times each year. From 1970 onward, however, the frequency increased sharply. The word appeared 50 times in 1970 (a tenfold year-on-year increase), 120 times in 1971 (a 2.4 fold increase), 362 times in 1972 (a threefold increase). In view of this distribution, I grouped the data into two phases: the first (1948–1969) and second (1970–1972) phases.

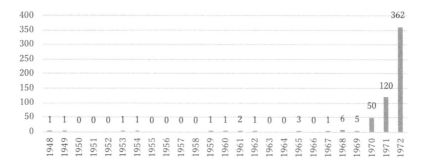

Fig. 1 Frequency of nanbyō references (number of times mentioned) by year

3.2 Diseases Referred to in Nanbyō Statements

Table 1 shows the frequencies for the diseases to which the speakers referred when they used the term nanbyō. As the table shows, in the first phase, the most frequent referent was tuberculosis (*kekkaku*), which accounted for 29 (48.3 percent) of the referents. Other referents in the first phase included cancer (*gan*), which was referred to six times (10.0 percent), and leprosy (*hansen-byō*), which was referred to five times (8.3 percent). In the second phase, there were two dominant referents, neither of which appeared in the first phase at all: SMON was the referent on 183 occasions (30.8 percent) and Behçet's disease (*beichetto*) on 127 occasions (21.3 percent). Referents from the first phase that appeared in the second phase as well were tuberculosis, cancer, leprosy, muscular dystrophy (*kin jisutorofī*), asthma (*zensoku*), epidemic (*densen-byō*), Minamata disease (*minamata-byō*), and the common cold.

Table 1—Diseases referred to in nanbyō statements (frequency)

First phase		Second phase	
Tuberculosis	29	SMON	183
Cancer	6	Behçet's disease	127
Leprosy	5	Cancer	90
Muscular dystrophy	4	Myasthenia	36
Asthma	4	Muscular dystrophy	24
Infectious disease	3	Kashin–Beck disease	12
Minamata disease	2	Minamata disease	12
Common cold	2	Tuberculosis	10
Whiplash	1	Autism	10
Filaria	1	"Adult disease" (i.e., lifestyle disease)	9
Gonorrhea	1	Yushō disease	7
Raynaud's phenomenon	1	Asthma	7
Pemphigus	1	Nephrotic syndrome	7
		Infectious disease	7
		Itai-itai disease	6
		Rheumatism	6
		Myositis	6
		Sarcoidosis	5
		Leprosy	5
		Mental illness	5
		Erythematosus	4
		Coralgil	3
		Renal failure	3
		Measles	2
		Stroke	2
		Leukemia	2
		Echinococcosis	1
		Common cold	1
		Hepatitis	1
		Arthritis	1
		Hemophilia	1

3.3 Who Made the Statements?

Table 2 shows the breakdown of statements by speaker categories in both phases. In the first phase, legislative speakers accounted for the largest share of the statements (70.8 percent), although the statements were few in number. In the second half, the total number of statements at 532, was 22 times higher than that in the first half.

The number of statements rose in the second half for each speaker category, but the legislative speakers' share of the statements declined by 18 percent. In contrast, the executive speakers' share doubled from 16.7 to 34.0 percent. The other speakers' share remained largely the same. Thus, the legislative speakers accounted for the largest shares in both phases, while the executive speakers doubled their share in the second phase.

Table 2—Nanbyō statements by speaker category

	Legislative speakers	Executive speakers	Other speakers	Total
First phase	17 (70.8)	4 (16.7)	3 (12.5)	24
Second phase	281 (52.8)	181 (34.0)	70 (13.2)	532
Total	298 (53.6)	185 (3.2)	73 (13.1)	556

Share (%) shown in parentheses

Table 3—Legislative speakers' nanbyō statements by party

First phase		Second phase	
Party	Frequency	Party	Frequency
Liberal Democrat	1 (5.9)	Komeito	84 (29.9)
Japan Socialist Party	11 (64.7)	Japan Socialist Party	148 (52.7)
Japan Communist Party	1 (5.9)	Liberal Democrat	17 (6.0)
Democratic Socialist Party	2 (11.8)	Japan Communist Party	31 (11.0)
Independent	2 (11.8)	Democratic Socialist Party	1 (0.4)

Share (%) shown in parentheses

Table 3 shows the breakdown of the legislative speakers' statements by party. In the first phase, the Japan Socialist Party accounted for the largest share (64.7 percent) with 11 statements. Members of other parties made statements too, but only once or twice. There were few statements overall. The Liberal Democratic Party (or its antecedent, the Liberal Party) dominated the Diet as the ruling party throughout the first phase. This might explain why 90 percent of the nanbyō statements came from opposition parties.

In the second phase, the Japan Socialist Party again accounted for the largest share (52.7 percent), with 148 statements. However, this share was 12 percent smaller than that in the first phase. This difference reflects a rise in the number of statements attributable to other parties. Komeito accounted for none of the statements in the first phase, but the party's members made

84 statements (29.9 percent) in the second phase, second only to the Japan Socialist Party. The Liberal Democratic Party had a roughly 6 percent share in both phases, but the ruling party accounted for 17 statements in the second phase as opposed to only one in the first phase.

Thus, in both phases, the Japan Socialist Party dominated both in terms of number and share of statements, and the opposition parties collectively accounted for 90 percent of the statements.

Table 4 shows the breakdown of the executive speakers' nanbyō statements. In both phases, most executive-speaker statements were attributable to the Minister for Health and Welfare and his civil servants. The Ministry of Health and Welfare eventually established a bureau for addressing nanbyō (the Bureau for Addressing Specified Diseases) in July 1972, just three months before the publication of the Guidelines on Measures to Address Nanbyō. The ministry had been tackling the nanbyō issue even before it had established a formal section dedicated to the issue, which may explain why it accounted for the vast majority of the statements in both phases.

In the first phase, there was one statement by a civil servant from the Ministry of Labor. This statement pertained to occupational diseases. In the second phase, there were four statements by civil servants from the Ministry of Finance. These statements concerned the budget for nanbyō.

Table 4—Executive speakers' nanbyō statements by party

	Minister of Health and Welfare	Civil servant in the Ministry of Health and Welfare	Civil servant in the Ministry of Finance	Civil servant in the Ministry of Labor
First phase	2 (50)	1 (25)	0 (0)	1 (25)
Second phase	83 (46)	94 (52)	4 (2)	0 (0)

Share (%) shown in parentheses

3.4 What were the Contexts for the Statements?

Table 5 shows the key phrases that appear in the statements in both phases. A key phrase exemplifies the category of text in which it appears. According to Higuchi (2014), a key phrase "has a very high probability of appearing in the relevant category of text relative to the text data as a whole." Table 5 shows the Jaccard similarity coefficients for the key phrases in both phases. As

Higuchi (2014, p.39) explained, "the Jaccard similarity coefficient is a value between 0 and 1, with a higher value indicating a stronger relationship." Thus, a key phrase is one that pertains to a certain category of text more than it does with other categories and thus offers insight into the context behind the category of text. In the first phase, the key phrase with the highest Jaccard coefficient was "patient" (*kanja*) followed by "called" (*iu*), and "Japan." The second phase featured a different set of top-three key phrases: "think" (*omou*), "issue" (*mondai*), and nanbyō.

Table 5—Key phrases in each phase

First phase		Second phase	
Patient (s)	.077	Think	.169
Called	.062	Issue	.139
Japan	.051	Nanbyo	.111
Special account	.045	Medical care	.103
Tuberculosis	.044	Consider	.090
National sanatorium (a)	.044	Measure (s) (to address)	.081
Hospital	.040	Now	.080
Nursing	.040	Health insurance	.066
Severe	.037	Research	.066
Individual (s)	.033	Very	.063

The first phase had too few statements to enable a speaker category-specific analysis. However, this analysis was possible in the second phase, which featured many more statements by both legislative and executive speakers. Figure 2 shows a collocation network for legislative speakers, while Figure 3 shows the same for executive speakers.

According to Higuchi (2012), a collocation network is one in which a thicker line indicates a stronger collocation between the phrases (i.e., a greater likelihood that the phrases will appear together). In such a network, "importance lies in whether phrases are interconnected by lines; if two phrases are close to each other in the network but have no line connecting them, they do not strongly collocate" (Higuchi, 2014, p.158). A collocation between phrases can suggest the context.

Figure 2 shows the collocation network for legislative speakers, while Figure 3 shows the same for executive speakers. The figures indicate trends that are common to the statements of both legislative and executive speakers.

First, nanbyō strongly collocated with "measures (to address)" (*taisaku*), "issue" (*mondai*), "rare and unusual disease" (*kibyō*), and "Consider" (*kangaeru*). Second, "treatment/therapy" (*chiryō*) collocated with "research" (*kenkyū*), "SMON," and "cause(s)" (*genin*). On the other hand, some trends were specific to each speaker category. Among the legislative speakers, "issue" (*mondai*) collocated with "now" (*ima*). The statements by legislative speakers also featured some collocating phrases that did not feature among the executive speakers' statements; these were "health insurance" (*hoken*) "health" (*kenko*), and "nationals" (*kokumin*). Conversely, the statements by executive speakers featured some collocating phrases that did not feature among the legislative speakers' statements; these were "establishment" (*kakuritsu*), "diagnostic" (*shindan*), "criteria" (*kijun*), and "disease(s)" (*shikkan*).

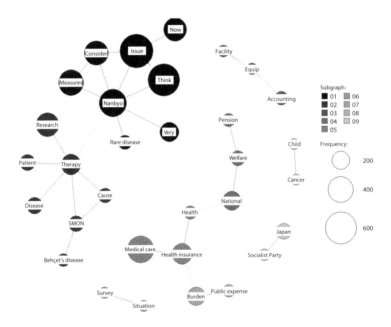

Fig. 2 Collocation network for legislative members' statements (second phase)

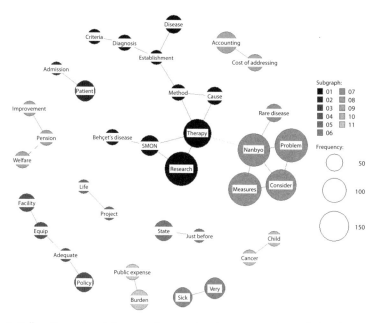

Fig. 3 Collocation network for executive members' statements (second phase)

4. Discussion

4.1 What is Nanbyō?

As Table 1 shows, in the first phase, nanbyō was most likely to refer to tuberculosis. This disease was the greatest cause of death in Japan between 1935 and 1950 (2017 population statistics published by Ministry of Health, Labour and Welfare). It was a top priority for the Japanese government in this period. In 1939, the government founded the Anti-Tuberculosis Association. In 1942, it started issuing BCG vaccines and in 1948, it toughened vaccination legislation. These measures coupled with postwar improvements in public hygiene resulted in a decline in the number of tuberculosis deaths in the 1950s. In 1951, tuberculosis fell from the first to the second greatest cause of death, having been displaced from the first position by cerebrovascular disease. By 1953, it dropped to fifth place.

To relate this historical trend to the analysis, tuberculosis collocated with nanbyō between 1954 and 1968, the time when the disease had fallen from second to fifth place among the major causes of death. I isolated the statements that featured the word tuberculosis but did not include nanbyō. These statements indicated that tuberculosis was mentioned as early as 1947, when it was still the deadliest disease in Japan. While tuberculosis remained the greatest killer, speakers mentioned the disease (in discussions about how to address it), but never described it as a nanbyō. The association between tuberculosis and nanbyō emerged once tuberculosis ceased to be the greatest killer.

These findings, coupled with the fact that tuberculosis was the main referent of nanbyō in the first phase (as shown in Table 1), suggest that describing tuberculosis as a nanbyō did not connote that tuberculosis was the deadliest disease. For the 15 years that tuberculosis remained the deadliest disease, the disease never collocated with nanbyō. Thus, during the first phase, nanbyō denoted a disease that was a common cause of death, rather than the top cause of death.

As Table 1 shows, whereas nanbyō had 13 referents in the first phase, it had as many as 31 in the second phase. Of these, 23 were exclusive to the latter. In the first phase, nanbyō denoted tuberculosis in about half of the cases. The situation in the second phase was completely different, since nanbyō denoted tuberculosis in only 1.7 percent of the cases.

The most frequent referent of nanbyō in the second phase was SMON. The first mention of SMON in the Diet records came up in 1967, during a meeting of the Committee on Social Affairs and Labor. A member of this government committee mentioned SMON as an example of a rare and unusual disease. From 1969, there was a dramatic increase in the use of the term, with Japan Socialist Party Diet member Kazutaka Ohashi and some government civil servants mentioning it regularly. Before 1969, the term had been mentioned only thrice, and on each occasion, it was mentioned during a meeting of the Committee on Social Affairs and Labor. In 1969, it was mentioned as many as 21 times, in each case by members of the Committee on Social Affairs and of other committees. These committee members frequently described SMON as a rare and unusual disease.

The first instance among the Diet statements where SMON is described as a nanbyō came in the second phase, in 1970. The speaker on that occasion was a minister (Fujio Uchida). Subsequently, a number of Diet members and government committee members mentioned SMON as a nanbyō-kibyō (a "nanbyō / rare and unusual disease") along with Behçet's disease. Thus, in the second phase, the predominant nanbyō referent was SMON, and nanbyō denoted a rare and unusual disease.

4.2 What were the Contexts in which the Statements were made?

In the first phase, few speakers mentioned nanbyō, and most of those who did were in the Japan Socialist Party (Tables 2 and 3). The first Diet member to mention the term was Shogetsu Tanaka, a member of this opposition party. Tanaka spoke about a study into the efficacy of acupuncture and anma massage in treating nanbyō. In the statement, he cited gonorrhea as an example of a nanbyō. As Table 1 shows, subsequent nanbyō statements referred to a range of other diseases, including leprosy and muscular dystrophy; but as discussed above, tuberculosis was the referent in most cases. The context for these statements on tuberculosis is evident from a number of key phrases in Table 5 (first phase)—namely, "national sanatorium(a)" (*kokuritsu ryoyojo*), "severe" (*jusho*), "tuberculosis," "patient(s)," and "nursing care" (*kango*). That is, the context concerned the "nursing care" of "patients" with "severe" "tuberculosis," a nanbyō requiring care at a "sanatorium."

Two other key phrases were "special account" (*tokubestu kaikei*) and "hospital" (*byōin*). These phrases were used in a 1968 Diet debate on whether to apply special accounting in national tuberculosis sanatoria. During this debate, legislators had highlighted an issue with special accounting in national hospitals, which did not willingly accept nanbyō. A minister and some civil servants used the two phrases while responding to the legislators' questions.

As discussed earlier, whereas tuberculosis was the dominant referent of nanbyō in the first phase, the situation was markedly different in the second phase, when the media ran stories on SMON, highlighting cases of numbness with no apparent cause. Against this backdrop, Komeito dubbed SMON, Behçet's disease, and other diseases with no known cause or treatment as "public diseases" (*shakai-byō*) and "nanbyō." The party also urged the government to provide welfare assistance to patients in addition to investing in research. However, the Health and Welfare Minister and his civil servants declined the request, citing the need to prioritize research spending. In response, Komeito members petitioned Prime Minister Eisaku Sato, proffering data that legislators had not previously presented. The petition convinced

Sato to signal a new policy direction, wherein he said:

SMON causes great suffering to patients. We cannot help patients simply by lamenting their suffering or by noting its unknown cause. We must take active measures to address the situation. The Ministry of Health and Welfare should actively explore countermeasures in parallel with research; research and the measures should be explored as a separate matter from the research.

(63rd Diet Session, Budget Committee, No. 18, March 30, 1970)

Before Sato's statement, the Minister of Health and Welfare together with his civil servants did not consider welfare subsidies (because they intended for research to be the priority). However, the Prime Minister's statement prompted a volte-face, and the ministry started considering welfare assistance in parallel to facilitating research. Emboldened by the statement, Komeito members pressed the minister and his civil servants to provide concrete measures for nanbyō, thus forcing them to respond. Thus, by the second phase, the context behind nanbyō had shifted from tuberculosis toward measures for addressing SMON and other nanbyō.

In the previous section, I discussed the flow of the discourse among all speakers in the second phase. In this section, I focus on the legislative speakers' statements.

As Figure 2 shows, the legislative speakers' statements prominently featured phrases that never appeared in the executive speakers' statements, including "health insurance," "health" (*iryo*), and "burden" (*futan*). These phrases reflect the discussions in the Diet about amending the health insurance system as a means of addressing SMON and other nanbyō. One legislator argued that the government should expand the scope of national health insurance to cover nanbyō (68th Diet Session, Committee on Social Affairs and Labor, No. 24, May 11, 1972; Legislator Kawamata). Another opposed this measure, arguing that the state should bear the entire burden of the costs associated with the nanbyō (68th Diet Session, Committee on Social Affairs and Labor, No. 27, May 18, 1972; Legislator Shimamoto). The topic of pensions came up during the debate, and one legislator discussed "welfare pensions" (*fukushi nenkin*; i.e., non-contributory pensions) in relation to nanbyō (I have underlined the key phrases):

What people want are stable prices, generous welfare, and an end to recession. When it comes to the matter of welfare, as the Health and Welfare Minister and Labor Minister discussed earlier, people are interested in whether or not the government will raise welfare pensions by 100 yen—or by 200 yen. People are very interested in whether the government will raise them by 100 yen, to 1,100 yen, and whether the government will bear the 10,000 yen burden in medical costs that nanbyō patients currently pay each month (68th Diet Session, Committee on Social Affairs and Labor, No. 2, January 25, 1972; Legislator Kodaira).

Statements like the above were mostly from members of the Japan Socialist Party. Komeito members accounted for the second greatest share of such statements, despite them having made no nanbyō statements at all in the first phase.

Although Komeito had formed in 1961 (which falls in the first phase), the party's members did not speak about nanbyō in the first phase. In the second phase, a statement by a Komeito member (Yamada) had prompted Prime Minister Sato to announce that the government would pursue measures as a matter distinct from research. The statement marked the first of a spate of Komeito statements on nanbyō, indicating that the party had started taking an active interest in the matter. Komeito became interested in nanbyō countermeasures, according to Eto (2005), because of the presence of SMON patients in the members' constituencies coupled with the party's desire to shed its religious trappings. Eto's claim that the party made a calculated decision to focus on nanbyō measures is corroborated by the change in Komeito's nanbyō statements, as seen in Tables 3 and 4.

In the first phase, the Japan Socialist Party members (who accounted for most nanbyō statements in both phases) occasionally referred to national hospitals and specific diseases in their nanbyō statements. However, they neither mentioned nanbyō as a generic/collective term for multiple diseases nor petitioned the government for countermeasures, as the Komeito members did in the second phase. In the second phase, Yamada and other Komeito members started using nanbyō and "public diseases" as generic/collective terms and successfully petitioned the government for measures. The Japan Socialist Party then echoed this trend. When Komeito urged the government to take action against nanbyō, the Japan Socialist Party joined these calls and pressed the government to address nanbyō, such as SMON. These findings imply that the flow of the discourse leading up to the publication of the Guidelines on Measures to Address Nanbyō was as follows: After Komeito kickstarted

183

the discussion on measures for addressing nanbyō, the Japan Socialist Party started using the term nanbyō in a context that was different from that of the first phase, while continuing to account for the most nanbyō statements in the second phase as in the first.

Another notable finding is that the Japan Communist Party became the third contributor of nanbyō statements in the second phase, following the Japan Socialist Party and Komeito. In the first phase, only one Japan Communist Party member mentioned nanbyō. The statement concerned efforts to eradicate filariasis. In the second half, the Communists mentioned nanbyō as many 31 times (11.0 percent). In these statements, the members used the term not to refer to a specific disease but rather to denote a disease with no cure. Collectively, Komeito, the Japan Socialist Party, and the Japanese Communist Party accounted for 95 percent of nanbyō statements in the second phase, indicating that the opposition parties led the discourse that culminated in the Guidelines on Measures to Address Nanbyō. Thus, in the second phase, nanbyō was predominantly used by those members in opposition parties and in the context of promoting countermeasures for nanbyō, particularly SMON.

Executive speakers' statements in the second phase. In this section, I discuss the trends in the statements made by the executive speakers in the second phase. As the collocation network in Figure 3 shows, the executive speakers' statements include collocating terms that never featured among the legislative speakers' statements ("establish," "diagnosis [diagnostic]," "criteria," and "disease"). One possible reason for this difference is that whereas the legislative speakers were pressing the government to take action against nanbyō, the executive speakers focused more on researching nanbyō, establishing diagnostic criteria, establishing therapeutic strategies, and identifying underlying causes. During the second phase, the Ministry of Health and Welfare came under pressure to explore measures for nanbyō following the announcement of Prime Minister Sato that I cited earlier. Just before Sato made this statement, the Minister of Finance had stated that the Ministry of Health and Welfare was prioritizing research into underlying causes: "The Minister of Health and Welfare is working flat out to examine the cause and research other aspects of the issue. Once this work is done, it should then be possible to come up with measures." This statement implies that although nanbyō measures had become a pressing matter in the second phase, the Ministry of Health and Labor continued to prioritize research over the countermeasures. The following statements by the Minister of Health and Labor underscored the ministry's focus on researching nanbyō and on establishing diagnostic criteria (The key phrases have been underlined):

With regards to the matter of nanbyō the member has raised, generally speaking, diagnosis is difficult in a great many cases. Unless and until we establish diagnostic criteria, we won't be able to identify and distinguish them from similar diseases (65th Diet Session, 4th Section of the Budget Committee, No. 2, March 24, 1971; Minister Uchida).

As part of measures for the elderly, some talk of establishing a project team to consider measures for addressing nanbyō. You are a doctor as is the head of public health, so you would surely understand how each of the diseases will have its own causes and pathology. Therefore, a project team may not be best for coming up with measures for the diseases. It would be better to have a research committee for each disease. As with SMON, a research team for each disease, with a set of experts and researchers, should explore the causes of the disease in question, as well as therapeutic strategies. These teams should also seek to establish the diagnostic criteria for the disease in question. This challenge is different in some respects to the challenge of addressing elderly issues. That's why our approach is to have independent, separate teams for each disease, as you know (65th Diet Session, 4th Section of the Budget Committee, No. 2, March 24, 1971; Minister Uchida).

During Diet deliberations, members repeatedly asked for updates about the progress in nanbyō measures. Although the executive speakers responded saying that progress was minimal, the Diet began discussing nanbyō measures in detail. Consequently, in the second phase, the government started examining nanbyō measures, and this development was accompanied by a sharp rise in government statements about the same. Having been unenthusiastic about engaging in the nanbyō matters theretofore, the government was now under pressure to do so. This sharp rise in government statements about nanbyō measures explains why executive speakers accounted for a much larger share of nanbyō statements in the second phase than they did in the first (see Table 2).

Thus, in the second phase, the nanbyō statements by executive speakers initially emphasized research, but the emphasis gradually shifted toward measures for addressing the issue.

5. Conclusion

5.1 What Diseases did Nanbyō Describe?

My analysis yielded the following conclusions. In the first phase, nanbyō typically referred to tuberculosis and connoted a disease that was prevalent, but was not the deadliest. In the second phase, the term primarily referred to SMON and connoted a rare and unusual disease.

5.2 Speakers

The breakdown by speaker category indicates that legislative speakers accounted for most nanbyō statements in both phases. The breakdown of legislative speakers' statements by party indicates that parties' engagement in the nanbyō issue depended on the phase. The Japan Socialist Party accounted for most statements in both phases, while in the second phase, there were also statements by legislators from the Komeito and the Japan Communist Party.

The statements by executive speakers were mostly from the Minister of Health and Welfare and his civil servants. Executive speakers referred to nanbyō twice as much in the second phase as they did in the first, suggesting that the second phase offered more opportunities for engaging in the issue.

5.3 What were the Contexts in which the Statements were Made?

In the first half, legislators generally mentioned nanbyō in the context of treating tuberculosis patients in national sanatoria. In the second half, legislators mentioned the term in the context of measures for addressing SMON and other nanbyō. Executive speakers initially used the term in statements that emphasized how the government was prioritizing research into nanbyō. When pressed by legislators, however, these speakers began mentioning the term in statements that expressed a willingness to consider nanbyō measures.

5.4 Summary

With text analysis, I was able to investigate who used the term nanbyō and how they used it in the national discourse that eventually culminated in the government formally defining the term—a matter that has not been studied before. Consequently, I could show the diseases to which the term referred, as well as how these diseases were described, in the course of this discourse.

Nanbyō was rarely mentioned in the Diet discussions between 1948 and 1970. In the few cases where it was, the speaker would typically be a legislative member, and the referent would usually be tuberculosis. The term was mentioned far more frequently from 1970 onward, wherein legislative members used it in discussions addressing SMON, Behçet's disease, and other nanbyō. During this phase, executive members initially mentioned nanbyō in the context of prioritizing efforts to establish diagnostic criteria. However, after legislative members steered the discussion toward measures for addressing nanbyō, the executive members' nanbyō statements shifted accordingly. Thus, I showed how the above contexts in which nanbyō featured in the above discourse, and how the discourse led to the publication of the Nanbyō Countermeasures Guidelines in October 1972.

However, in focusing on the speakers and contexts, I was unable to adequately investigate elements that do not appear in the text data, such as trends in policymaking or statements and actions that occurred outside of Diet discussions. Future research should build on the findings of this study and consider these other elements.

References

Akagawa, M. (2009). "Gensetsu bunseki wa shakai chōsa no shuhō tarieruka [Discourse analysis: Does it stand up as a social survey method?]." *Shakai to Chosa*, 3, 52–8.

Aoki, E. (1971). "Nanbyō to tatakau (beichetto-byō) [Fighting nanbyō (Behçet's disease)]." *Shimin*, 4, 98–101.

Eto, M. (2005). *Iryō no Seisaku Katei to Juekisha* [Medical policy process and beneficiaries]. Tokyo: Shinsansha.

Fruchterman, T. M. J., & Reingold, E. R. (1991). "Graph Drawing by Force-directed Placement," *Software-Practice and Experience*, 21(11), 1129–1164.

Fujimura, I., & Takizawa, N. (2001). *Gengo Kenkyū no Gihō* [Linguistic research techniques]. Tokyo: Hitsuji Shobo.

Fukuyama, M. (1973). "Nanbyō-sha undō no Dōkō [Trends in the nanbyō patient movement]." *Jūrisuto [Jurist]*, 548, 284–288.

Higuchi, K. (2004). "Tekisuto-gata deita no keiryō-teki bunseki: Futatsu no apurōāū-chi no shunbestu to tōgō [Quantitative analysis of text data: Distinction and integration]." *Riron to Hōhō [Theory and method]*, 19 (1), 101-115.

Higuchi, K. (2014). *Shakai Chōsa no Tame no Keiryō Tekiusuto Bunseki [Quantitative Text Analysis for Social Research]*. Kyoto: Nakanishiya Shuppan.

Horiuchi, K. (2006). *Nanbyō Kanja Fukushi no Keisei: Kōgenbyō-kei Shikkan Kanja o Tōshite [Formation of Welfare for Nanbyō Patients: Focusing on CTD Patients]*. Tokyo:Jichosha.

Ishida, M. & Kim, M. (2012). *Kōpasu to Tekisuto Mainingu [Corpus and Text Mining]*. Tokyo: Kyoritsu Shuppan.

Kawamura, S., Kinoshita, Y., & Yamate, S. (1975). *Nanbyō Kanja to Tomo ni [Together with Nanbyō Patients]*. Tokyo: Aki Shobo.

Kawamura, S. (1979). *Nanbyō ni Torikumu Josei-tachi [The Women who Tackled Nanbyō]*. Tokyo: Keiso Shobo.

Kawamura, S., Hoshi T. (1986). *Nanbyō e no Torikumi [Nanbyō Initiatives]*. Jūrisuto Sōgō Tokushū [Jurist special collection], 44.

Kobayashi, S., & Kojima, M. (1971). "Gendai no nanbyō to shingai-sha fukushi no atarashī kadai: Aru kin-jisu kanja no "ikirukoto" e no kiroku [New issues concerning today's welfare for individuals with nanbyō and disabilities: A record of what living means for someone with muscular dystrophy]." *Sunkan Chigin to Shakai Hoshō* [Wages and social welfare], 588(9), 10–19.

50th Anniversary editorial committee of the ministry of health and welfare. (1988). *Kōseishō 50 Nen Shi [Fifty-year history of the Ministry of Health and Welfare]* Ministry of Health and Welfare Committee for Researching Issues.

Kuzuhara, S. (2016). "Wa-ga-kuni no nanbyō taisaku no rekishi to nanbyō hō ka de no iryō to kenkyū (AYUMI shitei nanbyō to wa?) [History of Japan's measures for addressing nanbyō; medicine and research under the nanbyō law (What are specified diseases?)]." *Igaku no Ayyumi [Progress in Medical Care]*, 258(12), 1097–1103.

McMillan, S. J. (2000). "The Microscope and the Moving Target: The Challenge of applying Content Analysis to the World Wide Web," *Journalism and Mass Communication Quarterly*, 77, 80–98.

Nakamura, E. (1973). "Kōseishō no nanbyō taisaku: 48 nendo no tokutei shikkan tai-saku o chūshin ni [The Ministry of Health and Welfare's measures for addressing nanbyō: Focusing on measures for specified diseases in 1973]." *Rinshō to Kenkyū [Practice and research]*, 50(7), 1856–1860.

Serizawa, S. (1973). Nanbyō taisaku no genjō to ichi, ni no mondai-ten [The state of measures for addressing nanbyō, and 1, 2 issues]. *Jūrisuto [Jurist]*, 548, 261–267.

Shinohara, Y. (1999). "Nanbyō to wa, nanbyō taisaku to wa: Shō tokushū Nanbyō (tokutei shikkan) no genjō to taisaku [What are nanbyō, and what are the measures for addressing nanbyō?: The state of nanbyō <specified diseases> and the mea-sures for addressing them]." *JMA Journal*, 121(4), 481–485.

Shiokawa, Y. (1973). "Kongo no iryō no dōkō: Seijin-byō to nanbyō no shakai-teki igi o chūshin ni [Future developments in medicine: Focusing on the social implications of adult diseases and nanbyō]." *Juntendo Medical Journal*, 19(2), 270–271.

Takemura, S., & Ogata, H. (2010). "Nanjisei shikkan no shikkan gainen kakuritsu purosesu [The process for establishing the concept of difficult-to-treat disease]." *Journal of the National Institute of Public Health*, 59(3), 241–244.

Uono, M. (2009). "Iwayuru nanbyō no gainen to sono taisaku no mondaiten." *Kousyu eisei*, 37(3), 186-192.

Yamate, S. (1980). "Nanbyō to wa nani ka: Fukushi kara mita nanbyō to sono taisaku [What are nanbyō?: Nanbyō and the measures for addressing them, from a welfare perspective]." *Monthly Welfare*, 63(10), 8–13.

Regional Arrangement of City Functions in *Lugang* Town, Changhua Prefecture, Taiwan

Hideo Matsui

Abstract

Lugang, with a history dating back to the Qing dynasty, is a Taiwanese city that shares similarities with the old cities of Tainan and Taipei. *Lugang* Township (lù gǎng zhèn) is a central urban area that developed from *Lugang* port, and various attractive functions that emerged through the process of development and decline of the area are accumulated here. The turn of the century has seen a remarkable increase in the number of overseas visitors to Taiwan, a trend that is also visible in Changhua Prefecture, with many tourists visiting the historical sites of the *Lugang*. Consequently, in addition to functions supporting the *Lugang* as a regional center, functions supporting it as a historical tourist center have also proliferated, and the regional arrangement of city functions is now clearly visible. This study considers the distribution of the various functions in the central urban area of the *Lugang*, looking at both the functions that support a major regional center and the functions that support a historical tourist center. The study clarified that, among characteristics of the regional arrangement of the various relevant functions, is the fact that they are mainly located around *Zhongshan* Road, the axis of the central urban area of *Lugang*, centering especially on the area around its intersection with *Minquan* Road.

Introduction

The development of *Lugang* dates to the Qing dynasty (1662–1895); it is a Taiwanese town with a long history of expansion. *Lugang* got its start as a port town that developed at the mouth of the *Lugang* river. However, the functional deterioration of the bay due to silt accumulation and the subsequent distancing of railway transportation hubs have led to a decline in the vitality of the town. Using topographic maps and documents primarily from the Japanese colonial period to 2000, the author (2017) clarified that the town of *Lugang* expanded to the rural area by growing extensionally from an area centered on the old port town and radially along major roads.

Dapei Ye (1997) divides the history of *Lugang*'s expansion into four periods: 1. Rise 1681–1783; 2. Prosperity 1784–1839; 3. Decline 1840–1894; and 4. Collapse 1895–1945.[1] Additionally, Tianfu Shi (1998) discussed the topographical information and the history of *Lugang*'s expansion and decline in three chapters of *The Geography of Lugang Township*: "Natural Environment," "Urban Expansion" and "Places of Interest." Based on these sources, the Changhua Cultural Affairs Bureau (2008) later divided the transitions that *Lugang* experienced into 10 periods and discussed the defining characteristics of urban expansion in each period: 1. Qing Dynasty, 2. Early Colonial Rule, 3. Colonial Rule around 1904, 4. Colonial Rule in 1935, 5. Late Colonial Rule, 6. Postwar Period 1945–1946, 7. Republic from 1960 onward, 8. Republic from 1965 onward, 9. Republic from 1973 onward, and 10. Republic from 1973 to the present.

In 2004, Changhua Prefecture held the "Changhua Cross-strait Academic Research Conference: Research on Lugang" in *Lugang* and published the results in "The 2004 Changhua Cross-strait Academic Research Conference: Collected Research on Taiwan." This collection includes 27 research papers on *Lugang* that cover topics such as history, art, construction, and industrial expansion. Among these papers, Wenbin Huang and Hanhua Yan (2004) discuss *Lugang*'s expansion as a case study of the spatial expansion model. Additionally, Zhizhang Lai (2004) divides *Lugang*'s expansion into five historical periods: 1. Development as a Fishing Port (Ming Dynasty 1660 – Mid Qing Dynasty 1780), 2. River Shipping (Mid Qianlong Period 1780 – Daoguang Period 1840), 3. Continued Expansion Precariously Maintained[2] (Daoguang Period 1840 – Japanese Colonial Rule 1900), 4. Small Inland City Separated from Railway Transportation (Japanese Colonial Rule 1900 – Postwar 1980s), and 5. Comprehensive Reorganization Focused on Culture and Historical Sites (1980s – Present).

This is the process of expansion and decline that *Lugang* has experienced. The town did not experience the growth other historically significant cities went through from the Qing dynasty onward, leaving behind historical remnants that have become attractions today and allow *Lugang* to flourish as a tourist city visited even by overseas travellers. On the subject of the increasing number of tourists in Lugang, Xiuzhen Xu, Jinfa Cai, Shishuo Ye, and Zongcheng Huang (2004) predicted the number of visitors[3] using an estimation model.

To promote *Lugang*'s development as a tourist destination, Changhua Prefecture has been working to establish it as a National Scenic Area and, in 2015, it held an event called "Promoting a National Scenic Area in *Lugang*: 1st Regional Meeting." The conference proposed a plan for basic divisions in which the town of *Lugang* is positioned as a "core area," the surrounding inland area as a "local natural reconstruction zone," and the oceanside as the "Xibin Ecological Corridor." Furthermore, the event, "Promoting a National Scenic Area in *Lugang*: 2nd Regional Meeting," was held again in 2016, and five projects to be instituted for the National Scenic Area were announced: the Museum Project, Natural Scenery Project, Cultural Project, Tourism Project, and Transportation Project. *Lugang* is on the cusp of accelerating its efforts to become an even bigger tourist area.

The goal of this study is to determine the population changes in *Lugang* as it transforms into a tourist area following the process of expansion and decline described above. And this study elucidates the regional arrangement of the commercial and public city functions concentrated in the city center and the defining characteristics of such functions. For the purposes of the May to October 2017 study, dashboard cameras were used to record traffic along roadways and areas being studied in and around *Lugang*, and wearable cameras were used to record the exterior of shops for this study. In addition to determining city functions with the videos; such functions were confirmed using the Changhua Prefecture Commercial Phone Book and the Yellow Pages of the Republic of China.[4] City functions that were consistent in both records were considered real, plotted in a distribution map, and investigated in detail.

1. Population Changes in the Major Urban Areas of Lugang and Surrounding Areas

The total population of Taiwan was 23,539,816 at the end of 2016, while Changhua Prefecture[5] had a population of 1,287,146 and *Lugang* Town in Changhua had a population of 86,709.[6] The major business area of *Zhongshan*

Road passes through *Lugang*'s city center from the northwest to the southeast, and this major urban area also extends to the hamlets of *Fuxing*, *Qiaotou*, and *Xishi* in *Fuxing* Village (population of 47,479) along the southern side of *Lugang*.

Lugang is made up of 29 neighborhoods, and urban districts extend into 18 of these. Additionally, *Fuxing* Village is made up of 22 hamlets, and *Lugang*'s major urban areas extend into three of these. This study investigated population changes in these 21 neighborhoods and hamlets over a five-year period from the end of 2011 to the end of 2016 (Fig. 1-a, 1-b).

	District NO.	District Name		Population (person) 2011 The end of Dec.	Population (person) 2016 The end of Dec.	Annual average population change number (person) 2011-2016	Annual average population change rate (%) 2011-2016
Lungang Urban township (鹿港鎮)	1	Dongshi-li	（東石里）	5,072	5,293	44	0.87
	2	Pulun-li	（埔崙里）	5,504	6,106	120	2.19
	3	Dingcuo-li	（頂厝里）	8,999	9,752	151	1.67
	4	Yongan-li	（永安里）	5,430	5,526	19	0.35
	5	Jingtu-li	（景福里）	1,398	1,317	-16	-1.16
	6	Guocuo-li	（郭厝里）	695	641	-11	-1.55
	7	Yushun-li	（玉順里）	1,591	1,448	-29	-1.80
	8	Xingong-li	（新宮里）	1,123	1,017	-21	-1.89
	9	Shunxing-li	（順興里）	1,129	1,093	-7	-0.64
	10	Luojin-li	（洛津里）	1,076	1,018	-12	-1.08
	11	Zhongxing-li	（中興里）	624	596	-6	-0.90
	12	Dayou-li	（大有里）	1,401	1,373	-6	-0.40
	13	Caiyuan-li	（菜園里）	1,275	1,213	-12	-0.97
	14	Longshan-li	（龍山里）	916	883	-7	-0.72
	15	Xinghua-li	（興化里）	812	767	-9	-1.11
	16	Changxing-li	（長興里）	359	340	-4	-1.06
	17	Taixing-li	（泰興里）	1,582	1,525	-11	-0.72
	18	Jiewei-li	（街尾里）	2,825	2,802	-5	-0.16
Fuxing Rural township (福興鄉)	19	Qiaotou-cun	（橋頭村）	3,185	3,099	-17	-0.54
	20	Xishi-cun	（西勢村）	2,439	2,421	-4	-0.15
	21	Fuxing-cun	（福興村）	4,321	4,289	-6	-0.15
	Total			51,756	52,519	153	0.29

Fig.1-a

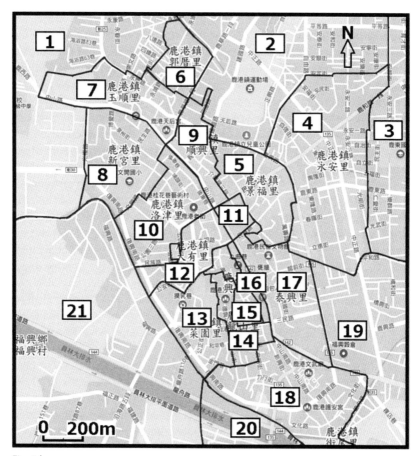

Fig. 1-b
Fig. 1-a,b Population change in the central urban area and its surrounding area, Lukang Township, Changhua Prefecture, Taiwan (2011-2016)
(Source: Created by author based on statistical data of Lukang Urban Township Government and Fuxing Rural Township Government)

Population increased overall in the 21 neighborhoods and hamlets, and the average annual rates of population change were positive as well. However, only four individual neighborhoods had positive annual rates of population change, while the remaining 14 neighborhoods and three hamlets had decreases in population and negative annual rates of population change.

The population increased in the neighborhoods of *Dongshi* (district no. 1), *Pulun* (district no. 2), *Dingcuo* (district no. 3), and *Yongan* (district no. 4). These four neighborhoods are primarily located in the northwest, north, and northeast sides of *Lugang*'s major urban areas, and the *Dongshi*, *Pulun*, and *Dingcuo* are on the periphery of urban areas. The neighborhood with the highest average annual rate of population change was *Pulun*, with growth exceeding 2.0%. This neighborhood includes *Lucao* Road, which passes through the major urban areas of *Lugang* and connects to Provincial Highway 17 (Western Coastal Highway), a highway that runs north along the coastline. After *Pulun*, the neighborhood with the second highest average annual rate of population change was *Dingcuo*, which is located in the northeast of *Lugang*'s major urban areas. This neighborhood includes *Luhe* Road, which connects to the major urban area of *Hemei* next to *Lugang* in the north, and *Ludong* Road, which connects to the National Freeway 1 (*Zhongshan* Freeway) interchange in the east. *Dongshi* is third in average annual rate of population change, and it serves as a connection point to *Luan* Bridge and *Lugong* Road, the two gateways to an industrial zone on reclaimed land called the Changbin Lugang Industrial Zone. *Yongan* is fourth in annual rate of population change. *Yongan* is adjacent to *Dingcuo* on the west and was developed relatively recently, compared to other urban areas. The wide Zhongzheng Road passes through it and is mostly traversing north-south.

Meanwhile, the neighborhood with the lowest average annual rate of population change was *Xingong* (district no. 8). *Xingong* is a district with a long history; it contains an area referred to as the *Quanzhou* Quarter because many of the people who lived there came from Quanzhou in mainland China during the Qing dynasty. After *Xingong*, the neighborhood with the second lowest average annual rate of population change was *Yushun* (district no. 7). The Lugang Mazu Temple in this district was built during the Qing dynasty (early years of Qianlong's reign) to celebrate the sea goddess Mazu, and it is both a major religious site for the people and a vital tourism resource for *Lugang* (Reiji Chubachi, 2015) (Photo 1).

Photo 1 Lukang Tianhou Temple（鹿港天后宮） (Taken by author on 10 May, 2017)

    The neighborhood with the third lowest average annual rate of population change was *Guozhuo* (district no. 6). This neighborhood is home to the Zhongyi Shurine in the Beitou area of *Lugang*. Zhongyi Shrine is an offshoot of a shrine in *Quanzhou*, China and is said to have begun religious services in the 55th year of Qianlong's reign during the Qing dynasty (1790). *Guozhuo* was also an important region for the fishing industry once referred to as *Beitou* fishing village. These three neighborhoods of *Xingong*, *Yushun*, and *Guozhuo* are located in the northwest of *Lugang*'s major urban areas and share a history of development dating back to the Qing dynasty. Their average annual rate of population change is -1.50% or lower, and they are experiencing the worst population declines of any of *Lugang*'s major urban areas.

    Furthermore, neighborhoods to the south that are located at the center of *Lugang*'s major urban areas such as *Jingfu* (district no. 5), *Xinghua* (district no. 15), *Luojin* (district no. 10), and *Changxing* (district no. 16) have average annual rates of population change from -1.50% to -1.00%, the second worst population decline after neighborhoods in the northwest of *Lugang*'s major urban areas. Additionally, neighborhoods in the central southern part of *Lugang*'s major urban areas such as *Caiyuan* (district no. 13), *Zhongxing* (district no. 11), *Taixing* (district no. 17), *Lungshan* (district no. 14), and *Qiaotou* (district no. 19) have average annual rates of population change from -1.00% to -0.50%. Even among *Lugang*'s major urban areas, some neighborhoods have average annual rates of population change from -0.50% to 0.00% and could be deemed areas with slight population decreases such as

Dayou (district no. 12), which includes areas along *Zhongshan* Road and along the southwestern part of the former *Lugang* Valley; *Jiewei* (district no. 18), which is located in the southernmost part of *Lugang*'s major urban areas; and *Fuxing* (district no. 21) and *Xishi* (district no. 20), which used to be on the left bank of the former *Lukang* Valley and became adjacent to one another when the river channels were replaced.

Generally, the five years of research (2011–2016) on population changes in the neighborhoods and hamlets of *Lugang*'s major urban areas shows notable population increases in the northwestern, northern, and northeastern areas on the outer edges of major urban areas, with the pattern being particularly strong in *Dongshi* and *Pulun*. Meanwhile, areas with drastic population decreases such as *Xingong* and *Yushun* are located in the northwest of major urban areas, a part of *Lugang* that has been developing since the late Qing dynasty. Population decline is not as intense in the central part of the major urban areas as it is in the northwest, and the decline is not even less intense in the south. This demonstrates that districts that urbanized since ancient times have more significant population decline, while districts that urbanized more recently have experienced less decline.

2. Changes in the Number of Tourists in Lugang, Changhua Prefecture

Inbound tourism from mainland China also has a powerful effect on the flow of tourists into *Lugang*, which is aiming to be a nationally recognized tourist area. According to the Taiwan Tourism Bureau's Tourism Statistics Database, 10,690,279 passengers traveled to Taiwan in 2016 (7,560,753 of whom came for tourism). When broken down by visitors' country and region of origin, mainland China rather than Japan has taken the top spot since 2011. In 2016, 3,511,734 people (about 33% of total visitors) came from mainland China. When the 1,614,803 visitors from Hong Kong and Macao are added, the number rises to 5,126,537 people (48%), about half of all visitors. In comparison, Japan is in second place at 1,895,702 visitors (18%).

Let us look at changes in the number of tourists in Changhua Prefecture (Fig. 2).

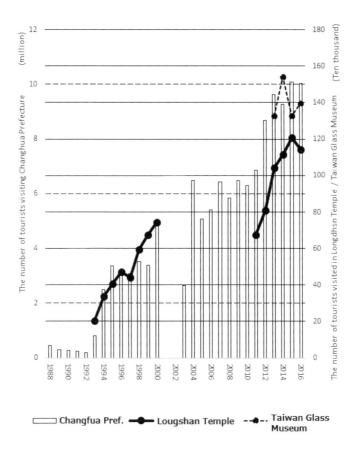

Fig. 2 Change in the number of tourists of Changhua Prefecture, Longshan Temple, Taiwan Glass Museum(1988-2016)
(Source: Created by author based on statistical data of Changhua County Government)

The precipitous drop in tourists in 2003 is attributed to the outbreak of the infectious disease SARS in about 30 countries around the world. Afterward, the total number of tourists grew at a steady rate, reaching 10,024,417 people in 2016.

Next, let us look at changes in the number of tourists visiting Lugang

Lungshan Temple and the Taiwan Glass Gallery, tourist attractions in *Lugang* with publicly available statistics on tourist numbers (Fig. 2). Statistics on tourist numbers for Lugang Lungshan Temple have been listed in the Annual Changhua Prefecture Statistics Report since 1993, and the Lungshan Temple Management Association is the source of the statistics from 1993 to 2000. In 1993, 205,278 tourists visited Lugang Lungshan Temple. From 2011 to 2016, data was compiled by the Tourism Bureau, and this data shows that 1,141,970 tourists visited Lugang Lungshan Temple in 2016. Although the sources of the data were different, a simple comparison shows that the number of tourists grew by about 5.6% over 23 years. Lugang Lungshan Temple was built on *Dayou* Street near the old harbor in the mid-17th century but was relocated to its current location on *Lungshan* Street in the 51st year of Qianlong's reign during the Qing dynasty (1786). Lugang Lungshan Temple is a well-known temple that was recognized as a first-class national important cultural asset in 1983 (Photo 2).

Photo 2 Lukang Longshan Temple(鹿港龍山寺) (Taken by author on 10 May, 2017)

A study by Shihui Huang, Minami Tanaka, Toshio Mitsuhashi, Junichiro Kato, and Kiyoshi Miyazaki (1996) examines Lugang Lungshan Temple's cultural value and role in regional development. It demonstrates that Lugang Lungshan Temple, which is primarily devoted to the Buddhist deity of mercy, Kannon, serves the wider Changhua area and functions as a place of relaxation and interaction for the many people who visit it. It also shows that temples and historical sites like Lugang Lungshan Temple are spread out around *Zhongshan* Road (Photo 3).

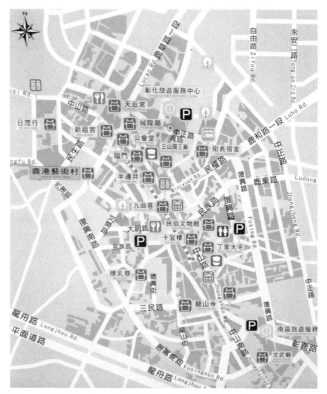

Photo 3 Lukang Guide Map (part)（鹿港導覧図　部分）(Taken by author on 13 Oct, 2017)

The Taiwan Glass Gallery is a relatively new tourist site within the Changbin Lugang Industrial Zone that was completed in March 2003. The gallery is one of 136 (as of June 2017) Tourist acceptance factories in Taiwan[7] and is a popular tourist facility, where visitors can tour the Taiwan Glass Gallery and purchase glassware as souvenirs. Furthermore, by attracting customers on large tour buses, the number of visitors to the Taiwan Glass Gallery has exceeded that of the Lugang Lungshan Temple since the gallery opened.

On the other hand, *Lugang*'s charm as a tourist attraction lies in its historical sites. Throughout the year, many tourists travel to *Lugang*, primarily visiting old streets[8] and temples. There are two old streets in *Lugang*'s main urban area. One is Lugang Old Street (Photo 4), which has been designated as a Historical Preservation Area. Lugang Old Street, which encompasses *Yuyao*

Photo 4 Lukang Traditional Wharf Street(鹿港老街埠頭街)(Taken by author on 10 May, 2017)

Street, *Putou* Street, and *Dayou* Street, represents what is left of an important district in the Qianlong years of the Qing dynasty, when *Lugang* was the most prosperous (Changhua Prefectural Society for the Promotion of Development in Lugang Old Street, 2008).

The other is Zhongshan Road Old Street. After Lugang Old Street developed, Zhongshan Road Old Street grew out of *Wufu* Street, which passed through a settlement of traditional longhouses that gradually developed along with *Lugang* Valley. At the time, Zhongshan Road Old Street was also referred to as a skyless street (City Office of Lugang, Changhua Prefecture, 2007). Keiichiro Mogi (1991) describes how skyless streets were constructed, stating that "a skyless street consisted of buildings with flat or gabled roofs on an extremely narrow pathway framed by markets on each side. Many skyless streets were apparently built in the mid-18th to mid-19th centuries, when *Lugang* was thriving". *Wufu* Street was widened during Japanese colonial rule in 1934 and was the forerunner to the present day *Zhongshan* Road. At the time, the facades of buildings were decorated with all kinds of subtle ornamentation, and the area became known as Zhongshan Road Old Street (Photo 5).

Photo 5 Lukang Traditional Zhongshan Street(鹿港中山老街)Taken by author on 25 Oct, 2017

Among the districts of *Lugang*, Zhongshan Road Old Street is the one that functions as a central shopping area. Hiromi Nishikawa and Osamu Nakagawa (2013) classified initiatives to preserve and maintain old streets. Based on classifications of old streets by Tomita Yoshiro, they also categorized Lugang's Zhongshan Road Old Street as a *Showa*-era (1926–1989) construction, which has "concrete or brickwork with cement spread on the exterior, presenting with a gray tone, and no buttresses with simple ornamentation" (Nishikawa & Nakagawa, 2014). Covered walkways referred to as "*Ting zi jiao*"[9] were built on the road-facing side of buildings in Lugang's Zhongshan Road Old Street as well, becoming one of the defining characteristics of historical streets described by Dongmin Li and Jun Hatano (2001).

In addition to such tourist sites, urban areas also offer access to many shrines and the remains of *sanheyuan*-style houses and houses of wealthy merchants. The area is also well known for its seafood (fried food, fried wraps, and omelets made with oysters, giant clams, clams, and shrimp) and noodles (stewed thin noodles). And it is even more appealing as a tourist destination because of its wide variety of traditional foods that can be taken home as gifts such as beef tongue rice cakes (pies in the shape of beef tongues), meat buns, steamed bread, and dried mullet roe.

3. Arrangement and Characteristics of City Functions in Major Urban Areas of Lugang

Lugang's major urban areas offer a mix of functions that support its character as a major regional city and a historical tourist city. As such, this study highlights 11 types of businesses and plots those shops, businesses, and facilities on a distribution map (Fig. 3).

The 11 types are public businesses/public services, finance/insurance businesses, real estate (intermediaries), trade, doctor's offices/hospitals, watches/eyeglasses, gold/silver/jewels (jewelry goods), eating establishments, bakery/rice cakes (bread/rice cake confections), religious products (Buddhist ritual implements), and religious facilities/temples.[10] Each of these shops, businesses, and facilities were categorized as having 1) the primary function of supporting a major regional city, 2) the primary function of supporting a historic tourist city, or 3) a function of supporting both a major regional city and a historic tourist city. Then, the arrangement of each function within *Lugang*'s major urban areas was considered.

3.1 Primarily a function supporting a major regional city

This section will discuss shops, businesses, and facilities that fall under the categories of public business/public service, finance/insurance business, real estate (intermediary), trade, doctor's office/hospital, watches/eyeglasses, and gold/silver/jewels (jewelry goods).

First, the distribution of shops, businesses, and facilities related to public business/public service will be investigated to determine the arrangement of administrative functions. Most of the governmental organizations in Changhua prefecture and *Lugang* are concentrated in an area northeast of the intersection of two main roadways, *Zhongshan* Road and *Minquan* Road. The Changhua branch of the Ministry of Labor Workforce Development Agency, a central governing body in Taiwan, is located along *Zhongzheng* Road in the bypass on the outermost side of the major urban areas. Other regional organizations are also distributed in this area, including the Lugang People's Congress, City Office of Lugang, Changhua Police Department's Lugang Office, Changhua Fire Department's Lugang Office, Lugang Government Office, and Lugang Administrative Office.

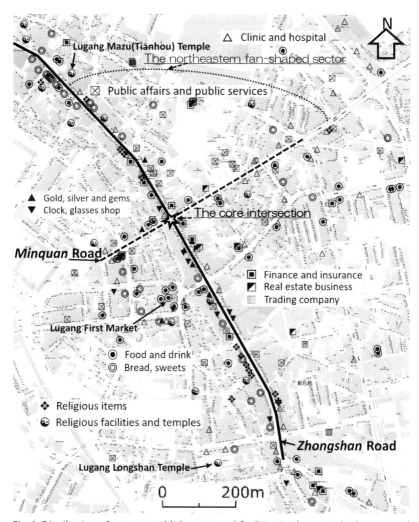

Fig. 3 Distribution of stores, establishments and facilities in the central urban area of Lukang Urban Township, Changhua Prefecture, Taiwan(2017)
Basic map: http://gissrv4.sinica.edu.tw/gis/twhgis_ja_JP.aspx (臺灣百年歷史地圖)
(Source: Created by author based on field survey)

Shops and businesses related to finance/insurance are mainly distributed within the main commercial area along *Zhongshan* Road. There is a concentration of financial institutions (banks), in particular, near the intersection of *Zhongshan* Road and *Minquan* Road. Credit unions, investment companies, and insurance businesses are scattered outside of the main area.

Most shops and businesses related to real estate (intermediaries) are distributed between the areas of population growth in the northeastern urban areas and the main commercial area, or along *Zhongzheng* Road in the bypass. Although there are few shops, businesses, and facilities related to trade, they are similarly located to a similar manner to real estate (intermediary) businesses.

Doctor's offices/hospitals are scattered in areas such as *Zhongshan* Road, *Zhongzheng* Road, *Minquan* Road, *Minzu* Road, *Sanmin* Road, and *Fuxing* Road. A major hospital is located along the wide *Zhongzheng* Road.

Shops offering watches/eyeglasses and gold/silver/jewels (jewelry goods) are concentrated near the intersection of *Zhongshan* Road and *Minquan* Road and near Lugang First Public Retail Market (shortened as Lugang First Market) on the southwestern side of the intersection. Other shops in this category are located in the main commercial area along *Zhongshan* Road.

3.2 Primarily a function supporting a historic tourist city

Tourism resources within the major urban areas of *Lugang* include Lugang Old Street, Lugang Zhongshan Road Old Street, side streets (*Jiuqu* Lane, *Moru* Alley, etc.), and the former homes of wealthy merchants (Yilou, the Ding Family home, etc.), as well as temples such as Lugang Mazu Temple, Xinzu Temple, Lugang Lungshan Temple, and Wenwu Temple. Shops, businesses, and facilities targeting tourists are distributed around such historical sites. Another aspect of *Lugang*'s appeal are the shops selling religious products (Buddhist ritual implements), as well as the religious facilities/ temples that people can visit, worship at, or travel between (when making the pilgrimage to the Baohu Dimu Temple, etc.). Zhaorong Li (2004) discusses the production of ritual furniture (ceremonial tables, altar cabinets, lamp holders, bell holders, and drum racks) in "A Historical Investigation of *Lugang*'s Wood Furniture Industry." The majority of shops offering religious products (Buddhist ritual implements) are concentrated in two districts along *Zhongshan* Road. One is the area along *Zhongshan* Road from where it intersects with *Minquan* Road to Lugang Mazu Temple, and the other is the area along *Zhongshan* Road from *Minzu* Road to *Sanmin* Road. This area that stretches along *Zhanglu* Road, which connects the major urban areas of *Lugang* to Changhua City, has a string of shops selling ceremonial tables, religious statues, Buddhist statues, Buddhist ritual implements, and Buddhist altars.

Although there are 59 temples[11] in *Lugang*, those designated as religious facilities/temples in this study are the ones with permanent custodians, according to phonebook data. Temples such as Lugang Mazu Temple and Xinzu Temple, dating to the Qing dynasty, are concentrated in the northwestern urban areas of *Lugang*. The majority of temples outside that area, including Lugang Lungshan Temple, which was moved out of the older part of town, are distributed in the area between the old *Lugang* Valley and *Zhongshan* Road.

3.3 A function supporting both a major regional city and a historic tourist city

The various shops, businesses, and facilities distributed around the city have never fulfilled just a single function supporting only a major regional city or a historic tourist city. However, due to their locations, there are shops that are used more frequently by local residents, those used more frequently by tourists, and those used frequently by both.

The eating establishment category includes frozen dessert shops, beverage shops, restaurants, cafeterias, and the like. These shops are distributed across a relatively broad area in the urban region. There is a particular concentration of these shops near Lugang First Market, its surrounding areas, and the area around Lugang Mazu Temple. Many worshippers visit on national holidays and during religious celebrations, and tourists look around these areas frequently as well. Although shops interspersed throughout *Minquan* Road, *Minzu* Road, *Ludong* Road, and *Zhanglu* Road are patronized by tourists, they are visited more often by Taiwanese, which has a culture of eating out frequently. As a result, eating establishments are distributed not only around tourist sites but also in residential areas.

Meanwhile, tourists purchase local snacks from stores selling baked goods and walk around eating them. There is an even more dense concentration of eating establishments in the areas around Lugang Mazu Temple and Lugang First Market. Additionally, from the intersection of *Zhongshan* Road and *Minzu* Road to the intersection of *Zhongshan* Road and *Sanmin* Road, shops are located along the southwestern side of *Zhongshan* Road at consistent intervals.

4. Conclusion

This study examined population changes in the major urban areas of *Lugang* as it attempts to become a tourist destination by investigating population trends in its urban areas. It also investigated the characteristics of the arrangement of city functions by studying 11 types of shops, businesses, and facilities that perform city functions. Below is a list of the findings.

1) The population in *Lugang*'s urban areas is growing in areas on the outskirts in the northwest, north, and northeast of central urban areas such as *Dongshi*, *Pulun*, and *Dingcuo*. Meanwhile, neighborhoods in major urban areas with intense population decline such as *Xingon*, *Yushun*, and *Guocuo* are located in the northwestern part of the major urban areas, a region whose development dates to the Qing dynasty. Additionally, population decline is not as intense in the central part as it is not in the northwest, and the decline is even less intense in the south.

2) The main tourist resources in *Lugang* are Lugang Lungshan Temple, Taiwan Glass Gallery, Lugang Old Street, and Lugang Zhongshan Road Old Street. Lugang Mazu Temple, which celebrates the goddess Mazu, and Lugang First Market are the core of central *Lugang*'s tourist district.

3) Characteristics of the Regional Arrangement of City Functions.

(1) Administrative functions of *Lugang* as a major regional city are concentrated in an area that extends from the intersection of *Zhongshan* Road and *Minquan* Road (hereinafter referred to as the core intersection) to the northeastern fan-shaped sector between *Zhongshan* Road and *Minquan* Road.

(2) As for financial and insurance businesses, banks are concentrated near the core intersection along Zhongshan Road. Additionally, insurance businesses are dispersed along major roadways around urban areas.

(3) Although shops selling high-end products such as gold/silver/jewels (jewelry goods) are concentrated near the core intersection, they are distributed in locations farther from the core intersection than the banks.

(4) Shops selling products such as eyeglasses/watches are located even farther out of the core intersection than the gold/silver/jewels (jewelry goods) shops, and there is also a comparatively large distribution of them around Lugang First Market.

(5) Eating establishments and shops selling bread or rice cake confections, well-known souvenirs of *Lugang*, are concentrated in two areas: around Lugang Mazu Temple and Lugang First Market.

(6) The majority of religious products (Buddhist ritual implements) are located along *Zhongshan* Road. There are two concentrations at the northwestern and southeastern tips of the commercial area along *Zhongshan* Road: the area from its intersection with *Minquan* Road to Lugang Mazu Temple and the area from its intersection with *Minzu* road to its intersection with *Sanmin* Road.

(7) Most traditional religious facilities/temples are distributed in the northwestern urban part of *Lugang*.

Looking at the regional arrangement of functions as in (1)–(7) demonstrates that functions are centered around *Zhongshan* Road. And various urban functions are located along the Zhongshan Road, with the intersection of *Zhongshan* Road and *Minquan* Road functioning as the core intersection. Additionally, in two directions (toward Lugang Mazu Temple due northwest from the core intersection along *Zhongshan* Road and toward Wenwu Temple due southeast), there is a transition from banks to jewelry stores, to watches/eyeglasses, to religious instruments. This is a transition from financial services to luxury shopping goods, to shopping goods, to shopping goods purchased once in a generation. This can be interpreted as a regional arrangement based on city centrality and the frequency of purchases by consumers.

Notes

1. "Japanese colonial rule" (1895–1945) can also be referred to as the "Japanese occupation," depending on the perspective and beliefs of the author. As a rule, this paper uses the phrasing of the original author.

2. The Japanese translation of the Chinese term "筍延殘喘" (subsequently

translated into English as "Precariously Maintained") is a nonliteral translation by the author.
3. "Visitor" has the same meaning as "tourist." The number of visitors from Taiwanese statistical tables that has been cited in this paper was rephrased as "number of tourists."
4. The Yellow Pages of the Republic of China is an online phone book. http://www.jyp.com.tw/ (Last viewed 11/29/2017)
5. Changhua Prefecture is made up of the municipalities of Changhua City and Yuanlin City, six towns, and eighteen villages.
6. Although Taiwanese population statistics (reporting of births and deaths totaled at the end of each month) are similar to the Japanese resident register ledger population, it is more appropriate to look at them as Japanese census of family register (natural variation) because they do not reflect population movement (social change).
7. The number of tourism factories comes from the Tourism Factory Registry on the Government Data Publication Platform. https://data.gov.tw/dataset/6848 (Last viewed 11/29/2017)
8. "*Laojie* (Old street)" is a general name used both in mainland China and in Taiwan to indicate a former urban area and can also refer to a historical neighborhood, similar to the usage of the term "traditional architectural area" in Japan. Unlike mainland China, even the oldest of Taiwan's cities formed in the Qing dynasty such as *sanheyuan* and *siheyuan*. And Taiwan is attempting to develop tourist areas by creating old streets through the preservation and *restoration* of Meiji-era (1868–1912) buildings and districts (prefectural offices, stations, etc.) and buildings or collections of buildings that preserve historical architectural methods.
9. "*Ting zi jiao*" resemble Japan's covered alleys and passages under the eaves of houses.
10. Although clothing/apparel sales are considered an appropriate indicator for measuring how urban a city is, they were left out of this study because there is still room to investigate differences in purchasing behavior based on time period and generation in Taiwan.
11. The source for the number of temples is the "Changhua Prefecture: Lugang Township Revitalization and Environmental Integration Plan."

References

Changhua Prefectural Lugang Old Street Development Promotion Association. (2008). *Readings on Lugang Old Street.*
City Office of Lugang, Changhua Prefecture. (2007). *Paradise on Lugang Old Street.*

Changhua Cultural Affairs Bureau. (2008). *Changhua Prefecture: Lugang Township Revitalization and Environmental Integration Plan.*

Chubachi, R. (2015). The shrine and culture sightseeing in Taiwan ; The religion that became the fashion and local turnout. *Journal of Hokkaido Tourism Research, 2*(1), 10–18.

Chunhua Telecom Co., Ltd. (2016). *105–106th Annual Changhua Prefecture Commercial Phone Book.* pg. 353.

Xu, X., Cai, J., Ye, S., & Huang, Z. (2004). Forecasting the number of tourists: A case study of Lugang. *The 2004 Changhua Cross-strait Academic Research Conference: Collected Research on Taiwan*, 385–396.

Huang, S., Tanaka, M., Mitsuhashi, T., Kato, J., & and Miyazaki, K. (1997). Role and Possibility of Long−Shan Temple in Regional Development of Lu−Gang, Taiwan −Methodology of Regional Development by Utilizing Temple Culture. *Design Research, 43* (6). 51–60, 1459–1468.

Lai, Z. (2004). Study of the Interface between Historical Changes on Lugang Streets. *The 2004 Changhua Cross-strait Academic Research Conference: Collected Research on Taiwan.* 341–359.

Li, D., & Hatano, J. (2001): The Formation and Changes of The Town -Houses with Arcade in Di-Hwa Street, Taipet City. *The Architectural Institute of Japan's Journal of Architecture and Planning*, (457), 237–242.

Li, Z. (2004). A Historical Investigation of Lugang's Wood Furniture Industry. *The 2004 Changhua Cross-strait Academic Research Conference: Collected Research on Taiwan.* 429–454.

Matsui, H. (2017). Expansion of build-up area Lugang Town, Changhua County, Taiwan. *Geo-environmental Science Research (Rissho University), 19*, 95–102.

Mogi, K., Katayama, K., Daxing, Z., Toyota, T., & Tejima, N. (1991). Research on the Barracks-style Residences. *Journal of Housing Research Foundation, Annual Research Report No. 18*, 1–15.

Nishikawa, H., & Nakagawa, O. (2013). Rows-of-Houses Preservation Project in Taiwan Lao-jie. *Architecture and Planning, 78*(685), 725–733.

Nishikawa, H., & Nakagawa, O. (2014). The Spread of Townscape of Roofed Walkway over Local Towns of Taiwan During Japanese colonial Period — Focus on the relation with the city improvement planning. *Journal of Architecture and Planning, 79*(700), 1459–1468.

Lugang Maintenance Committee, led by Tianfu Shi (ed.). (1998). *Geography of Lugang (Changhua Prefecture).* Lugang: City Office of Lugang, Changhua Prefecture.

Huang, W., & Yan, H. (2004). Study of the Construction of Spatial Structural Models in the Streets of Taiwan's Early Riverbank Cities: A Case Study of Lugang. *The 2004 Changhua Cross-strait Academic Research Conference: Collected Research on Taiwan.* 127–143.

Ye, D. (1997). *The History of Expansion in Lugang.* Zuo Yang Publishing House.

Covariance Structure Analysis of GIS Use Motivation at the Kumagaya Uchiwa Festival

Shintaro Goto

Abstract

The purpose of this study is to analyze the characteristics of Web GIS (Geographic Information System) users of the festival float location system that was implemented at the traditional Kumagaya Uchiwa Festival in Saitama Prefecture, Japan. We will clarify the factors which contributed to the appearance of regional expectations and effects brought about by Web GIS. There were not any significant associations between the users of this system; the only common attribute among them was their sex. The results of the analysis were derived from the relationships between factors; from attributes such as age; actions such as the willingness to put out the information on the Internet by Web GIS; and regional effects such as the improvement of security. The expectations concerning regional effects realized by Web GIS use were much more influenced by the willingness to put out the information on the Internet than by the frequent use of it. We also found that the willingness to put out the information on the Internet by Web GIS was influenced by age.

Introduction

The results of the proliferation of cell phones and the Internet is that now most person-to-person (point-to-point) communications occur in cyberspace. Common Internet communication tools used to be the electronic conference room and bulletin board applications, but now blogs and SNS (Social Networking Service) are taking their place. Each community formed by such means was expected to contribute and stimulate their particular region. It is thought that GIS (Geographic Information System) would be used to help people express their concerns for, as well as promote, their region (area). GIS is a tool that visualizes information, thereby prompting interest in regions to form links between people (points) and the region (area).

The use of GIS as a tool for sharing critical information has been observed during disasters and other emergencies (Goto et al., 1997; Goto, 1998; Goto, 2004). Following the Great East Japan Earthquake of March 2011, GIS was used to share vital information. For example, it was used to validate specific information such as instructions for support personnel sent to the disaster region as well as the confirmation of the status of survivors. It was also used then in 2011 to release the results in detailed report format along with maps using the "Great East Japan Earthquake/Restoration Support Platform created by everyone" (sinsai.info). Additionally, in 2011, the "ALL311: Great East Japan Earthquake Joint Support Platform" was launched and used to release maps needed to clarify the state of damage or to support volunteer rescuers. This was a program from the National Research Institute for Earth Science and Disaster Resilience (http://www.bosai.go.jp/e/), which is an organization that collects, prepares, and sends out trustworthy information regarding disaster response, restoration, and recovery. Additionally, GIS is commonly used to collect and disseminate regional activity information (Sakai et al., 2005, Sakai & Goto; 2005; Tsuboi et al., 2007; Nakagawa et al., 2007) as well as a tool to link individual people with their regions.

In more recent years, Twitter and other social media have become communication tools. They have also attracted attention as ways of supplementing existing communication methods during the Great East Japan Earthquake. For example, Twitter has been used for various forms of communication such as situational documentation, opinions, and conversations regarding Twitter postings. Furthermore, it offers services which display a user's location on a map in response to submissions accompanying provided location information; cases of use in parallel with spatial information are also available. During the Great East Japan Earthquake, these features were used to send damage information and to confirm the safety and status of people. Similar to day-to-day use at it has used as an effective information-sharing tool during emergencies. For example, regional governments released hazard maps based on GIS, but it still is important to encourage the day-to-day use of GIS so that it can be used effectively for emergencies.

GIS is an excellent way to visualize location information because it represents spatial information on maps. In particular, it can be used to control each natural feature in layer units as well as superimpose multiple layers to prepare maps adapted to each user's purpose. Additionally, commonalities are embedded in a regional society, and visualizing these to the greatest possible degree is counted on for contributing to consensus formation or local information discovery. In this way, GIS has functions that permit for a high and wide clarification of regional information. For example, it can confirm a user's surroundings in addition to objects of their interest. It can discover relationships between connected information and so on, and will probably permit its use as a tool to link people with their region.

While GIS is being expanded for purposes outside of its standard footprint, an effort is being undertaken to popularize it at the national government level via the 2010 "GIS Action Program" from the Commission for the Promotion of the Utilization of Geographical Spatial Information (http://www.cas.go.jp/jp/seisaku/sokuitiri/index.html). This involves the standardizing and improving of spatial information and metadata. They are building and publicly releasing a digital clearing house to simplify the acquisition of this data as well as developing the Electronic National Land Web System that will be compatible with Web GIS. There will be no charge for the high-quality administrative GIS services and the seminars given to popularize the program and enlighten the public. Through these efforts, it will improve the environmental aspect of GIS use which will in turn promote its further implementation. Outside of this progress, a further challenge remains: the study of the methods of how to encourage the spontaneous and continuous use of GIS by citizens in the course of their daily lives and regional activities.

Additionally, studies of GIS activity at the regional level have shown its usefulness for activities related to community creation (Takeyama and Nakase, 2005; Tanaka and Uchihira, 2008), as well as for residents and administrative bodies to exchange views (Oba, 2005). These studies evaluated the utilization of GIS systems at event sites such as experimental operations which showed the effects of and functional challenges facing such systems. These are important initiatives in that they evaluate the results of citizens using GIS. The one challenge in the future is for citizens to use GIS in their daily lives instead of only in circumstantial events. Our goal then is to conduct studies to find out what elements we should focus our analysis on in order to spread the use of GIS.

This study clarifies the relationships of user attributes by evaluating the implementation and functionality of a system employing Web GIS in transmitting parade float locations during the Kumagaya Uchiwa Festival, which is held in Kumagaya City, Saitama Prefecture.

Furthermore, we think that there are widespread opportunities for GIS outside of the festival experience. There are opportunities for GIS in varieties of regional situations. Therefore, we must spread awareness that GIS is a technology that can be effective for regional societies. So, along with organizing factors that contribute to the spread of GIS, this study is also intent on analyzing and studying the structure of relationships concerning the following question.

How are expectations of effects on a region such as regional activation or increasing interest in the region ("regional effects") manifest in light of the relationships between the use of spatial information that is distributed by Web GIS with users' attributes?

1. Outline of the survey

The Kumagaya Uchiwa Festival is a lively summer event held at the end of July. Floats representing twelve districts parade through the streets. It is held in the Northern Kanto Region and it attracts about 750,000 visitors over its three-day period. A Web-based system displaying the present locations of every float was constructed and announced for this festival.

A questionnaire was conducted at two places—inside the grounds of JR Kumagaya Station and at the Community Plaza, the center of the festival—during the festival which took place from July 20 to 22, 2007. Visitors to the festival were asked at random to fill in a questionnaire by themselves. They received assistance only if they needed some clarifications. The major items were "frequency of visit"; "reason for visit"; "age (20s, 30s, 40s etc.)"; "address"; "sex"; whether or not they had used the float location confirmation system; their assessment of how easy it was to use and of its usefulness; and "frequency of use of, expectations of, and evaluation of usefulness of Web GIS." A total of 265 responses were received. Table 1 shows the basic attributes of the persons who responded to the questionnaire. In regard to the "frequency of use of, expectations of and evaluation of usefulness of Web GIS," they were asked about "maps that can be used from a cell phone or PC," which is the definition of Web GIS for this paper.

In 2006, the provision of information about the present locations of floats using Web GIS at the festival was publicized at the time of a proving test of the system. This was the year before this questionnaire, and the announcement was well-received. Then in the beginning of 2007 the results of the proving test were incorporated into preparations for the festival and the questionnaire was conducted assuming that it would be important to evaluate the state of use of and usefulness of GIS in this way.

Additionally, a study was done to analyze the relationship between people's expectations of whether or not distributing regional information through Web GIS could promote the region. Another topic of this study was whether or not it would improve the safety and feeling of security of its residents with consideration to their individual attributes such as their age or their Web GIS usage behavior. The "region" is "an area where daily life and daily activities are conducted centered on residential districts."

Table 1—*Basic Attributes of Respondents*

	Item	Number		Percentage
Sex	Male	127		48.7%
	Female	134		51.3%
	No answer	4		-
Age	20s or younger	58		22.3%
	30s	50		19.2%
	40s	41		15.8%
	50s	55		21.2%
	60s	46		17.7%
	70s or older	10		3.9%
	No answer	5		-
Length of Residence (years)	Less than 5	62		23.6%
	5 or longer, less than 10	34		12.9%
	11 or longer, less than 20	56		21.3%
	21 or longer	111		42.2%
	No answer	2		-

2. Structure and evaluation of the float location information system

2.1 Outline of the float location information system

For this study the float location information system that uses Web GIS to transmit the present locations of 12 floats as they parade through the streets was constructed and then announced. Based on the results of the questionnaire, trends in use of this system and evaluations of the system were studied. Two versions of this system were put forth. The first was a PC browser system which permitted people to check on the present locations of the floats from their homes. The other was an application based on a QR code which allowed them to confirm the present locations of floats by using the Internet on their cell phones while at the festival. The two systems were announced in the official festival pamphlets and on a custom banner on the official festival web page. Additionally, when the systems were introduced, the job of providing devices and dealing with their specific problems was handled by a collaboration of concerned organizations. These groups in charge of these tasks had close links to the Kumagata Gion-kai, which is the organization that manages the festival. They are assisted in their festival management through the mutual provision of ideas by industry, academia, government, and the people. The PC browser system was built by preparing a large 40+ inch TV screen with PC connectivity. It was then installed in an open space facing the exit gate at JR Kumagaya Station during the festival. This system displayed the current locations of the floats in an effort to increase awareness of the system and induce visitors' interest in using it.

The PC browser system used Portable Site GPS made by I-O Data Device Inc. to obtain present locations of floats. It periodically used the email functions of cell phones connected to GPS to automatically transmit the email input with latitudes and longitudes. The transmission of present locations of floats to clients by Web GIS was done using Electronic National Land provided by the Geographical Survey Institute. *Figure 1* shows a display screen of the PC browser float location information system.

Fig.1 PC Browser System display screen. (Background map uses "Electronic National Land" from the Geographical Survey Institute).

Figure 2 shows the float present position display screen of this system.

Fig.2 Cell phone system display screen (Nakagawa et al., 2007) from Doko-iruka Service.

2.2 System use trends and evaluation of the system

The results of the analysis of the access data showed that about 20,000 page-views per day were recorded by both systems, indicating a high degree of interest.

The results of totaling the answers to the questionnaire confirmed that 30 of the people in the entire sample used the system. Table 2 shows the system usage rate according to a comparison of people using the system by basic attribute with the numbers of people with similar ones. Respondents who did not answer questions about their use or non-use of the system were omitted.

Table 2—*Number of Users of the System by Basic Attributes and Usage Rates*

	Item	Number	Usage rate
Sex	Male	20	17.9%
	Female	10	8.8%
Age	20s or younger	4	8.5%
	30s	4	9.3%
	40s	9	24.3%
	50s	6	13.3%
	60s	7	16.7%
	70s or older	0	0.0%
Reason for visit	Advertised	1	4.8%
	Friend/acquaintance	4	10.0%
	Tradition	11	13.3%
	Hometown	12	18.2%
	Present resident	8	16.7%
Number of visits	1st	3	4.8%
	2nd to 5th	12	17.1%
	6th to 10th	2	8.7%
	11th or more	13	18.1%

The results of verifying independence based on the χ^2 distribution of the relationship between attributes and system use show that by sex, the usage rate of men was, at a significant level of 5%, significantly higher than that of women. In regard to age, no significant difference was observed, but the usage rate of people in their 40s or older was higher than that of young people in their 30s and younger.

There was no significant difference between reasons for visits and system use; the highest usage rate was found for the attribute giving "hometown" as reason for a visit. This was followed by the attributes giving "present residence" and "tradition."

Although significant differences by frequency of visits were not seen, a high usage rate appeared among visitors who visited 11 times or more. High use was also clearly shown among visitors who visited from 2-5 times.

Next, evaluations of ease of use and usefulness by actual users of the system was studied. Table 3 shows the results of the cross-analysis.

Table 3—*Evaluations of the PC and Cell Phone Systems by Actual Users*

Machine	Item	Low evaluation		Medium evaluation		High evaluation	
		Number	%	Number	%	Number	%
PC	Ease of use	2	11.1%	5	27.8%	11	61.1%
	Usefulness	0	0.0%	3	30.0%	7	70.0%
Mobile	Ease of use	1	5.6%	12	66.7%	5	27.8%
	Usefulness	3	42.9%	1	14.3%	3	42.9%

No significant difference was shown by verification of independence based on the χ^2 distribution, but judging from the table, both ease of use and usefulness were evaluated highly by a larger percentage of the PC browser system users than the cell phone system users. Regarding this, although 18 of the 30 subjects were cell phone users, as a result of interviewing them during the survey, it can be pointed out that the evaluations of usefulness among them tend to be slightly lower because of their concern about fees etc. required for connection, operation, etc.

Then we looked at the relationship of the frequency of use of Web GIS in the respondents' daily lives. The frequency was obtained based on responses selected from: "I don't think so (subjective evaluation: low)," "Can't say either way (subjective evaluation: medium)," or "I think so (subjective evaluation: high). These choices were offered as possible answers to the question, "Do you or do you not usually use it often?" which was positioned under the previous question: "What do you think of sightseeing maps, gourmet restaurant maps, event maps, crime prevention maps, and other maps you can access and use from your cell phone or PC?" No significant differences were seen in the relationship between frequency of daily use of Web GIS and the use or non-use of the system, but a tendency was found for the system usage rate to be higher among respondents who use Web GIS often in their daily lives (subjective evaluation) than respondents who infrequently use it (Table 4).

Table 4—*Frequency of use of Web GIS in Daily Lives by Users and Non-Users of the System*

	Subjective evaluation	Users		Non-users	
		Number	Percentage	Number	Percentage
Frequency of use of Web GIS in daily life	Low	7	10.1%	62	89.9%
	Medium	11	12.6%	76	87.4%
	High	12	18.2%	54	81.8%

Among the reasons for non-users not using the system the responses "Didn't know about it" (76.9%) and "Seemed difficult to operate" (13.9%) were often expressed. This shows that inducing use by advance advertising is a methodological challenge. Among non-users of the system, 129 (61.7%) "want to use it" the next time, but the percentage who answered "Don't know" remained high at 68 (32.5%). We believe that in publicizing the convenience of using the system, it will be necessary to present incentives by adding information such as histories of the floats or city traffic regulations in the city to the present positions of the floats.

3. Regional Stimulation Effects of Using Web GIS

3.1 Expectations of regional stimulation effects of Web GIS

The implementation of Web GIS to regional citizens' activities is expected to promote and stimulate understanding of the region by visualizing its information. The system functions as a hub that strengthens the relationship between the people and their region. It is also expected to promote the dissemination of information by residents, share regional information and contribute to safety as well as security. In recent years, GIS has come into use for exchanging information about environmental protection activities; raising of children; sharing of information about regional safety; and presumably, it can become a device which forms links between "people and their region" and between "actual space and information space."

In order for this study to find out what kind of expectations visitors have of Web GIS not just at traditional events, but on its value in their daily lives, a cross-analysis of the users and the non-users of the float location information system was done with "expectations of regional stimulation effects (=regional stimulation)" and "expectations of increasing interest in and concern with the region effects (=interest in the region)" as the indices (*Figure 3*).

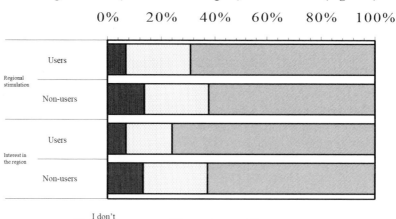

Fig.3 Regional effects anticipated by users/non-users
      p>0.05 (No significant difference).

The question concerning expectations of regional effects asked whether or not using spatial information through Web GIS would or would not have effects on regions where it is used. Three possible answers were "I don't think so," "I think so," and "normal (cannot say either way)." As a follow-up, familiar examples of the use of Web GIS were cited after the question. The respondents were asked what they thought of sightseeing maps, gourmet restaurant maps, event maps, crime prevention maps, and other maps they could access and use from their cell phone or PC. This clearly showed how GIS is used in a variety of situations, which made the respondents aware that Web GIS can be utilized in other ways other than the float location information system.

The figure shows that both users and non-users of the system expressed high expectations of stimulation of interest in the region. The results of the χ^2 verification of independence did not show any difference between them at a significance level of 5%. For this reason, regardless of use or non-use of the system, Web GIS can become a device for stimulating a region or garnering interest in the region.

3.2 Determinant analysis of regional effects of Web GIS

The results concerning the float location information system showed no trends in use according to specific attributes aside from sex. They revealed that people have expectations of regional effects of Web GIS regardless of whether or not they used the float location information system. As this shows, no trends indicating a relationship of the state of use of this system under the specified conditions with feelings of expectations of regional effects were found, but it is necessary to study relational structures that will contribute to generalizations based on attributes and usage behavior focused on the regional effects of Web GIS whose range of acceptance has broadened in recent years.

Therefore, assuming that in order to encourage residents to use GIS, it will be necessary to make them aware that it is a technology that can impact regional society. Factors that stimulate expectations about how using Web GIS will improve regional effectiveness should be studied. Here, the relationships between individual attributes, Web GIS usage behavior, and regional effects are analyzed using covariance structure analysis in an effort to perform an overall interpretation of the relationships found between each of these items.

For this analysis, variables were set for the hypothesis that individual attributes which were age, residence history, and sex impact Web GIS usage behavior. Additionally, the contents of this behavior are expressed as feelings of expectations that using it will have regional effects. Table 5 shows the contents of observable variables used for the model.

Figure 4 shows a model representing the relationships between individual attributes, Web GIS usage behavior, and the expectations of regional effects of its use.

In modeling by the covariance structure analysis, the following assumptions were used and paths were set between variables. Factors that lead to the use of PCs and cellular. Age, residence history, and sex were set as variables concerning individual attributes. "GIS daily use frequency (frequency of daily use of Web GIS)" and "information put out willingness (willingness to put out information by Web GIS)" were set as variables concerning Web GIS usage behavior. "Improving convenience (improving convenience of behavior)," "stimulation improvement (improving stimulation of the region)," "safety and security (improving feelings of safety and security)," and "interest in the region (improving interest in and concern with the region) were set as variables concerning the latent variable, which was the variable concerning expectations of regional effects.

Table 5—*Variables and Contents of Questions*

Items	Contents	Evaluation criteria
Variables concerning individual attributes	Age	Eight 10-year periods ranging from teens (1) to 80s (8).
	History of residence in the region (residence history)	4 levels: 5 years (1), 6–0 years (2), 11–20 years (3), 21 years and longer (4)
	Sex	Two levels: male (0) and female (1) (dummy variable with male as the standard)
Variables concerning Web GIS usage behavior	What do you think about the following items related to maps such as tourism maps, gourmet food maps, event maps, and crime prevention maps that you can use with your cell phone or PC? · I use them often in my daily life (frequency of daily use of GIS). · I want to put out information myself (willingness to put out information).	Three levels: I don't think so (1), Cannot say either way (2), I think so (3)
Variables concerning effects of Web GIS on the region (regional effects)	What do you think about the following items related to maps such as tourism maps, gourmet food maps, event maps, and crime prevention maps that you can use with your cell phone or PC? · Will increase interest in or concern with the region (interest in the region). · Will improve feelings of safety and security (Safety-security). · Will stimulate exchanges between the city and people (improving stimulation). · Behavior becomes more convenient (improvement of convenience).	Three levels: I don't think so (1), Cannot say either way (2), I think so (3)

(Of all 265 responses, 240 used as valid responses)

Shintaro Goto

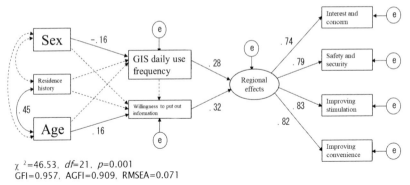

χ^2=46.53, *df*=21, *p*=0.001
GFI=0.957, AGFI=0.909, RMSEA=0.071

Solid lines: significant paths at 5% level, Dotted lines:
Insignificant paths at 5% level

Fig.4 Determinants of expectations of regional effects of Web GIS.

The relationship of individual attributes with Web GIS usage behavior was examined using Internet Overview Statistical Collection from the Ministry of Internal Affairs and Communications (Institute for Information and Communications Policy, 2015, Revised). It was shown that the individual Internet usage rate by age period in 2004 was, in the age groups from teens to 40s, higher than 80%, which is far higher than among people in other age groups. GIS introduces the behavior using a PC or a cell phone, so it is assumed that degree of mastery of and low resistance to machine operation according to age are related to frequency of daily use of GIS. Regarding sex, males (usage rate of 75.1%) show a usage rate 11 points higher than that of females (usage rate 64.0%), so it is assumed that similarly, sex is related to daily use of GIS. Additionally, regional SNS has begun to attract interest as a way to distribute regional information using PCs or cell phones. However, when the "Handbook on the use of resident participation systems –Regional SNS public individual certification compatible electronic questionnaire system—" (Reference document 2. Outline of corroborative experiment, http://www.soumu.go.jp/denshijiti/ict/pdf/index.html) is examined, it shows that among regional SNS in the corroborative experiment districts—Chiyoda Ward in Tokyo and Nagaoka city in Niigata Prefecture—the percentages by age group of SNS registrants are less than 3% among people in their teens and in their 60s or older. It is 20% or higher among people from their 20s to their 40s, and even 10% among those in their 50s, which shows that age-based gaps in SNS registration exist. For this reason, it is thought that the behavior—putting out information about one's region using Web GIS—is related to age. While a relationship with residence history is not reported, it is thought that the longer a person's residence history, the greater that person's concern with their region of residence. This impacts their behavior of putting out information. Furthermore, it is reported that more men than women are users of regional SNS, and it is thought that collecting and putting out regional information using the Internet is also related to sex. Based on this, we set the impact on the variables, "Frequency of daily use of GIS" and "Willingness to put out information" which present Web GIS usage behavior according to the individual attribute variables of age, residence history, and sex.

Regarding the two variables related to Web GIS usage behavior, it is thought that by putting out information by Web GIS as part of our life experience—using GIS—subsequently, the more a person uses GIS in his or her daily life, the lower that person's resistance to using GIS becomes. Conversely, the stronger the person's awareness of the convenience of GIS, it is hypothesized that willingness to put out information is impacted, and a path is set from "Frequency of daily use of GIS" to "willingness to put out information."

Regarding expectations of "regional effects," considering examples of acceptance of Web GIS in recent years, four variables have been added to the set. They are "improving convenience (improving convenience of behavior)," "safety and security (improving safety and security)," "improving stimulation (improving stimulation of the region)," and "interest and concern (improving interest in and concern with the region)."

Regarding the relationship of Web GIS usage behavior with "regional effects," because of the goal of measuring expectations of regional effects of GIS, it is assumed that more Web GIS is used in daily life. Therefore, the greater the awareness of the convenience of GIS, the greater the expectations of regional effects from the use of it. Assuming that there are more people who are willing to personally put out regional information in hopes of increasing interest in their region, the greater people's expectations of regional effects of GIS will be. Furthermore, the impact on "regional effects" of "frequency of daily use of GIS" and "willingness to put out information" was set.

Figure 4 represents the results of the analysis. Coefficients which appear on significant paths represent standard solutions. In this model, GFI and AGFI are 0.957 and 0.909 respectively, which shows high fidelity. Additionally,

RMSEA (*Root Mean Square Error of Approximation*) that indicates the gap between distribution of a model and actual distribution has reached 0.071. This number exceeds 0.05, which is the criterion for the adaptation standard value. Nevertheless, a value that is not higher than 0.1 whose applicability is considered poor was obtained, so it can be said that it represents a degree of fidelity. In the verification based on the χ^2 value, at the 5% level, the model is abandoned and good fidelity was not shown. But for the χ^2 value, the larger the number of samples, the more likely the model will be abandoned. In this analysis, there were 200 samples, which is considered to be a medium quantity of examples. It was thought that the model was discarded, but the other fidelity indices were good, so it was judged that this model is suitable (Asano et al., 2005).

We believe the causal relationship between variables is considered to be based on analysis results, and so we found in the relationship between individual attributes and Web GIS usage behavior, the path from "sex" to "daily use of GIS" shows a negative result of (-0.16). Additionally, the more men there are, the higher the frequency of daily use of GIS. Additionally, the variable that impacts "willingness to put out information" is age, and its path coefficient shows a positive relationship (0.16) so it can be concluded that as age increases, willingness to put out information using Web GIS increases.

The path coefficient from Web GIS usage behavior to "regional effects" is 0.28 for "frequency of daily use of GIS", and it is 0.32 for "willingness to put out information." Both numbers indicate positive relationships, showing that the higher the frequency of daily use of GIS and the higher the willingness to put out information by Web GIS, the greater the expectations for the regional effects of it. The higher the frequency of daily use of GIS, the more people feel the benefits of using it for spatial information, and the higher people's willingness to put out information by Web GIS. The stronger the determination of residents to encourage interest in their region by putting out information, the more they will feel the benefits of the use of GIS as a method in which they can visualize the attractiveness of the region and as well as the challenges it faces. Finally, this means that they will manifest expectations that it will be possible for use of Web GIS to improve regional effects.

Regarding "regional effects," all of the observable variables which were set show almost equal high-positive correlations. Notably, "improving convenience" and "improving stimulation" obtained results which surpassed the parameter value of 0.8.

For these reasons, the more men involved, the higher the frequency of daily use of GIS and the higher their age; the greater their willingness to use Web GIS to put out information. This result suggests a relationship that increases expectations of regional effects of GIS. This fact can be said to show that individual attributes impact Web GIS usage behavior, and that multiplies feelings of expectations for regional effects.

Focusing on the two variables concerning Web GIS usage behavior can reveal that although neither necessarily obtain a high parameter to improve regional effects, "willingness to put out information" has a greater impact than "frequency of daily use of GIS." Although it is hypothesized that at the present time, the spread of PCs and cell phones are expanding the daily use of Web GIS, it is thought that in order to strengthen people's expectation of regional effects of this system it will be important to, for example, introduce literacy and education opportunities that will support the "putting out of information."

Therefore, expectations of regional effects of Web GIS use are manifest through its usage behavior according to individual attributes, and of these, the impact of willingness to independently put out information on Web GIS is greatest. Willingness to put out information is a behavior impacted by age, and providing opportunities to put out information jointly by using SNS and GIS as is seen in regional SNS. Encouraging the willingness to put out information by introducing opportunities for education concerning this matter to residents who, as they age, are increasingly willing to put out regional information using Web GIS will presumably be one method that demonstrates how GIS technology can effectively contribute to a region.

4. Conclusions and Challenges

This study evaluated the state of use, usefulness, and ease of use of a system that releases the present locations of traditional festival floats using Web GIS. Next, a relational structure analysis as well as a study of the relationship of people's individual attributes with usage behavior of Web GIS was conducted. Web GIS is coming into wide use and is being improved to find out how expectations of regional effects of this system are manifest.

The study clarified the following points.

1) The relationship between the use and non-use of the system that confirms

the present locations of floats during the festival. The basic attributes of re-spondents to the questionnaire did not reveal any significant relationships except in the category of sex. This was evaluated under the limited conditions of a regional festival, but it is thought that it was accepted by a wide range of people in addition to those with specific attributes who showed interest in this system.

2) The PC browser system was evaluated as easier to use and more useful than the cell phone system. The cell phone system was evaluated as less useful because of the concern with the plan charges that must be paid for its connection and operation.

3) It was confirmed that regardless of whether or not they used this system, people held high expectations that the use of Web GIS would im-prove regional awareness and stimulate interest in and concern for the region. This finding has suggested that Web GIS can gain potential as a device with regional effects.

4) It was confirmed that among the variables set for the study model, among Web GIS usage behaviors, the "willingness to put out information" is significantly impacted by age." It can be stated that this shows the possibility that advancing age increases people's willingness to put out information by Web GIS and brings about the expectations that GIS is a technology that can have effects on regional societies. Additionally, we think that in order to strengthen people's willingness to put out information, it will be important to create opportunities to put out regional information and to create mechanisms to make this happen—for example, by improving support systems.

SNS that enables communication with other users who mutually dissemi-nate information on the Internet or the use of GIS on blogs are considered as ways to put out information about Web GIS usage behavior. Nevertheless, a future challenge that must be tackled in order to strengthen people's willing-ness to put out information is to study ways to handle regional information. Ways of letting citizens feel affection for their region or consider how it can be improved for example must be examined. This will focus their attention on and strengthen their interest in the region. It will probably also be necessary to study specific methodologies that introduce information dissemination ed-ucational opportunities, such as building a support system which includes seminars regarding the use of such systems. Another future challenge will be to verify if improving people's expectations of GIS affecting their region by promoting willingness to put out information could contribute to the wider use of GIS.

Cell phones are versatile as Internet service use terminals and can be used not only for Web GIS but for SNS or blogs. They offer a way for people to immediately post information about discoveries they make in their own towns to Web GIS or to SNS, etc. and can be used to build GIS utilization environments that make daily life feel like a series of special events. Cell phones serve to strengthen people's willingness to use these methods, but evaluations of the cell phone use version of this system revealed concerns with plan fees and operability, so it is probably necessary to study the hardware environment for GIS use. On the other hand, according to the Communication Use Trends Survey Report (Ministry of Internal Affairs and Communications, 2008), a survey conducted in 2008—the same year as this study—found that 14.3% (n = 7,233 people) accessed individual websites or blogs with cell phones during the previous one year period. A 2009 survey found that this site access figure had increased by two points in two years to 16.2% (n = 9,410), showing a rising trend in the percentage of those who used cell phones to access websites thought to charge heavier plan fees than email. Also it is expected that the promotion of environments that reduce concerns about plan charges and operability will appear as, for example, cell phone service providers offer fixed-plan rates services and devices that can be connected to the Internet through wireless LAN. Soon, cell phones with intuitive interfaces permitting users to operate them by directly touching buttons displayed on their screens will arrive.

References

Asano H., Suzuki T., & Takaya, K. (2005). *Introduction: Truth of Covariance Structure Analysis*. Kodansha.

Goto S., Kitagawa J., Takeuchi W., Oyama H., & Higashi Y. (1997). Study of GIS on the Internet during a disaster –application to the heavy oil spill accident by the Nakhodka. *Proceedings of 1997 Conference of the Japan Society of Photogrammetry and Remote Sensing,* 75–78.

Goto, S. (2004). Front line of Web-GIS. *Monthy Kaiyo, 36*(5), 355–59.

Goto, S. (1999). Construction of Oil-Spill Warning System based on Remote Sensing/ Numerical Model and Its application to the Natural Resource Damage Assessment and Restoration System. *Proceedings of International Symposium on Remote*

Sensing, 243–48.

Sakai, T., Goto, S., & Kawamura, H. (2005). Case of the application of GIS to a full survey of water quality of the Arakawa River. *Proceedings of 2005 Conference of the Japan Society of Photogrammetry and Remote Sensing,* 217–220.

Institute for Information and Communications Policy. (2015). Internet Overview Statistical Collection. Retrieved from: http://www.soumu.go.jp/iicp/chousaken-kyu/data/research/survey/telecom/2006/2006-1-01-2.pdf

Ministry of Internal Affairs and Communication. (2008). Communications use trends and survey report. Retrieved from http://www.soumu.go.jp/johotsusintokei/statis-tics/pdf/HR200700_001.pdf & http://www.soumu.go.jp/johotsusintokei/statistics/pdf/HR200900_001.pdf

Nakagawa, M, Sakai T., Goto S., & Tsuboi, S. (2007). Study of the use of GIS at a regional traditional event – case of its application at the Kumagaya Uchiwa Festival. *Proceedings of the Second National Conference of the Japan Personal Computer Application Technology Society,* 9–12.

Oba, T. (2005). Experimental exchange of views between citizens and administration by electronic conferencing using Web-GIS. *GIS—theory and application, 13*(1), 99–196.

Sakai, T., & Goto, S. (2005, July). Application of GIS to citizens' activities. *Global Environment Research*, 79–85.

Secretariat of the Stable GIS Utilization Project. (2007). Okabe A., & Imai O. (Eds.). Kokon, S. GIS and resident participation.

Takeyama H. & Nakase, I. (2005). Building and studying the effects of a conscious-ness-raising system related to city planning based on GPS equipped cell phones and Web-GIS. Shinshu Elementary School, Collected Papers on Urban Planning, 40(3). 199–204.

Tanaka T. & Uchihira, T. (2008). Study of the use of GPS equipped mobile GIS for resident-participation type city planning inspections –Through practice in the Muko District of Amagasaki City. *Collected technical reports of the Architectural Institute of Japan, 14*(27), 199–204.

Tsuboi S., Sakai T., & Goto S. (2007). Study of citations of and willingness to use GIS in a regional traditional event: Taking the float location information system at the Kumagaya Uchiwa Festival as a sample case. *Proceedings of the Second National Conference of the Japan Personal Computer Application Technology Society,* 13–16.

Effect of Depressive Tendencies and Individual Differences in Imagery Ability on Imagery Experiences

Abstract

The purpose of this study is to examine (1) the relationship between imagery vividness and controllability and depressive tendencies; and (2) the effect of depressive tendencies and imagery vividness on imagery experience. The shortened form of Betts' Questionnaire Upon Mental Imagery (QMI), the Test of Visual Imagery Control (TVIC), and the Beck Depression Inventory (BDI) were administered to participants. I asked participants to recall imagery of a successful examination (positive image) and an unsuccessful examination (negative image) for 3 minutes with their eyes closed. I counterbalanced to present the image and evaluated the participants' imagery experiences after each and every one of their recollections. To evaluate the imagery experiences, I used an 18-item scale that asked about the vividness of the imagery for each sensory modality, physical sensation, and sense of reality. The results showed a weak positive correlation between the vividness of imagery of physical sensations and depressive tendencies. Those expressing high depressive tendencies and high imagery vividness strongly felt tensed cheeks (straining) when recalling the negative image. Although imagery autonomy decreased, imagery of physical movements became stronger. Those with a high depressive tendency and low imagery vividness experienced a decreased sensation of physical movement when recalling the negative image. Participants who have depressive tendencies exhibit them through imagery, particularly with physical sensations. The manner in which such characteristics are exhibited may be influenced by the content of the recalled image and individual differences in imagery vividness.

Introduction

Clinical psychology is inconceivable without understanding the psychological world of clients. Such psychological worlds and experiences reflect the overall lives as perceived by clients through imagery (Mizushima, 1984). In actual clinical settings, imagery is used to understand and assess clients or as a medium to achieve successful psychological treatment. While imagery has a sensory and perceptual basis, it represents an overall experience that flexibly projects one's inner world in response to the outer world (Mizushima, 1984), presenting diverse phases. Considering the different sensory and perceptual aspects, not only visual, of basic imagery itself, but there is also imagery that exists for each sensory modality, such as auditory and gustatory.

If we consider imagery to be responsible for individual differences in one's ability to recall and experience, several dimensions emerge, such as vividness and controllability of imagery, and imaginative involvements. In particular, the extent to which imagery can be recalled vividly and the degree to which imagery one can control have an impact on the success or failure of psychological treatments that utilize imagery (Lazarus, 1961; Lazarus, 1964; Taneda, 1988; Koizumi, 2009; Tamura, Okuno, and Aoki, 2016, etc.).

From the perspective of recalled imagery and imagery experiences, the emotional values of imagery, such as comfort or discomfort, and the emotions aroused by imagery, have been examined. In general, imagery accompanied by positive emotions are recalled vividly, while the opposite is true for imagery that are associated with negative emotions (Matsuoka, 2006).

Factors that influence the recollection and experience of imagery, including personality traits and emotions have been examined, including those beset with anxious and depressive tendencies, and a thickness of boundaries in the mind which has effects on one's relationship with imagery. It is reported that when anxious tendencies are strong, imagery become suppressed, and the overall vividness of imagery decreases (Euse & Haney, 1975). Likewise, Tucker, Stenslie, Roth, and Shearer (1981) showed that when depressive tendencies are high, the vividness of visual imagery diminishes. The relationship between having a thin boundary and unregulated fluid imagery has already been indicated (Okuma and Suzuki, 1983).

Martin and Williams (1990) showed that under conditions in which a depressive mood is aroused, the group with the higher depressive tendencies experiences higher vividness of visual imagery regarding negative words. In general, when one experiences negative emotions, the vividness of imagery tends to decrease; however, it has been confirmed that a "mood congruency effect of imagery" occurs in which some people with specific personality traits such as depression experience higher vividness of imagery that match their mood.

Thus, the relationship between personality traits such as depressive tendencies and vividness/controllability of imagery has been examined; however, when considering the mood congruency effect of imagery indicated by Martin and Williams (1990), it is assumed that associated aspects will vary depending on the type of emotional values associated with the imagery, particularly with regard to whether the emotional values of the imagery and the mood impacted by personality traits are consistent.

Therefore, in this study, (1) I examined the relationship between depressive tendencies and imagery vividness/controllability, and (2) on the basis of this relationship, I aimed to examine the effect of depressive tendencies and individual differences in imagery on the imagery experience of positive and negative images. In terms of imagery controllability, I measured the controllability of visual imagery on the basis of previous studies that discuss changes in visual imagery.

1. Methods

1.1 Participants:

Participants included 69 university students who provided consent to the experiment (16 male and 53 female, average age 22.1 years).

1.2 Scale:

1.2.1 Vividness of imagery
I used a shortened form of Betts' Questionnaire upon Mental Imagery (QMI; Sheehan, 1967), which measures imagery vividness. It consists of 35 questions, with five questions for each sensory modality: visual, auditory, cutaneous, kinaesthetic, gustatory, olfactory, and organic (physical) sensation. Participants were asked to recall imagery of "the sun going down below the horizon" for visual; a "cat's meow" for auditory; "sand" for cutaneous;

"reaching for a high shelf" for kinaesthetic; "salt" for gustatory; "leather" for olfactory; and "hunger" for organic sensation. The score for each area was summed for the total score.

I used a 7-point scale ranging from "there is no imagery at all. I've only thought about the subject" to "the imagery is as vivid as the actual experience." Higher scores indicated higher imagery vividness.

1.2.2. Controllability of Imagery

I used the Test of Visual Imagery Control (TVIC; Gordon, 1949), which is a scale that measures visual imagery control. It consists of 12 items that require a series of imagery operations associated with the shape and movement of a vehicle, such as "Can you see the vehicle on the road in front of the house?"; "Can you see the color of the vehicle?"; "Can you see a beautiful couple in the vehicle as it drives by?"; and "Can you see the vehicle becoming old, taken apart, and being discarded at a junkyard?" I used a 3-point scale—"no," "unsure," and "yes"—for each item. Higher total scores indicated higher visual imagery control.

1.2.3. Depressive tendencies

I used a Japanese version of the Beck Depression Inventory (BDI: Hayashi, 1988; Hayashi and Takimoto, 1991), prepared by Beck, Ward, Mendelson, Mock, & Erbaugh (1961) and Beck, Rush, Shaw, & Emery (1979). I used a 4-point scale for the total of 21 items. Higher scores indicated more depressive tendencies.

1.2.4. Evaluation of imagery experience

According to the scale prepared by Miyazaki and Hishitani (2004), I used a total of 18 items—vividness, outline, color, details, auditory, olfactory, cutaneous, movement, operability, responsiveness, autonomy, participation, loosened cheeks (smiling), tensed cheeks (straining), body warmth, body coolness, sense of reality, and being absorbed—on a 5-point scale to examine the imagery and experiences when recalling imagery.

1.3 Recalled imagery situations:

I presented situations using the following scripts:

Effect of Depressive Tendencies and Individual Differences in Imagery Ability on Imagery
Experiences

1.3.1 Positive image

"You are at an examination venue. When the written examination begins, you find that you can solve the problems. You can think clearly and answer calmly with a steady hand."

1.3.2 Negative image

"You are at an examination venue. When the written examination begins, you find problems that you do not understand. You cannot think clearly, your hands shake, and you answer frantically."

1.4 Procedures:

The experiment was conducted on all groups at the same time. Prior to the experiment, I obtained responses to the QMI, TVIC, and BDI. Next, I had participants recall imagery of a positive image (a successful exam) and a negative image (an unsuccessful exam) for 3 minutes, each with eyes closed. I counterbalanced the image presentation, and participants evaluated the imagery experience after each recollection.

2. Results

2.1 The relationship between imagery vividness and controllability with depressive tendencies

To examine the relationship between imagery vividness (QMI) and imagery controllability (TVIC) with depressive tendencies (BDI), I calculated the Pearson's correlation coefficient between the QMI scores of each sensory modality, the total score, the TVIC total score, and the BDI total score (Table 1).

Table 1—The correlation between vividness of imagery (QMI). controllability of imagery (TVIC), and depressive tendencies (BDI).

	TVIC	QMI							
		Visual	Auditory	Cutaneous	Kinaesthetic	Gustatory	Olfactory	Organic	total
TVIC		.36**	.25*	.41**	.44**	.21*	.23*	.35**	.41**
BDI	.01	-.09	.08	.11	-.03	-.00	-.05	.28*	.06

* $p<.05$ ** $p<.01$

A moderate-to-weak positive correlation was found between all sensory modalities of imagery vividness and controllability ($r = .21 \sim .44$). If I focus on the correlation between each sensory modality and controllability, then cutaneous, kinaesthetic, and the total had stronger correlations when compared with those of the other modalities.

In terms of imagery vividness and depressive tendencies, there was a weak positive correlation in the range of organic sensations ($r = .28$).

No significant correlation was found between imagery controllability and depressive tendencies.

2.2 Effect of imagery vividness and depressive tendency on imagery experience

I looked at depressive tendencies and imagery vividness, and a significant correlation with depressive tendency was confirmed. To examine the impact of positive and negative images on imagery experience with the mean depressive tendency (BDI) of 12.13 ($SD = 7.64$) as the reference, I assigned participants to a high-depression group (BDI-H: 33 people with a mean BDI of 18.79 and with SD of 4.70) and a low-depression group (BDI-L: 36 people with a mean BDI of 6.03 and with SD of 3.64). Similarly, for the total score of imagery vividness, on the basis of the mean of the QMI of 168.43 ($SD = 30.87$), I assigned participants to a high-vividness group (QMI-H: 36 people with a mean QMI of 193.50 and with SD of 17.61) and a low-vividness group (QMI-L: 33 people with a mean QMI of 141.10 and with SD of 14.44). Table 2 shows the mean and standard deviation of each item of the imagery experience.

Table 2—The mean and standard deviation of each item of the imagery experience.

		Positive image		Negative image	
		QMI-L	QMI-H	QMI-L	QMI-H
vividness	BDI-L	3.39 (0.95)	3.72 (1.15)	3.28 (0.99)	4.00 (0.67)
	BDI-H	3.13 (1.36)	3.89 (1.10)	3.07 (1.24)	3.72 (0.93)
outline	BDI-L	3.33 (1.00)	3.56 (1.12)	2.83 (1.07)	3.50 (1.17)
	BDI-H	2.93 (1.06)	3.56 (1.07)	3.20 (1.17)	3.33 (1.15)
color	BDI-L	2.67 (0.67)	2.56 (1.21)	2.06 (0.85)	2.50 (1.21)
	BDI-H	2.60 (0.88)	2.56 (1.12)	2.53 (1.09)	2.28 (1.04)
details	BDI-L	3.06 (1.03)	3.33 (1.29)	2.78 (1.03)	3.00 (1.11)
	BDI-H	2.93 (1.00)	3.11 (1.10)	2.93 (1.06)	3.22 (1.08)
auditory	BDI-L	1.89 (1.20)	2.67 (1.60)	1.94 (1.08)	2.89 (1.41)
	BDI-H	2.60 (1.40)	2.39 (1.46)	2.33 (1.40)	2.28 (1.28)
olfactory	BDI-L	1.22 (0.42)	1.39 (0.49)	1.28 (0.56)	1.61 (0.95)
	BDI-H	1.40 (0.49)	1.50 (0.96)	1.53 (0.81)	1.44 (0.96)
cutaneous	BDI-L	1.67 (0.47)	2.72 (1.37)	1.78 (0.79)	2.67 (1.20)
	BDI-H	2.00 (1.03)	2.17 (1.46)	2.13 (1.09)	2.06 (1.39)
movement	BDI-L	2.94 (1.18)	3.61 (1.25)	2.83 (1.26)	3.22 (1.18)
	BDI-H	3.20 (1.22)	3.00 (1.15)	2.27 (1.29)	3.39 (1.16)
operability	BDI-L	3.17 (1.21)	3.17 (1.26)	2.94 (1.22)	3.17 (1.17)
	BDI-H	3.13 (1.15)	3.50 (1.17)	2.87 (1.26)	3.61 (1.11)
responsiveness	BDI-L	3.17 (0.90)	3.56 (0.90)	3.06 (1.03)	3.50 (0.83)
	BDI-H	3.20 (1.05)	3.28 (1.04)	3.07 (1.00)	3.06 (0.97)
autonomy	BDI-L	2.94 (1.08)	3.39 (1.34)	2.72 (1.33)	3.22 (1.31)
	BDI-H	2.80 (1.11)	3.33 (1.11)	3.13 (1.26)	2.56 (1.26)
participation	BDI-L	3.83 (0.90)	4.06 (0.97)	3.72 (1.04)	3.94 (0.85)
	BDI-H	3.40 (1.02)	4.00 (1.15)	3.33 (1.14)	3.61 (1.06)
loosened cheeks	BDI-L	2.06 (1.18)	2.44 (1.34)	1.56 (0.60)	1.61 (0.68)
	BDI-H	2.87 (1.20)	3.06 (1.35)	1.60 (0.49)	1.50 (0.96)
tensed cheeks	BDI-L	1.56 (0.76)	1.83 (0.83)	3.89 (0.99)	3.61 (1.11)
	BDI-H	1.87 (0.81)	1.94 (1.03)	3.60 (1.14)	4.33 (0.82)
body warmth	BDI-L	2.17 (1.21)	2.33 (1.05)	1.89 (1.05)	1.78 (0.79)
	BDI-H	2.27 (1.29)	2.83 (1.21)	2.27 (1.12)	1.56 (0.83)
body coolness	BDI-L	1.44 (0.50)	1.78 (0.71)	2.67 (1.29)	2.94 (1.22)
	BDI-H	1.80 (0.65)	1.67 (0.58)	3.33 (1.14)	3.17 (1.30)
sense of reality	BDI-L	2.94 (0.97)	3.72 (1.19)	3.50 (1.01)	3.89 (0.87)
	BDI-H	3.13 (1.20)	3.72 (1.19)	3.73 (0.85)	3.67 (1.05)
absorbed	BDI-L	2.72 (1.10)	3.28 (1.15)	2.17 (0.76)	3.06 (1.03)
	BDI-H	3.00 (1.10)	3.72 (1.10)	2.80 (1.05)	3.11 (1.15)

note: (SD)

As the structure of the imagery experience changes with the emotional values of the imagery (Miyazaki and Hishitani, 2004), I did not perform factor analysis for the imagery experience items. I used an evaluation of each imagery experience as the dependent variable and performed three-way analysis of variance (ANOVA) for depression (BDI-H and -L) × imagery vividness (QMI-H and -L) × image (positive and negative).

With regard to vividness, the main effect of imagery vividness ($F(1,65)$ = 7.17, $p < .001$) was significant, and the high-vividness group had a significantly higher score than the low-vividness group.

Similarly for the outline, the main effect of imagery vividness ($F(1,65)$ = 3.10, $p < .10$) showed a significant trend, and the high-vividness group had a significantly higher score than the low-vividness group.

In terms of color, the secondary interaction ($F(1,65) = 3.92$, $p < .10$) showed a significant trend. The result of examining the simple interaction of vividness × image for each depressive tendency showed that for the low-depression group, the interaction between vividness × image ($F(1,65) = 4.33$, $p < .05$) was significant. A simple main effect test showed that for the low-vividness group, the positive image had a significantly higher score than the negative image ($F(1,65) = 10.47$, $p < .01$). The difference in images for the high-vividness group was not significant. In the high-depression group, no significant interaction or main effect was found. These results showed that those with a low depressive tendency and low vividness reported less color when recalling the negative image.

With regard to auditory, the interaction between depressive tendency × vividness ($F(1,65) = 2.89$, $p < .10$) had a significant trend. I performed a simple main effect test of vividness for each depressive tendency and found that for the low-depression group, the high-vividness group scored significantly higher than the low-vividness group ($F(1,65) = 12.83$, $p < .01$). In addition, I examined the simple main effect of depressive tendency for each vividness group and found that for the low-vividness group, the high-depression group scored significantly higher than the low-depression group ($F(1,65) = 5.24$, $p < .05$). In contrast, for the high-vividness group, the low-depression group scored significantly higher than the high-depression group ($F(1,65) = 3.42$, $p < .10$). These results indicate that when the depressive tendency was low, those with high vividness experienced sounder imagery, and when vividness was low, those with a high depressive tendency experienced sounder imagery. Finally, when vividness was high, those with a low depressive tendency experienced sounder imagery. In particular, when depression was low and vividness was high, the auditory imagery was recalled.

Concerning the cutaneous modality, in what is similar to the case of the auditory modality, the interaction between depressive tendency × vividness ($F(1,65) = 3.22, p < .10$) reflected a significant trend. I performed a simple main effect test of vividness for each depressive tendency and found that for the low-depression group, the high-vividness group scored significantly higher than the low-vividness group ($F(1,65) = 31.80, p < .01$). I also performed a simple main effect test of depressive tendency for each vividness and found that for the low-vividness group, the high-depression group scored significantly higher than the low-depression group ($F(1,65) = 3.99, p < .10$), and for the high-vividness group, the low-depression group scored higher than the high-depression group ($F(1,65) = 11.45, p < .01$). These results indicate that when the depressive tendency was low, those with high vividness experienced more cutaneous imagery, and that when vividness was low, those with a high depressive tendency experienced more cutaneous imagery. Finally, when vividness was high, those with a low depressive tendency experienced more cutaneous imagery. This specifically shows that when depression was low and vividness was high, cutaneous imagery were recalled.

In terms of movement, the secondary interaction ($F(1,65) = 5.69, p < .05$) was significant. I examined the simple interaction of vividness × image for each depressive tendency and found that in the high-depression group, the interaction between vividness × image ($F(1,65) = 7.42, p < .01$) was significant. A simple main effect test showed that for the negative image the high-vividness group scored significantly higher than the low-vividness group ($F(1,65) = 10.69, p < .01$). For the positive image, no significant difference in vividness was found. For the low-vividness group, the positive image scored significantly higher than the negative image ($F(1,65) = 7.39, p < .01$). There was no difference between the images for the high-vividness group. For the low-depression group, no significant interaction or main effect was found. These results indicate that when recalling the negative image, those with a high depressive tendency and high vividness experienced stronger motor imagery, and when recalling the positive image, those with a high depressive tendency and low vividness experienced stronger motor imagery.

In terms of autonomy, the secondary interaction ($F(1,65) = 3.64, p < .10$) had a significant trend. I examined the simple interaction of vividness × image for each depressive tendency and found that for the high-depression group, the interaction between vividness × image ($F(1,65) = 6.31, p < .05$) was significant. I performed a simple main effect test and found that for the high-vividness group, the score for the positive image was significantly higher than the negative image ($F(1,65) = 6.19, p < .05$). For the low-vividness group, there was no difference between the images. For the low-depression group, no significant interaction or main effect was found. These results indicate that those with a high depressive tendency and high vividness experienced declined autonomy for imagery in the negative image.

In terms of loosened cheeks (smiling), the interaction between depressive tendency × image ($F(1,65) = 4.60, p < .05$) was significant. I performed a simple main effect test of the images for each depressive tendency and found that for the low-depression and high-depression groups, the positive image scored significantly higher than the negative image ($F(1,65) = 7.37, p < .01$; $F(1,65) = 33.02, p < .01$). In addition, I examined a simple main effect of depressive tendency for each image, and I found that in the positive image, the high-depression group scored significantly higher than the low-depression group ($F(1,65) = 5.03, p < .05$). These results indicate that when recalling the positive image, participants strongly felt loosened cheeks (smiling), which was particularly strong in those with a high depressive tendency.

In the case of tensed cheeks (straining), the secondary interaction ($F(1,65) = 3.14, p < .10$) had a significant trend. I examined the simple interaction between depressive tendency × vividness for each image and found that for the negative image, the interaction between depressive tendency × vividness ($F(1,65) = 3.97, p < .10$) had a significant trend. I performed a simple main effect test and found that for the high-vividness group, those with a high depressive tendency scored significantly higher ($F(1,65) = 4.06, p < .05$). Likewise, for the high-depression group, those with high vividness scored significantly higher ($F(1,65) = 4.18, p < .05$). No significant interaction or main effect was found for the positive image. These results indicate that participants with a high depressive tendency and high vividness strongly experienced tensed cheeks (strain) when recalling the negative image.

As for the body warmth modality, the interaction between vividness × image ($F(1,65) = 4.97, p < .05$) was significant. I performed a simple main effect test of the images for each type of vividness and found that for the high-vividness group, the positive image scored significantly higher than the negative image ($F(1,65) = 13.80, p < .01$). I also performed a simple main effect test of vividness for each image and found that for the negative image, the low-vividness group had a significantly higher trend than the high-vividness group ($F(1,65) = 3.02$, $p < .10$). These results show that in the positive image, those with high vividness experienced imagery of body warmth, whereas in the negative image, those with low vividness experienced imagery of body warmth.

Regarding body coolness, the main effect of the images ($F(1,65) = 62.12$, $p < .001$) was significant, with the negative image's effect being significantly higher than that of the positive one.

As for the sense of reality, the main effect of vividness ($F(1,65) = 4.21$, $p < .05$) was significant, where the high-vividness group scored significantly higher than the low-vividness group. The main effect of the scenes ($F(1,65) = 3.80$, $p < .10$) had a significant trend, where the negative image tended to score higher than the positive image.

In terms of feeling absorbed, the main effect of vividness ($F(1,65) = 8.20$, $p < .01$) was significant, where the high-vividness group scored significantly higher than the low-vividness group. The main effect of the images ($F(1,65) = 7.02$, $p < .05$) was significant, with the positive image significantly outscoring the negative one.

No significant interaction or main effect of details, olfactory, operability, responsiveness, or participation was found.

3. Discussion

I examined the relationship between imagery vividness and controllability and found a moderate-to-weak positive correlation between all the sensory modalities of imagery vividness with controllability. These results were consistent with the works by Tamura (2011, 2017). Specifically, the correlation between cutaneous and kinaesthetic with vividness and controllability was strong. The scale of controllability dealt with imagery associated with vehicles and driving; hence, it might have been more prone to association with cutaneous and kinaesthetic.

Imagery vividness in the range of organic sensations was linked with depressive tendency. In terms of the relationship between depressive tendency and imagery, it is known that when the depressive tendency is high, the vividness of visual imagery decreases (Tucker et al.,1981); however, in the present study, no significant negative correlation was found. On the other hand, there

Hanae Tamura

was a relationship between vividness of organic sensation, but considering the use of the depression scale, with many items associated with physical symptoms, the experience of the physical symptoms of depression had an impact, thereby causing the link between vividness of organic sensation. No significant correlation was found between visual imagery controllability and depressive tendency.

I analyzed each imagery experience item in terms of the effect of imagery vividness and depressive tendency on imagery experience. The result showed that the main effect of imagery vividness was confirmed for vividness, out-line, sense of reality, and feeling absorbed. For all of these, the high-vividness group scored higher than the low-vividness group. That is to say, regardless of the image experienced or the degree of depressive tendency, these items were easily influenced by individual differences in vividness, whereby higher imagery vividness resulted in a clearer and more realistic recollection of im-agery, allowing for participants to be absorbed in the recollected imagery. These results indicate that those with a high depressive tendency could recall imagery with vividness and with a sense of reality for the negative image as long as the image's vividness was high.

There was a main effect of the images on body coolness, sense of reality, and feeling absorbed. For the negative image, participants strongly experi-enced coolness and a sense of reality, making it difficult to be absorbed in recollection. This is an item in which the impact of the emotional values of the imagery appeared strongly. Considering that the high-vividness group scored high while recalling the positive image in terms of body warmth and that the score for loosened cheeks (smiling) was high when recalling the pos-itive image, it can be said that the image operated appropriately. In respect of loosened cheeks (smiling), it is worth noting that those with a high depressive tendency felt this strongly with the positive image.

Those with a low depressive tendency and high vividness scored high with auditory and cutaneous, indicating that if imagery vividness is high and depressive tendency is low, more sounds and tactile imagery could be ex-perienced. In terms of color, those with a low depressive tendency and low vividness reported less color when recalling the negative image. In general, when there is more information included in the imagery, the imagery can be experienced more vividly. Therefore, auditory, cutaneous, and color imagery experiences may have impacts on imagery vividness and the sense of reality, and their connection with items where the main effect of imagery vividness has been confirmed should be considered. However, even those with a low depressive tendency experienced auditory, cutaneous, and color differently on the basis of imagery vividness. I conclude that for auditory, cutaneous, and color—particularly the experience of imagery of auditory and cutaneous—experience is influenced by the interaction between depressive tendency and imagery vividness.

The results of items in which the secondary interaction was significant indicated that those with a high depressive tendency and high vividness strongly felt tensed cheeks (straining) when recalling the negative image, and although imagery autonomy also became low, physical movement imagery became strong. Those with a high depressive tendency and low vividness felt less physical movement when recalling the negative image.

When recalling the negative image in which the mood is consistent with depressive tendency, those with a high depressive tendency and high vividness strongly felt the sensation of tensed cheeks and physical movement. In contrast, those with a high depressive tendency but without high vividness experienced a stiffening of their bodies. The presentation of the negative image included scripts such as "inability to think," "shaking hands," and "frantic response." Among those with a high depressive tendency, those with high vividness had an increased sensation of physical movement—answering frantically while shaking their bodies—in the imagery, and thus, those with low vividness had less sensation of physical movement. When the scripted sensation was captured as movement, those with a high depressive tendency and high vividness clearly recalled the negative image with physical movements. When I compared our results with the mood congruency effect of the imagery indicated by Martin and Williams (1990), not only did the consistency or inconsistency of mood tend to be associated with depressive tendency with recalled imagery but also individual differences in imagery vividness had an impact on imagery experience.

Items on which there was an impact of high depressive tendency included loosened cheeks (smiling), tensed cheeks (straining), physical movement, and autonomy of imagery. Among these, loosened cheeks (smiling), tensed cheeks (straining), and physical movement can be considered to be physical sensations, indicating the strength of the relationship between depressive tendency and imagery of physical sensation. This relationship is consistent with the result confirmed in the correlation analysis. Specifically, depressive tendency readily shows its characteristics through imagery of physical sensations. The way these characteristics appear may be influenced by the degree of vividness that each person can achieve or the content of the recalled image.

If I consider the present results in terms of clinical practice, clients with a high depressive tendency and high imagery vividness may be making their depression worse by recalling negative images and memories vividly. On the other hand, when recalling positive images, the sensation of loosening the cheek (smiling) was more notable in those with a higher depressive tendency, which may indicate that it is possible to ease depression using physical sensations and their imagery. These points require additional examination and could become future topics of study.

Thus, the present results showed that the experience of imagery is influenced by the interaction of three factors: individual difference in imagery, different personality traits, and the content and emotional values of imagery. When using imagery in clinical settings, it is necessary to examine how individual differences in imagery recollection, individual personality traits, and associated emotions and the content and emotional values of the recollected imagery interact to create the imagery experience in clients. Furthermore, the question as to whether such imagery experiences could ease or treat problems and symptoms must be examined.

References

Beck, A. T., Ward, C. H., Mendelson, M., Mock, J. E., & Erbaugh, J. K. (1961). An inventory for measuring depression. *Archives of General Psychiatry, 4*, 561-571.

Beck, A. T., Rush, A. J., Shaw, B. F., & Emery, G. (1979). *Cognitive Therapy of depression.* NewYork : The Guilford Press.

Euse, F., & Haney, J.N. (1975). Clarity, controllability, and emotional intensity of image : Correlations with introversion, neuroticism, and subjective anxiety. *Perceptual and Motor Skills, 40*, 443-447.

Gordon, R. (1949). An investigation into some of the factors that favour the formation of stereotyped images. *British Journal of Psychology, 39*, 156−167.

Hayashi, T. (1988). Treatment to students' depressive tendencies based the Beck's cognitive therapy. *The Japanese Journal of Student Counseling, 9*, 97-107. (in Japanese)

Hayashi, T., & Takimoto, T. (1991). An examination of Beck Depression Inventory (1978) and an analysis of relation between depressive tendencies and grade of self-efficacy. *Memoirs of Shiraume Gakuen College, 27*, 43-52. (in Japanese)

Koizumi, S. (2009). *Experimental clinical psychology studies on the sharpness of emotional imagery*. Tokyo : Kazamashobo. (in Japanese)

Lazarus, A. A. (1961). Group therapy of phobic disorders by systematic desensitization. *Journal of Abnormal and Social Psychology, 63*, 504–510.

Lazarus, A. A. (1964). Crucial procedural factors in desensitization therapy. *Behaviour Therapy and Research, 2*, 65–70.

Martin, M., & Williams, R. (1990). Imagery and emotion: Clinical and experimental approaches. In P. J. Hampson, D. F. Marks, & J. T. E. Richardson (Eds.), *International library of psychology. Imagery: Current developments* (pp. 268-306). New York and London : Routledge.

Matsuoka, K. (2005). Emotion and imagery. In Hatakeyama, T., Nihei, Y., Obuchi, K., Gyoba, J. & Hatakeyama, M. (Eds.), *Emotion psychology perspective's - rich world of emotions* (pp.80-89). Kyoto : Kitaohjisyobo. (in Japanese)

Miyazaki, T., & Hishitani, S.(2004). Structures of positive/negative emotional imagery. *The Japanese Journal of Mental Imagery, 2*, 35-49. (in Japanese)

Mizushima, K. (1984). Clinical psychology and imagery. In Mizushima, K., & Ogawa, K. (Eds.), *Clinical psychology of imagery* (pp. 1-16). Tokyo : Seishinshobo. (in Japanese)

Okuma, Y., & Suzuki, A. (1983). Imagery and emotion/motivation. In Mizushima, K., & Uesugi, T. (Eds.), *Basic psychology of the image* (pp. 219-238). Tokyo : Seishinshobo. (in Japanese)

Sheehan, P.W. (1967). A shortened form of Betts' questionnaire upon mental imagery. *Journal of Clinical Psychology, 23*, 386–389.

Taneda, M. (1988). *Introduction of cognitive psychiatry*. Tokyo : Kongoshuppan. (in Japanese)

Tamura, H. (2011). The relationship among vividness of imagery, controllability of visual imagery, and imaginative involvements. *Rissho University Bulletin of clinical psychology, 9*, 31–37. (in Japanese)

Tamura, H., Okuno, S., & Aoki, S. (2016). Effect of heaviness and warmth suggestions on the vividness and the controllability of mental imagery. *Japanese journal of applied psychology, 41*, 264-270. (in Japanese)

Tamura, H. (2017). The relationship among vividness of imagery, controllability of visual imagery, and verbalizer-visualizer. *Rissho University Bulletin of clinical psychology, 15*, 19-23. (in Japanese)

Tucker, D. M., Stenslie, C. E., Roth, R. S., & Shearer, S. L. (1981). Right frontal lobe activation and right hemisphere performance decrement during a depressed mood. *Archives of General Psychiatry, 38*, 169-174.

Trajectories of Mindfulness and Anger Rumination

Masaya Takebe
Hiroshi Sato

Abstract

The purpose of this study was to investigate a longitudinal relationship between trait mindfulness and anger rumination. To date, previous cross-sectional studies have reported that trait mindfulness may be effective for alleviating anger rumination. Few studies, however, have examined the associations between these variables in a longitudinal design. In this study, a sample of 81 Japanese undergraduates was followed over four months, and a latent growth curve model was used to examine the longitudinal relationship. Results indicated that the slopes of mindfulness and anger rumination were negatively covariant to a moderate degree ($r = -.54$, $p = .095$). Furthermore, the estimated correlation between the intercepts of mindfulness and anger rumination was negatively correlated, and its strength was small ($r = -.26$, $p = .049$). The current study may support the idea that interventions to cultivate mindfulness skills could be effective for alleviating anger rumination.

Introduction

The regulation of angry feelings is a major focus in anger treatment. Cognitive-behavioral therapy (CBT) has been focused on anger regulation through both a behavioral component (e.g., acquiring adaptive alternative behaviors to aggression) and a cognitive component (e.g., modifying dysfunctional thoughts about anger; Del Vecchio & O'Leary, 2004). In this field, anger rumination has generated considerable recent research interest. Rumination about anger episodes, known as anger rumination, is a tendency to engage in unintentional re-occurring thoughts about anger episodes (Sukhodolsky, Golub, & Cromwell, 2001). Several experimental studies reported that anger rumination exacerbates or maintains angry feelings (Denson, Moulds, & Grisham, 2012; Fabiansson, Denson, Moulds, Grisham, & Schira, 2012). Ruminating about anger episodes does not allow feelings of anger to dissipate naturally, increases the probability of anger being aroused in various situations, and predisposes individuals to both reactive and proactive aggression (White & Turner, 2014).

Mindfulness has been demonstrated to have effects on rumination. Mindfulness is defined as the quality of consciousness or awareness that arises through intentionally attending to the present moment experience in a nonjudgmental and accepting way (Kabat-Zinn & Hanh, 2009). It has been found that mindfulness-based interventions (MBIs) are efficacious for treatment of a variety of mental disorders, especially major depressive disorder and anxiety disorders (e.g., Khoury et al., 2013). Mediation analysis has been growing in this field as well. Gu, Strauss, Bond, and Cavanagh (2015) reviewed various studies that systematically tested mediators of MBIs and tried to verify which proposed underlying mechanisms had evidence that is more convincing. In their study, there was moderate and consistent support for rumination as the underlying mechanism of MBIs. Furthermore, rumination was a significant mediator of the effects of MBIs. These results are consistent with theoretical models of mindfulness-based cognitive therapy (MBCT), and rumination is considered a treatment target of MBIs, both theoretically and empirically.

However, attempts to apply mindfulness to anger rumination have lagged far behind. Anderson, Lau, Segal, and Bishop (2007) provided the initial evidence for the effects of mindfulness on anger rumination, and this has been the only intervention study to investigate the impact of MBIs on ruminating anger episodes. Healthy adults were randomly assigned to eight-week Mindfulness-Based Stress Reduction (MBSR) or a wait-list control group. The results indicated that participants assigned to MBSR significantly reduced their tendency to ruminate about angry episodes compared to participants assigned to the wait-list control. Subsequently, Wright, Day, and Howells (2009) systematically reviewed the treatment of anger problems and explored the applicability of mindfulness to anger problems. The review suggested that interventions focused on a non-judgmental stance and de-centering attention to one's thoughts might be helpful to change cognitive reactivity such as rumination. After this review was published, some studies investigated anger rumination as an underlying mechanism of the effect of mindfulness on anger problems. It has been reported that anger rumination mediated the relationships between mindfulness and anger problems, including some forms of aggression, hostility (Peters et al., 2015), trait anger, and maladaptive suppression of anger (Takebe, Takahashi, & Sato, 2015). These findings supported the suggestion of Wright et al. (2009) and advanced the application of mindfulness to anger problems by suggesting the mediating role of anger rumination.

Previous studies, however, have had a limitation in their study design and statistical methodology. First, most of these studies investigated the relationship between mindfulness and anger rumination adopting a cross-sectional survey; thus, longitudinal changes in these variables remain unclear. The chronic effects of anger regulation are very different from experimentally-induced or cross-sectional effects (Szasz, Szentagotai, & Hofmann, 2011). Although there was one intervention study (Anderson et al., 2007) that was helpful in understanding longitudinal change, it did not directly verify the relationship between the changes in mindfulness and anger rumination.

The current study followed mindfulness and anger rumination for four months. This approach allowed us to explore the longitudinal relationship between these variables. Previous studies reported that some of the mindfulness skills (e.g., "non-react") changed spontaneously (Taylor, Strauss, Cavanagh, & Jones, 2014). Like Taylor et al., we decided to follow the spontaneous changes of mindfulness.

1. Methods

Participants and procedure
Japanese undergraduates ($N = 81$; 76.5% female) completed questionnaires every month for 4 months (Time 1-Time 4). The age range of the participants was 19 to 24 years ($M = 20.67$, $SD = .99$ years, Range = 19-24). All participants completed an informed consent form before participating in the study.

1.1 *Measures*

1.2 *Mindfulness*

The Five Facets of Mindfulness Questionnaire (FFMQ; Baer, Smith, Hopkins, Krietemeyer, & Toney, 2006) is a 39-item self-report questionnaire assessing five facets of mindfulness: *Acting with awareness* (e.g., "I find myself doing things without paying attention"), *Nonjudging of inner experience* (e.g., "I think some of my emotions are bad or inappropriate and I should not feel them"), *Nonreactivity to inner experience* (e.g., "I perceive my feelings and emotions without having to react to them"), *Observing* (e.g., "I notice the smells and aromas of things"), and *Describing* (e.g., "I am good at finding words to describe my feelings"). Total scores of the FFMQ were used for analysis in this study, and the items utilize a Likert scale ranging from 1 (*never or very rarely true*) to 5 (*almost always or always true*). The FFMQ has adequate reliability, adequate convergent, and discriminant validity (Baer et al., 2006). The Japanese Version of the FFMQ (Sugiura, Sato, Ito, & Murakami, 2012) was used in the current study. The alpha coefficients in this sample were .79, .82, .85, and .85, respectively.

1.3 *Anger rumination*

The Anger Rumination Scale (ARS; Sukhodolsky et al., 2001) is a 19-item self-report questionnaire examining the degree to which individuals tend to focus on angry moods. There are four subscales, including "*Angry afterthoughts*" (e.g., "I re-enact the anger episode in my mind after it has happened"), "*Thoughts of revenge*" (e.g., "I have long-living fantasies of revenge after the conflict is over"), "*Angry memories*" (e.g., "I ponder about the injustices that have been done to me"), and "*Understanding of cause*" (e.g., "I think about the reasons people treat me badly"). The total score of the ARS was used in analysis in this study. Responses are made on a Likert scale ranging from 1 (*almost never*) to 4 (*almost always*). The ARS has adequate reliability, and convergent and discriminant validity is also adequate (Sukhodolsky et al., 2001). The Japanese Version of the ARS (Hatta, Ohbuchi, & Hatta, 2013) was used in the current study. The alpha coefficients in this sample were .94, .95, .95, and .96, respectively.

1.4 *Data analysis*

Our analytic approach to testing the hypothesis had two steps. The first step involved testing one-way repeated ANOVAs using IBM SPSS ver.23 to examine overall changes in mindfulness and anger rumination. The second step involved testing latent growth curve models, estimated using IBM SPSS AMOS ver.23, which can describe individual differences in changes. We examined the association between the slopes of mindfulness and anger rumination.

In the latent growth curve model, we employed criteria from Hu & Bentler (1999) to estimate the model. Goodness of fit of the models to data was evaluated with chi-square statistics (χ^2), the comparative fit index (CFI), and root-mean-square error of approximation (RMSEA). A model is considered to have a good fit when the χ^2 is not significant, the CFI is greater than 0.95, and RMSEA is less than .06.

2. Results

As indicated in the data analysis section, initial overall changes in mindfulness and anger rumination were examined as a preliminary analysis. Next, the relationship between the slopes of these variables was estimated by a latent growth curve model. The results of the preliminary analysis were compared with those of Anderson et al. (2007), who reported that the wait-list control group reported no changes of mindfulness and anger rumination over eight weeks.

2.1 *Preliminary analysis*

Means, standard deviations, and the correlations for the FFMQ and ARS can be found in Table 1 and 2. A one-way repeated ANOVA was conducted to examine a main effect of Time on mindfulness and anger rumination. This analysis revealed that although the main effect of Time on mindfulness is marginally significant, $F (2.65, 211.88) = 2.24$, $p = .093$, $\eta^2 = .027$, multiple comparison revealed that there is no significant difference between times. In addition to mindfulness, the main effect of Time on anger rumination is also marginally significant, $F (2.62, 209.76) = 2.40$, $p = .078$, $\eta^2 = .029$,

Masaya Takebe Hiroshi Sato

but multiple comparison revealed that there is no difference between times. Figure 1 illustrates the estimated and observed trajectories of mindfulness and anger rumination. Mindfulness showed a downward trend and anger rumination showed an upward trend over time.

These results appear to indicate that the total mindfulness score spontaneously decreased and anger rumination spontaneously increased from time 1 to time 4. This differs from the results of Anderson et al. (2007). However, given that effect sizes were small, Type I error inflation may have occurred. Caution should be taken when drawing conclusions regarding the spontaneous changes in mindfulness and anger rumination.

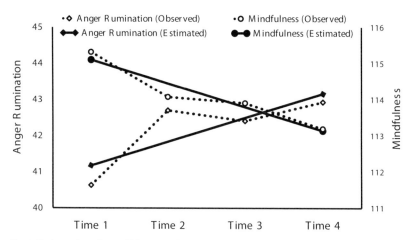

Fig. 1 Trajectories of mindfulness and anger rumination over four months

Table 1—Means and standard deviations of FFMQ and ARS

	Time 1	Time 2	Time 3	Time 4	F value	Multiple Comparison	Effect Size (η^2)
FFMQ	115.31 (11.78)	114.07 (12.30)	113.90 (12.06)	113.19 (12.70)	2.24[†]	n.s.	.027
ARS	40.63 (12.29)	42.70 (13.75)	42.41 (13.78)	42.93 (13.75)	2.40[†]	n.s.	.029

$N = 81$, FFMQ = Five Facets of Mindfulness Questionnaire, ARS = Anger Rumination Scale ( ) = Standard deviation, † = $p < .10$

Table 2—Correlations for FFMQ and ARS

	FFMQ T$_1$	FFMQ T$_2$	FFMQ T$_3$	FFMQ T$_4$	ARS T$_1$	ARS T$_2$	ARS T$_3$	ARS T$_4$	α
FFMQ T$_1$	—	.77**	.76**	.76**	-.18	-.16	-.13	-.12	.79
FFMQ T$_2$		—	.87**	.84**	-.21†	-.29**	-.22*	-.21†	.82
FFMQ T$_3$			—	.88**	-.22*	-.26*	-.23*	-.21†	.85
FFMQ T$_4$				—	-.19†	-.23*	-.18	-.24*	.85
ARS T$_1$					—	.79**	.75**	.73**	.94
ARS T$_2$						—	.80**	.81**	.95
ARS T$_3$							—	.89**	.95
ARS T$_4$								—	.96

$N = 81$, FFMQ = Five Facets of Mindfulness Questionnaire, ARS = Anger Rumination Scale

T$_1$ = Time 1, T$_2$ = Time 2, T$_3$ = Time 3, T$_4$ = Time 4,

** $= p < .01$, * $= p < .05$, † $= p < .10$

2.2 *Slopes and intercepts of mindfulness and anger rumination*

In order to describe the individual differences in changes, a latent growth curve model was constructed to examine the relationship between the slopes of mindfulness and anger rumination. The latent growth curve model of mindfulness and anger rumination (see Fig. 2) provided an acceptable fit to the data; $\chi^2 = 46.57$ ($df = 29$), $p = .021$; CFI $= .97$; RMSEA $= .09$ (90%CI $= .03$-$.13$). The estimated correlation between the slopes of these variables was marginally significant, and the strength of the relationship was moderate ($r = -.54$, $p = .095$). The estimated correlation between the intercepts of mindfulness and anger rumination was significant and the strength of the relationship was small ($r = -.26$, $p = .049$). All other relationships were not significant and omitted from Figure 2. Although the sample size was relatively small in this study, these results suggest that mindfulness and anger rumination are negatively covariant over time.

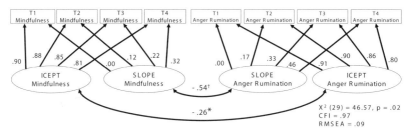

Fig. 2 Latent growth curve model of mindfulness and anger rumination
* $p < .05$, † = $p < .10$

3. Discussion

Previous studies (e.g., Anderson et al., 2007) have demonstrated the effects of MBIs on anger rumination. However, few studies has verified the longitudinal relationship between changes in mindfulness and anger rumination. In our study, the results were consistent with both analysis of overall change and considering individual differences with a latent growth curve model. As expected, this analysis revealed that the slopes of these variables were negatively covariant over four months, and this relationship was moderate. Overall changes in these variables appear to reflect the individual differences, but we need to view this result with care.

The latent growth curve model revealed that mindfulness and anger rumination were negatively and moderately covariant over time. Although mindfulness has already been negatively correlated with anger rumination in a cross-sectional study (e.g., Peter et al., 2015), this study may complement such knowledge from a longitudinal perspective. This study included no control of variables; therefore, there is no suggestion of causal links between mindfulness and anger rumination. Combined with the intervention study, however, their covariant relationship over time might be more clear. MBIs have been shown to cultivate mindfulness skills (Gu et al., 2015), leading to the reduction of anger rumination (Anderson et al., 2007). This is the first study to our knowledge to investigate the longitudinal relationship between these variables using a latent growth curve model.

The results indicated that mindfulness decreased and anger rumination spontaneously increased overall over time. This differs somewhat from results of previous research. Anderson et al. (2007) reported that there was no significant change in the anger rumination score from pre to post in the wait-list control group, which suggested that anger rumination was been stable over the eight weeks. There are two possible reasons for the discrepancy in results. First, given the small effect sizes, Type I error inflation could occur. In other words, our findings may be due to chance and the findings of the previous study, which reported the stability of mindfulness and anger rumination may be true. Second, both studies lacked control of numerous other variables, causing difficulty in identifying the variables that influence changes in mindfulness and anger rumination, so further research is necessary.

The intercepts of mindfulness and anger rumination negatively correlated and the strength of the relationship was small. This result supported the cross-sectional study (e.g., Borders, Earleywine, & Jajodia, 2010), which reported the negative correlation between mindfulness and rumination. The current study may reinforce the idea that interventions to cultivate mindfulness skills could be effective for alleviating anger rumination (e.g., Wright et al., 2009).

However, this study is an exploratory investigation with some notable limitations. First, this study included no control of numerous variables; therefore, we cannot deny the possibility that there is a third variable influencing mindfulness and anger rumination. Trait anger, for example, has been demonstrated to influence both mindfulness and anger rumination (e.g., Takebe, Takahashi, & Sato, 2015). Thus, it would be useful to control for trait anger. Second, the sample was composed entirely of Japanese undergraduate students and was relatively small, thus generalizations beyond this population must be tentative. Third, cultural differences regarding anger (Matsumoto et al., 2008; Gross, 2014) and mindfulness (Christopher et al., 2009) have been discussed. Further work is needed to assess cultural differences and collect a larger sample. Finally, goodness of fit of the models to data was acceptable, but insufficient. Although the current study was an early exploratory one, another model should be examined in the future.

It is necessary to accumulate knowledge about mindfulness and anger rumination because mindfulness may have great potential to improve treatments for anger. We hope that this study serves to encourage future studies on anger treatment and the development of better anger treatment.

4. Compliance with Ethical Standards

This research did not receive any specific grant from funding agencies in the public, commercial, or not-for-profit sectors. Informed consent was obtained from all individual participants included in the study.

References

Anderson, N. D., Lau, M. A., Segal, Z. V., & Bishop, S. R. (2007). Mindfulness-based stress reduction and attentional control. *Clinical psychology and psychotherapy, 14*(6), 449.

Baer, R. A., Smith, G. T., Hopkins, J., Krietemeyer, J., & Toney, L. (2006). Using Self-Report Assessment Methods to Explore Facets of Mindfulness. *Assessment,* 13(1), 27-45. doi:10.1177/1073191105283504

Borders, A., Earleywine, M., & Jajodia, A. (2010). Could Mindfulness Decrease Anger, Hostility, and Aggression by Decreasing Rumination? *Aggressive Behavior, 36(1),* 28-44.

Del Vecchio, T., & O'Leary, K. D. (2004). Effectiveness of anger treatments for specific anger problems: a meta-analytic review. *Clinical Psychological Review, 24*(1), 15-34. doi:10.1016/j.cpr.2003.09.006

Denson, T. F., Moulds, M. L., & Grisham, J. R. (2012). The effects of analytical rumination, reappraisal, and distraction on anger experience. *Behavior Therapy, 43*(2), 355-364. doi:10.1016/j.beth.2011.08.001

Fabiansson, E. C., Denson, T. F., Moulds, M. L., Grisham, J. R., & Schira, M. M. (2012). Don't look back in anger: neural correlates of reappraisal, analytical rumination, and angry rumination during recall of an anger-inducing autobiographical memory. *Neuroimage, 59*(3), 2974-2981. doi:10.1016/j.neuroimage.2011.09.078

Gu, J., Strauss, C., Bond, R., & Cavanagh, K. (2015). How do mindfulness-based cognitive therapy and mindfulness-based stress reduction improve mental health and wellbeing? A systematic review and meta-analysis of mediation studies. *Clinical Psychological Review, 37*(0), 1-12. doi: http://dx.doi.org/10.1016/j.cpr.2015.01.006

Hatta, T., Ohbuchi, K., & Hatta, J. (2013). Development of Japanese version of anger rumination scale. *Japanese Journal of Applied Psychology*, 38, 231-238 (In Japanese with English abstract).

Hu, L. t., & Bentler, P. M. (1999). Cutoff criteria for fit indexes in covariance structure analysis: Conventional criteria versus new alternatives. *Structural equation modeling: a multidisciplinary journal, 6*(1), 1-55.

Kabat-Zinn, J., & Hanh, T. N. (2009). *Full catastrophe living: Using the wisdom of your body and mind to face stress, pain, and illness*: Delta.

Khoury, B., Lecomte, T., Fortin, G., Masse, M., Therien, P., Bouchard, V., . . . Hofmann, S. G. (2013). Mindfulness-based therapy: A comprehensive meta-analysis. *Clinical Psychological Review, 33*(6), 763-771.

Peters, J. R., Smart, L. M., Eisenlohr - Moul, T. A., Geiger, P. J., Smith, G. T., & Baer, R. A. (2015). Anger rumination as a mediator of the relationship between mindfulness and aggression: The utility of a multidimensional mindfulness model. *Journal of Clinical Psychology, 71*(9), 871-884. doi:10.1002/jclp.22189

Sugiura, Y., Sato, A., Ito, Y., & Murakami, H. (2012). Development and Validation of the Japanese Version of the Five Facet Mindfulness Questionnaire. *Mindfulness, 3*(2), 85-94. doi:10.1007/s12671-011-0082-1

Sukhodolsky, D. G., Golub, A., & Cromwell, E. N. (2001). Development and validation of the anger rumination scale. *Personality and Individual Differences, 31*(5), 689-700. doi: http://dx.doi.org/10.1016/S0191-8869(00)00171-9

Szasz, P. L., Szentagotai, A., & Hofmann, S. G. (2011). The effect of emotion regulation strategies on anger. *Behavior Research and Therapy, 49*(2), 114-119. doi:10.1016/j.brat.2010.11.011

Takebe, M., Takahashi, F., & Sato, H. (2015). Mediating Role of Anger Rumination in the Associations between Mindfulness, Anger-In, and Trait Anger. *Psychology, 6*(8), 948-953. doi:10.4236/psych.2015.68093

Taylor, B. L., Strauss, C., Cavanagh, K., & Jones, F. (2014). The effectiveness of self-help mindfulness-based cognitive therapy in a student sample: A randomised controlled trial. *Behaviour Research and Therapy, 63*, 63-69.

Wright, S., Day, A., & Howells, K. (2009). Mindfulness and the treatment of anger problems. *Aggression and Violent Behavior, 14*(5), 396-401. doi:10.1016/j.avb.2009.06.008

Contributors

Hiroshi Yoshikawa, Ph.D., President of Rissho University

Eichi Terao, Ph.D., Professor, Faculty of Buddhist Studies, Rissho University

Kyoko Tanji, Ph.D., Associate Professor, Faculty of Buddhist Studies, Rissho University

Daiki Kanda, Ph.D., Assistant Professor, Faculty of Buddhist Studies, Rissho University

Yasushi Hayashi, M.A., Professor, Faculty of Economics, Rissho University

Tetsuya Utashiro, Ph.D., Part-time lecturer, Faculty of Economics, Rissho University

Hazime Mizoguchi, Ph.D., Professor, Faculty of Social Welfare, Rissho University

Kentaro Kawamoto, Ph.D., Associate Professor, Faculty of Social Welfare, Rissho University

Takatsugu Watanabe, M.A., Assistant Professor, Faculty of Social Welfare, Rissho University

Miwa Sakai, M.A., Assistant Professor, Faculty of Social Welfare, Rissho University

Hideo Matsui, Ph.D., Professor, Faculty of Geo-Environmental Science, Rissho University

Shintaro Goto, Dr.Eng., Professor, Faculty of Geo-Environmental Science, Rissho University

Hanae Tamura, M.A., Associate Professor, Faculty of Psychology, Rissho University

Masaya Takebe, Ph.D., Assistant Professor, Faculty of Psychology, Rissho University

Hiroshi Sato, Ph.D., Professor, School of Humanities, Kwansei Gakuin University

The Rissho International Journal of Academic Research in Culture and Society 3

The Academic Canon of Arts, Humanities, and Sciences

発行日………… 2020 年 3 月 11 日　初版第 1 刷

編集……………… 立正大学学術英文叢書編集・刊行委員会
発行……………… 立正大学
　　　　　　　　〒 141-8602　東京都品川区大崎 4-2-16
　　　　　　　　電話 03-3492-2681（代表）
発売……………… 株式会社平凡社
　　　　　　　　〒 101-0051　東京都千代田区神田神保町 3-29
　　　　　　　　電話 03-3230-6570（代表）
　　　　　　　　　　　03-3230-6573（営業）
装丁……………… 馬面俊之
印刷……………… 株式会社東京印書館
製本……………… 大口製本印刷株式会社

落丁・乱丁本のお取り替えは平凡社読者サービス係までお送り下さい（送料小社負担）。
© 立正大学 2020 Printed in Japan
ISBN978-4-582-47443-5
NDC 分類番号 040.3　A5 判（21.6cm）　総ページ 264